# THE DICHOTOMY
## OF LEADERSHIP

BALANCING THE CHALLENGES OF EXTREME
OWNERSHIP TO LEAD AND WIN

**Also by Jocko Willink and Leif Babin**

*Extreme Ownership: How U.S. Navy SEALs Lead and Win*

Task Unit Bruiser SEALs, explosive ordnance disposal bomb technicians, and Iraqi soldiers conduct a clearance operation in the Malaab District of eastern Ramadi alongside U.S. Soldiers of Task Force Red Currahee, the legendary "Band of Brothers" of the 1st Battalion, 506th Parachute Infantry Regiment (1/506th), 101st Airborne Division. A 1/506th company commander, "Gunfighter Six," an outstanding warrior and professional Soldier, is in the foreground at right.

(Photo courtesy of Todd Pitman)

# THE
# DICHOTOMY
## OF LEADERSHIP

BALANCING THE CHALLENGES OF EXTREME
OWNERSHIP TO LEAD AND WIN

JOCKO WILLINK

AND

LEIF BABIN

ST. MARTIN'S PRESS ✿ NEW YORK

THE DICHOTOMY OF LEADERSHIP. Copyright © 2018 by Jocko Command LLC and Leif Babin LLC. All rights reserved. Printed in the United States of America. For information, address St. Martin's Press, 175 Fifth Avenue, New York, N.Y. 10010.

www.stmartins.com

The Library of Congress Cataloging-in-Publication Data is available upon request.

ISBN 978-1-250-19577-7 (hardcover)
ISBN 978-1-250-19578-4 (ebook)

Our books may be purchased in bulk for promotional, educational, or business use. Please contact your local bookseller or the Macmillan Corporate and Premium Sales Department at 1-800-221-7945, extension 5442, or by email at MacmillanSpecialMarkets@macmillan.com.

First Edition: September 2018

10  9  8  7  6  5  4  3  2  1

*Dedicated to the Big Tough Frogmen of
SEAL Team Three, Task Unit Bruiser, especially:
Marc Lee, Mike Monsoor, and Ryan Job, who laid down their lives;
Chris Kyle, a friend and a Legend;
and Seth Stone, the Delta Platoon commander, our brother.
May we honor them always.*

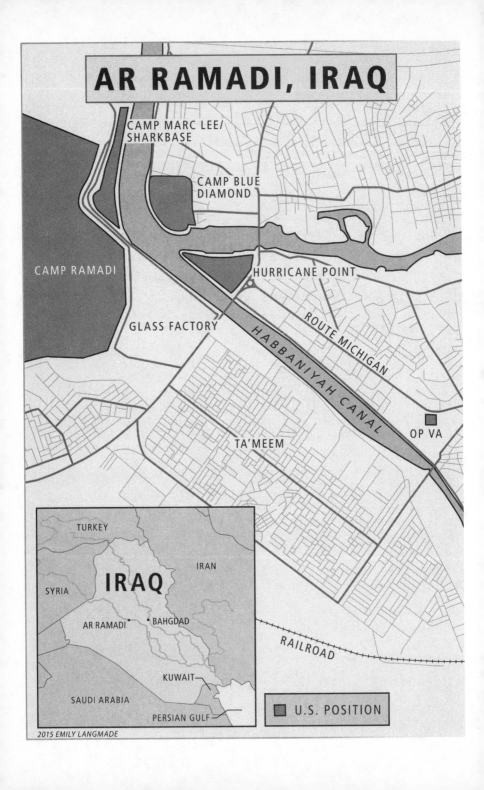

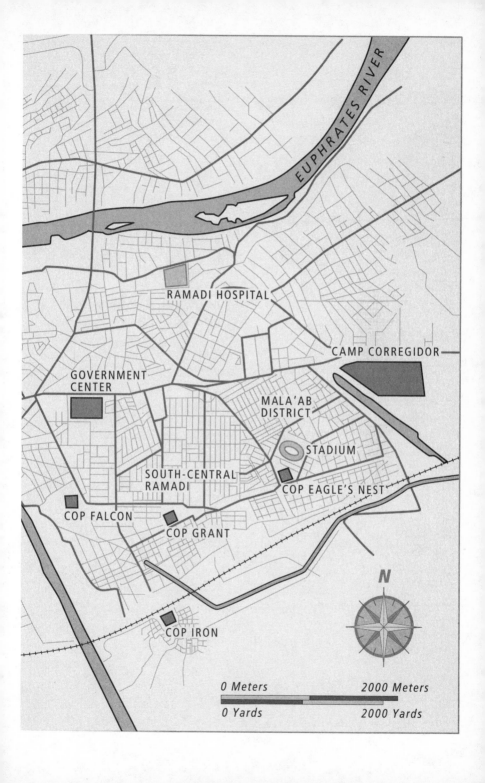

# CONTENTS

# PREFACE

War is a nightmare. It is awful, indifferent, devastating, and evil.
War is hell.

But war is also an incredible teacher—a brutal instructor. We learned lessons in war, written in blood, about sorrow, loss, and pain. We also learned about the fragility of human life and the power of the human spirit.

Of course, we learned about strategy and tactics. We learned how to most effectively take the fight to our enemies. We learned how to analyze targets, gather and exploit information, find our enemy's weaknesses, and capitalize on them. We applied these lessons and made the enemy pay for their transgressions.

But of everything we learned, nothing is as universal and transferable as how we came to truly understand the power of leadership. We saw how successful leaders could create victory where victory seemed impossible. We also witnessed how poor leadership could bring defeat upon teams that seemed invincible.

We discovered firsthand that the principles of leadership are "simple, but not easy." There are strategies, techniques, and skills that take time and practice to utilize effectively. The foremost requirement for potent leadership is humility, so that leaders can fully understand and appreciate their own shortfalls. We learned much on the battlefield and have tried to pass those lessons on, but we are still humbled every day by our mistakes and all that we continue to learn.

This book builds upon our first book, *Extreme Ownership: How U.S. Navy SEALs Lead and Win*. It is the follow-on book that so many readers of *Extreme Ownership* asked us to write. We have laid out the concepts in *The Dichotomy of Leadership* with clear descriptions and context so that it can be read and understood independently of the first book. For further explanation of the overviews given in the following pages, readers may want the deeper understanding and background provided in *Extreme Ownership*. But, while it may be helpful to understand the first book for greater enlightenment, it is not essential.

In both books, we reference our experiences in the military, where we both served as SEAL officers. The bulk of our lessons learned draw from the Battle of Ramadi in 2006, where we served as the leaders of SEAL Team Three, Task Unit Bruiser. During that battle, the SEALs from Task Unit Bruiser fought with incredible bravery and tenacity. They delivered huge impact on the battlefield. But Task Unit Bruiser also suffered severe casualties. Those sacrifices will never be forgotten.

Upon our departure from active duty in the U.S. Navy, we launched a company, Echelon Front, to share the lessons we learned with leaders in every capacity. In 2015, we published *Extreme Ownership*. Through that book, leaders all over the world embraced its fundamental principles—the mind-set of Extreme Ownership and the four Laws of Combat: Cover and Move, Simple, Prioritize and Execute, and Decentralized Command. More than a million readers have taken those tenets and implemented them in their professional and personal lives with extraordinary results.

But employing these principles to the fullest proves challenging. The nuances, if neglected or misunderstood, create obstacles difficult to overcome. We wrote this book to provide the granular insight and understanding that often render the difference between success and failure. This book will enable you to better process, analyze, and apply these leadership principles to *your* battlefield, in whatever arena that might be, whether leading in combat, business, or life.

The format of *The Dichotomy of Leadership* mirrors that of *Extreme Ownership:* there are three parts to the book, four chapters in each part, and three sections to each chapter. The first section of each chapter describes an experience from combat or SEAL training; the second section discusses the relevant principle; and the third provides the direct application of the concept to the business world.

*The Dichotomy of Leadership* is not a memoir or a history of the Iraq War. As we said in *Extreme Ownership,* "This book is about leadership. It was written for leaders of teams large and small, for men and women, for any person who aspires to better themselves. Though it contains exciting accounts of SEAL combat operations, this book is . . . a collection of lessons learned from our experiences to help other leaders achieve victory. If it serves as a useful guide to leaders who aspire to build, train, and lead high-performance winning teams, then it has accomplished its purpose."

The combat and training experiences we describe are all true stories. But they are not meant for historic reference. The dialogues we have written are intended to impart the message and meaning of conversations. They are imperfect and subject to the passage of time and the shortfalls of memory. We have also concealed specific tactics, techniques, and procedures and ensured that no classified information about when and where specific operations took place and who participated in them is revealed. In accordance with U.S. Department of Defense requirements, the manuscript was submitted and approved through the Pentagon's security review process. We do not use the names of our SEAL teammates, unless they are the names of our fallen or they are SEALs already in the public eye. Our brothers still on active duty in the SEAL Teams are silent professionals who seek no recognition, and we treat our responsibility to protect them with the utmost seriousness.

We have taken the same precautions to protect the incredible Soldiers and Marines* we served with in the Battle of Ramadi and elsewhere. Their names fill our memories with the extraordinary leadership, sacrifice, and heroism they demonstrated. But to ensure their privacy and security, we do not use their names in this book unless they are already known to the public.

Similarly, we have taken every measure to protect confidentiality for the clients of our leadership consulting company, Echelon Front. We have refrained from using company names, changed the names and titles of individuals, and in some cases abstained from using industry-specific information or altered it. As in *Extreme Ownership,* while the stories we tell from the business world are based directly on real experiences, in some cases we have combined situations, condensed timelines, and modified details to protect confidentiality or more clearly emphasize the underlying principles we are trying to illustrate.

It has been gratifying to witness the worldwide reach and impact of *Extreme Ownership,* particularly in the success that so many readers have achieved through its guiding principles. But there are those who misunderstood the title of that book and its powerful foundational principle: the mind-set and attitude of Extreme Ownership. In most cases, rather than extremes, leadership requires balance. Leaders must find the equilibrium between opposing forces that pull in opposite directions. Being aggressive but cautious, disciplined but not rigid, a leader but also a

---

* In accordance with U.S. Department of Defense policy, the term "Soldier" will be capitalized for "U.S. Soldier" as will "Marine" for "U.S. Marine" throughout the book.

follower—it applies to almost every aspect of leadership. Achieving the proper balance in each of the many dichotomies is the most difficult aspect of leadership.

We wrote *The Dichotomy of Leadership* to help leaders understand this challenge and find the balance needed to most effectively lead and win. No matter the arena, balance must be achieved for optimal performance. If a leader imposes too much authority, the team becomes reluctant to execute; not enough, and the team has no direction. If leaders are too aggressive, they put the team and the mission at risk; yet if they wait too long to take action, results can be equally catastrophic. If a leader trains his or her people too hard, they may burn out; yet without challenging and realistic training, the team remains unprepared for real-world situations they may face. The dichotomies go on and on, each one requiring balance.

Since the release of *Extreme Ownership,* as we worked with thousands of leaders from hundreds of companies and organizations, the majority of the questions we received were around this concept, this struggle: achieving balance in the Dichotomy of Leadership.

We wrote this book to specifically address those questions. Just as we described in the preface of *Extreme Ownership,* we don't have all the answers. No one does. But we learned extremely humbling and valuable lessons as battlefield leaders—from both our failures and our successes. Often our mistakes and failures provided the most valuable lessons that helped us learn and grow. We continue to learn and grow to this day.

As *The Dichotomy of Leadership* builds upon the concepts in *Extreme Ownership,* the words from the preface of our previous work are applicable:

> We wrote this book to capture those leadership principles
> for future generations, so that they may not be forgotten,
> so that as new wars begin and end, such crucial lessons
> will not have to be relearned—rewritten in more blood.

We wrote this so that the leadership lessons can continue to impact teams beyond the battlefield in all leadership situations—any company, team, or organization in which a group of people strives to achieve a goal and accomplish a mission. We wrote this book for leaders everywhere to utilize the principles we learned to lead and win.

# THE DICHOTOMY
## OF LEADERSHIP

U.S. Army M2 Bradley Fighting Vehicles and M1A2 Abrams tanks from Team Bulldog (Bravo Company), Task Force Bandit (1st Battalion, 37th Armored Regiment of the 1st Brigade, 1st Armored Division) led by Captain "Main Gun" Mike Bajema, provide crucial fire support to their dismounted U.S. and Iraqi infantry troops and Charlie Platoon SEALs on a combat operation in South-Central Ramadi. Team Bulldog and Task Force Bandit were outstanding, aggressive, and professional Soldiers whose courageous response saved Task Unit Bruiser SEALs on scores of combat operations.

(Photo courtesy at Mike Bajema)

# INTRODUCTION

Finding the Balance

*Leif Babin*

## J-BLOCK, SOUTH-CENTRAL RAMADI, IRAQ: 2006

"Stand by to get some," someone said over the intersquad radio, in the calm demeanor you might expect of a flight attendant telling airline passengers to stow their tray tables for landing. The street in front of us had emptied of people. Like magic, the local citizens had all suddenly disappeared. And we knew what that meant: enemy attack was imminent. The hair on the back of my neck stood at rigid attention.

After many a vicious gunfight in Ramadi, "stand by to get some" was a running joke that eased the tension right when we knew trouble was coming. The more nonchalantly it could be said under the direst of circumstances, the funnier it was.

It was broad daylight as our patrol of SEALs and Iraqi soldiers made its way on foot down the narrow city street, bordered by high concrete walls on either side.

Suddenly, the world exploded. Dozens of bullets snapped through the air, each with a sharp supersonic *crack,* and smashed into the concrete wall next to me with thunderous impact. Shards of concrete flew everywhere. The heavy volleys of incoming fire sounded like multiple jackhammers simultaneously chewing up the street and the walls all around us.

We had walked right into an enemy buzz saw. Insurgent fighters hit us from multiple directions with belt-fed machine guns. I couldn't see them or where they were shooting from, but the number of enemy bullets flying through the air around us was crazy.

There was no place to hide. With high walls on both sides, the narrow South-Central Ramadi street provided no cover. The only thing between us and the enemy machine guns was a single parked car on the side of the road some distance up the block and the typical trash strewn about. The patrol was in a dual-column formation—each column split on opposite sides of the street, hunkered close to the walls. There was nothing to get behind that could protect us from bullets. But we did have something on our side: devastating firepower. We fully expected a firefight on every patrol into this enemy-held neighborhood and we rolled in heavy. Each squad of eight SEALs packed at least four belt-fed machine guns to suppress any enemy attack we encountered. When we came under fire, our immediate response with violent and overwhelming gunfire provided the only answer: Cover and Move. Having learned through the humbling experience of months of urban combat, Task Unit Bruiser had had plenty of practice in this fundamental gunfighting principle.

Within nanoseconds, the SEALs with the big machine guns up front unleashed the most ruthless and lethal barrage of fire you could imagine. Despite the intensity and violence of close urban combat, I couldn't help but smile.

Damn, I loved those guys—the Big Tough Frogmen who carried the heavy Mk48* and Mk46 machine guns (pronounced "Mark Forty-Eight" and "Mark Forty-Six") and the weight of hundreds of rounds of ammunition in addition to their body armor,

---

* Mk48: Mark 48, a 7.62mm NATO medium machine gun designed specifically for the U.S. Navy SEAL Teams, and the big brother of the Mark 46, a lighter medium machine gun in the smaller caliber of 5.56mm NATO.

helmet, radio, water, and everything else they had to carry, all in the blistering heat of the Iraqi summer sun.

Those SEAL machine gunners kept us alive. Our snipers killed a lot of bad guys and received many well-deserved accolades for it, but every time we were attacked, it was the SEAL machine gunners who suppressed the threat of enemy fire. Standing or kneeling, they fired their machine guns from the shoulder, with incredible accuracy. That machine gun fire eliminated the insurgent fighters shooting at us or forced them to take cover (meaning they couldn't accurately engage us), which enabled us to maneuver, flank, or simply get off the street and out of harm's way.

Despite the dozens of bullets hitting the street and the walls near us, no one was hit. That was the beauty of Cover and Move.

As the commander of Charlie Platoon and the senior man on the ground, I was itching to make a call, pass a verbal command to peel back and choose a nearby building for a "strongpoint" where we could find protection behind concrete walls, set security, and take the high ground on the rooftop. From there, we could locate our attackers, send out a squad to flank them, or call in the tanks to blast them into oblivion. I had dreamed of being a combat leader since I was kid. I had wanted to be a SEAL since at least middle school, when I learned about the legendary Navy special operations unit. Leading intense combat operations in a place like Ramadi was the ultimate fulfillment of that dream. Every bone in my body wanted to step up and take charge, bark a verbal command that could be heard over the sound of intense gunfire.

*But I wasn't in charge.*

The leader of this particular combat operation was Charlie Platoon's most junior assistant platoon commander (or assistant officer in charge, AOIC), the least experienced officer in the platoon. It was his operation, and it was his call.

I would certainly step in and make a call if he or others needed me to, when the situation called for it. But he was a great officer and paired with Tony Eafrati, our outstanding and highly experienced platoon chief, I had total faith in my AOIC and he proved himself time and again.

Rapidly, the AOIC pointed out a larger building in which to strongpoint. As the SEALs up front laid down suppressive fire, other SEALs moved to the entrance gate—the pathway off the street—and entered the compound.

From my position toward the middle of the patrol, I observed at least one enemy firing position a few blocks in front of us and I lobbed several 40mm grenades from the M203 grenade launcher mounted below my M4 rifle. I sent the high-explosive "golden eggs" up over the heads of our patrol and down onto the enemy position, where they exploded with a fiery blast. It was a small contribution, but an effective way to keep the bad guys' heads down, complementing our machine gun fire.

I then moved up to the entrance gate of the compound and took position in the street just outside, directing guys inside the gate as they ran to catch up. Marc Lee, with his big Mk48 machine gun, stood in the street just ahead of me, laying down belt after belt of devastating fire. Marc was a badass. He had us covered. Enemy rounds were still cracking by us and flying down the street, but with Marc laying the hammer down, the enemy fire was less accurate.

I swiveled to face the rear of the patrol. One of the last SEALs still on the street was running hard in my direction.

"Let's go!" I yelled at him, waving him over with a hand motion toward the gate.

Suddenly, only feet from me and the safety of the concrete walls, the SEAL fell violently forward and landed hard, facedown in the street. I rushed over to him in horror.

*Man down,* I thought. *He must have taken a round to the chest or head.*

I darted over, expecting to find him a bloody mess. I was surprised to see him lying there, smiling back up at me.

"Are you alright?" I yelled over the sound of the gunfire.

Bullets were still whizzing past us, kicking up dirt just a few feet away and ricocheting off the nearby walls.

"I'm good," he replied. "I tripped."

I smiled back in relief, thankful that he wasn't gravely wounded or dead.

"Bro!" I yelled over the noise of the firefight. "I thought you got your head shot off!" We both chuckled.

Quickly, I grabbed his hand and helped him to his feet. We sprinted the rest of the way back to the gate. As the SEAL ducked into the gate, I ran forward and slapped Marc on the back.

"Last man!" I yelled, letting him know we had everyone accounted for. I covered for Marc as he pulled back, pointed his big gun, barrel smoking, to the sky, and we ducked inside the gate together. Finally, everybody was off the street, out of the enemy line of fire, and inside the compound behind the cover of concrete walls. Thanks to Marc and our other machine gunners, supported by SEAL shooters with their M4 rifles, despite the vicious enemy attack with substantial firepower, none of us had been hit.

I made my way to the rooftop, where SEAL shooters had taken up firing positions. As the enemy fighters moved from building to building and continued their attack, we engaged them. The AOIC was there on the roof, with our Charlie Platoon radioman, assessing the situation.

"What do you want to do?" I asked him.

"Let's call in the tanks for fire support," he said calmly. The AOIC was cool under fire—a great quality that every leader should work toward.

"Roger that," I said. It was exactly the right call. We had the high ground on the rooftop. We had good security behind the concrete walls. The SEAL radioman contacted the U.S. Army company Team Bulldog (Bravo Company, 1st Battalion, 37th Armored Regiment of the 1st Brigade, 1st Armored Division) and got the M1A2 Abrams tanks rolling our way with their massive firepower. We loved those Soldiers, under the command of Captain "Main

Gun" Mike Bajema. Despite the deadly threat of IEDs* that destroyed a number of tanks in this South-Central Ramadi neighborhood, every single time we called for help, Main Gun Mike personally loaded up in his tank and fearlessly came to our aid, accompanied by another Bulldog tank. We could take great risk and patrol deep into dangerous enemy territory only because we knew that when we got into trouble, Team Bulldog had us covered. Mike and his Soldiers were outstanding, aggressive warriors. They would do everything in their power to get to us, no matter how dangerous or difficult. And when they arrived in their tanks, they *brought the thunder.*

It took several minutes for the tank crews to mount up and drive out to our location. We continued to take enemy fire from several directions. One SEAL operator peeked his head above the roof wall to determine where the bad guys were. As he did so, his head snapped back violently and he fell backward. He sat up, unharmed, wondering what the hell had just happened. When the SEAL took off his helmet to examine it, he found a deep gash where an enemy bullet had ricocheted off the night-vision mount on the front of his helmet. Just an inch or two lower and that round would have taken his head off.

"What happened?" a SEAL next to him asked.

"I got shot," he said with a smile, pointing to his helmet.

It was a close call, but thankfully one we could laugh about.

As we waited on the rooftop, I switched my radio over to monitor Bulldog's company communications net. I heard Main Gun Mike ask if we could mark the buildings from where the enemy fighters were still shooting at us.

"Do you have any red smoke grenades?" the radioman asked. I didn't have any.

"We've got tracers," I suggested. The SEAL radioman had a

---

* IED: U.S. military acronym for improvised explosive device, the deadly roadside bombs that were the insurgency's primary and most effective weapon.

full magazine of tracer rounds, which emitted a visible orange glow along the bullet path as they zipped through the air. Marc Lee also had tracers every fifth round in his ammunition belt. We relayed to Main Gun Mike and his tankers the plan. As the heavy Abrams tanks approached, tank tracks clattering on the concrete city street, I heard the word over the radio to mark the target and relayed the order via verbal command.

"Mark the target!" I yelled. Marc and the SEAL radioman lit up the enemy position with tracer fire.

*Stand by to get some,* I thought as Mike's Abrams tank rotated its huge turret and trained the mighty 120mm cannon at the building from where we had been receiving fire. The tank unleashed its thunderous fury into the building and ended the enemy attack. The insurgent fighters who hadn't been obliterated beat a hasty retreat. We received no more fire from the enemy that day, thanks to Mike and his Team Bulldog Soldiers. Once again the tanks had been our deliverance. The combined team of SEALs and U.S. Army Soldiers had given the insurgents more than they could handle. And my AOIC had proven once again that he was a solid leader, competent and coolheaded, even under the stress of close combat.

But just as my assistant platoon commander had to be ready to lead, in this situation I had to be ready to follow. The goal of all leaders should be to work themselves out of a job. You never quite get there, but by putting junior leaders and frontline troops in charge, our SEAL platoon and task unit were far more effective. It created a culture of leaders at every level of the team. Trying to navigate between leadership and followership was an example of the Dichotomy of Leadership, the balance that every leader must find between two opposing forces in leadership. Ready to lead, but also knowing when to follow. Taking Extreme Ownership of everything that impacts the mission, but also empowering others to lead with Decentralized Command. The recognition of the many dichotomies and the ability to balance these opposing forces provide a powerful tool that enables leaders at every level to lead and win.

### The Dichotomy: Balancing the Challenges of Extreme Ownership

*Jocko Willink and Leif Babin*

Our first book, *Extreme Ownership*, struck a chord with many readers. The idea that leaders must take ownership—Extreme Ownership—of everything in their world, everything that impacts their mission, has changed the way people view leadership. If mistakes happen, effective leaders don't place blame on others. They take ownership of the mistakes, determine what went wrong, develop solutions to correct those mistakes and prevent them from happening again as they move forward.

Even the best teams and the best leaders never deliver flawless performances. No one can achieve perfection. What makes the best leaders and best teams great is that when they make mistakes, they acknowledge them, take ownership, and make corrections to upgrade their performance. With each iteration, the team and its leaders enhance their effectiveness. Over time, that team runs circles around its competition, particularly against other teams with a culture of excuses and blame casting, where problems never get solved and thus performance never improves.

Our four Laws of Combat have helped radically improve the performance of teams and organizations—large and small—across the United States and internationally, in nearly every industry in the business world, as well as military units, police and fire departments, charity organizations, school administrations, and sports teams.

The first Law of Combat: Cover and Move. This is teamwork—every individual and team within the team, mutually supporting one another to accomplish the mission. Departments and groups within the team, and even those outside the immediate team that are nevertheless crucial to success, must break down silos and work together to win. It doesn't matter if one element within the group does its job: if the team fails, everybody fails. But when the overall team wins, everybody wins. Everyone gets to share in that success.

The second Law of Combat: Simple. Complexity breeds chaos and disaster, especially when things go wrong. And things always go wrong. When plans and orders get too complex, the people charged with executing those plans and orders do not understand them. When team members don't understand, they can't execute. Therefore, plans must be simplified so that everyone on the team recognizes the overall "commander's intent"—the greater purpose behind the mission—and understands their role in achieving mission success. Orders must be communicated in a manner that is "simple, clear, and concise." The true test for whether plans and orders have been communicated effectively is this: The team gets it. When the people on the team understand, then they can execute.

The third Law of Combat: Prioritize and Execute. When multiple problems occur simultaneously (which happens often), taking on too many problems at once results in failure. It is imperative that leaders detach themselves—pull back from the details—and assess to determine the highest priority to the strategic mission. Then, once that highest-priority task has been determined, leaders must clearly communicate that priority to the team and ensure the team executes. Then the leaders and the team can move on to the next priority. Then the next. Training and proper contingency planning assist greatly to better prepare teams and leaders to most effectively Prioritize and Execute under pressure, in real time.

The fourth Law of Combat: Decentralized Command. No one leader can manage it all or make every decision. Instead, leadership must be decentralized, with leaders at every level empowered to make decisions, right down to the frontline troopers in charge of no one but themselves and their small piece of the mission. With Decentralized Command, everyone leads. To empower everyone on the team to lead, team members must understand not just what to do but *why* they are doing it. This requires clear and frequent communication up and down the chain of command—and most importantly: trust. Junior leaders must have confidence that they clearly understand the strategic mission, the commander's intent of their boss, and the parameters within which they can make decisions. Senior leaders must trust that their junior leaders will make the right decisions and encourage them to do so. This requires training and frequent communication to implement with maximum effectiveness.

There was one big problem with the book *Extreme Ownership:* the title. While it drove home the most important leadership foundation in the book, it was also slightly misleading. Extreme Ownership is the foundation of good leadership. But leadership seldom requires *extreme* ideas or attitudes. In fact, quite the opposite is true: leadership requires balance. We addressed that concept in chapter 12 of *Extreme Ownership,* "Discipline Equals Freedom—The Dichotomy of Leadership." But as we assessed legions of leaders in companies, teams, and organizations as they implemented the principles we taught in the book, many struggled to find that balance. This struggle represents the biggest challenge we observed as we trained and advised hundreds of companies and thousands of leaders over the past few years with our leadership consulting company, Echelon Front.

In the final chapter of *Extreme Ownership,* we wrote:

> Every leader must walk a fine line. . . . Leadership requires finding the equilibrium in the dichotomy of many seemingly contradictory qualities, between one extreme and another. The simple recognition of this is one of the most powerful tools a leader has. With this in mind, a leader can more easily balance the opposing forces and lead with maximum effectiveness.

Every behavior or characteristic carried out by a leader can be taken too far. Leaders can become too extreme and upset the balance required to effectively lead a team. When balance is lost, leadership suffers and the team's performance rapidly declines.

Even the fundamental principles of combat leadership in Extreme Ownership can get out of balance. A leader can Cover and Move too much and step on the toes of other leaders, departments, or divisions. A plan can be too Simple and fail to cover likely contingencies. A team can go too far with Prioritize and Execute, resulting in target fixation and loss of situational awareness on newly emerging problems and threats. Decentralized Command can also be taken too far, when too much autonomy is given to subordinate leaders who then don't fully understand strategic goals and how to execute in support of those goals.

And this idea continues on with just about everything a leader does. Leaders must be close with their people, but not so close that it becomes a problem. They must hold the line with discipline but not become tyrannical. A leader can even become too extreme with Extreme Ownership, when a leader takes so much ownership of everything in his or her world that members of the team feel there is nothing left for which they can take ownership. When this happens, team members will execute only at the boss's specific direction without any root ownership or buy-in themselves, resulting in a team far less capable of overcoming obstacles and accomplishing the mission.

Therefore, balance in leadership is crucial to victory. It must be monitored at all times and it must be modulated to specific situations as they arise. If a team member fails to perform adequately, for example, a leader must get down in the weeds and micromanage that member until he or she executes correctly. But once the team member gets back on track and resumes effective performance, the leader must maintain the ability to back off and give that team member room to take greater ownership and manage tasks on his or her own.

It is not easy to maintain the constant shift, continual modulation, and frequent adjustment necessary to balance all the dichotomies across every spectrum of leadership characteristics. Yet this skill is essential for effective leadership.

We have observed these struggles continuously in good leaders striving to be better. That is what drove us to go deeper into the concept of the Dichotomy of Leadership. The goal of this book is to help leaders overcome that struggle through examples of how to find the right balance in leadership—to moderate the idea of leading from the extremes and focus on maintaining balance—within teams, among peers, and both up and down the chain of command. Every good leader must develop the ability to recognize, understand, and adjust that balance. While it isn't easy, through knowledge, disciplined practice, and sustained effort, anyone can master finding the equilibrium in the Dichotomy of Leadership. Those who do will dominate their battlefield and lead their teams to victory.

# PART I

## BALANCING PEOPLE

Marc Lee's combat gear—helmet, boots, and his carefully painted Mark 48 machine gun—staged to honor him on the roof of the tactical operations center at Sharkbase, Task Unit Bruiser's camp, which was renamed Camp Marc Lee in his honor. While it was technically against regulations to fly the American flag in Iraq, Task Unit Bruiser marked its headquarters with Old Glory. Marc fought for the flag and his brothers-in-arms and was the first SEAL killed in action in Iraq. Task Unit Bruiser also lost Michael Monsoor and, eventually, Ryan Job, who died from medical complications following a surgery to repair his combat wounds.

(Photo courtesy of the authors)

# CHAPTER 1
## The Ultimate Dichotomy

*Jocko Willink*

### CHARLIE MEDICAL FACILITY, CAMP RAMADI, IRAQ: 2006

"Sir," the young SEAL whispered in a faint voice, "come here." Our hands were clasped in a handshake. Not a formal handshake like two businessmen, but palm to palm with thumbs wrapped around the back of the hand like an arm-wrestling contest—a handshake of brotherhood. The young SEAL was feeling the morphine. I saw it in his eyes, but he was still there, still conscious and aware. He was everything a young man should be: smart, brave, athletic, funny, loyal, and tough. He had been shot in the leg about half an hour before. I found out later that Mikey Monsoor, a young SEAL machine gunner, had run out into heavy enemy gunfire and dragged this SEAL out of a war-torn street in the Malaab District in the city of Ramadi, the violent heart of the insurgency in Iraq.

The wounded SEAL now lay on a gurney in Charlie Med, the Camp Ramadi field hospital where U.S. military surgical teams worked furiously to save the lives of gravely wounded troops almost every day. The bullet, a mammoth armor-piercing 7.62 × 54 millimeter round with a steel core, had entered his leg at the lower thigh, ripped apart flesh and bone inside his leg, and exited in his upper thigh, close to the groin. It was hard to say if he would keep his leg. From the looks of the wound, my guess was no, he would lose it.

The wounded SEAL's grip on my hand tightened and he pulled me in, drawing me just inches from his face. I could tell he wanted to say something to me, so I turned my head and put my ear next to his mouth. I wasn't sure what to expect. Was he scared or angry or depressed that he might lose his leg? Was he nervous about what might happen next? Was he confused?

He took a breath and then whispered, "Sir. Let me stay. Let me stay. Please. Don't make me go home. I'll do anything. I'll sweep up around the camp. I can heal here. Please, please, please just let me stay with the task unit."

There you go. Not scared. Not angry. Not depressed that he might lose his leg. Only concerned that he might have to leave our task unit.

Task Unit Bruiser. Our task unit. Our lives. This SEAL was our first significant casualty. We had had guys catch some frag on previous operations. We had had some very close calls. But this was the first wounded SEAL from Task Unit Bruiser whose life would be forever changed by a grave combat injury. Even if he kept his leg, the damage was so substantial that it didn't seem possible he would ever fully regain the extraordinary athleticism he had displayed previously. And yet this SEAL was only concerned that he would let me down, let the task unit down, let his platoon—his team—down.

This was a man. This was a true friend—a brother. This was a hero: young, brave, and without question more concerned for his friends than for his own life.

I was moved. I felt tears welling up in my eyes. I fought them back and swallowed the lump in my throat. This was no time to break down. I was "the Leader." He needed me to be strong.

"It's alright, brother. We've got to get you healed up first," I whispered. "As soon as you heal up, we'll get you back over here. But you have to get healed up first."

"I'll be okay," the wounded SEAL replied. "Just let me stay . . . let me stay."

"Brother," I told him earnestly, "I'll bring you back as soon as you can stand. But you have to go and get yourself healed up."

"I'll heal up here. I can work in the TOC," he argued, referencing our tactical operations center, where we monitored combat missions via radio and television screens that displayed overhead video feed from aircraft, both manned and unmanned.

"Listen," I told him, "that won't work. This wound is no joke. You're going to need real rehab—and we don't have that here for you. Go home. Heal up. Get back on your feet and I'll get you back over here. I promise."

I meant it. Whether he kept his leg or not, once he was stable enough, I would do all I could to bring him back.

"Okay, sir," he replied, convinced that it wouldn't take long, "I'll be back soon."

"I know you will, brother. I know you will," I told him.

Soon he was being loaded onto a medevac* helicopter and flown to a more advanced medical facility where he would get the surgery he needed—a place where they might be able to save his leg.

I went back to my camp, a compound of tents and buildings we called Sharkbase sandwiched between the large U.S. military base of Camp Ramadi and the Euphrates River.

I went to my room on the second floor of the building that housed our TOC, a once lavish structure with ornate columns that had previously belonged to members of Saddam Hussein's regime.

---

\* Medevac: stands for *medical evacuation*, the movement and en route care provided by medical personnel to the wounded being evacuated from the battlefield to a medical treatment facility, or the transfer of patients from one medical treatment facility to another by medical personnel. Similar but slightly different from casevac, or *casualty evacuation*.

Now it was our headquarters and barracks, with sandbagged windows and makeshift furniture. I sat down on my crude bed, constructed of plywood and two-by-fours.

Reality set in: we were only one month into our deployment. My guys were getting in gunfights on a daily basis. The city of Ramadi, where we operated, was crawling with insurgents. And the insurgents were good: they were well equipped, well trained, and well disciplined. They fought with tenacity and ruthlessness.

Of course, we were better. Our training, gear, and attitude were among the best of any combat troops in the world. We were in Ramadi to make the city safe for the local populace by taking the fight to the enemy—to hunt the evil insurgents down in the streets and kill them. All of them.

But we weren't bulletproof. We couldn't run around this city day in and day out and not expect to take casualties. If you cut wood, you get sawdust. When you wage war, especially in violent urban combat, you take casualties. That was the nature of the business. Oddly enough, up until this point, SEALs in Iraq had been very lucky. Three years into the war, only a handful of SEALs had been wounded—and none had been killed. The incidents were fairly random, often more bad luck than anything else.

But we weren't going to get lucky this whole deployment. The proof was evident, as I'd just witnessed, seeing my wounded SEAL, pale from blood loss, hazy from morphine, and lucky—so extremely lucky—to be alive.

The wounded SEAL was a young man. This was only his second SEAL platoon and his second deployment to Iraq. He was an excellent SEAL operator and a crucial member of the team. A great guy to be around: Faithful. Loyal. Funny.

Although all the SEALs in the task unit were different, they were also, in many ways, the same. Sure, they had quirks and little personality traits that made them individuals. Of course, they were far from perfect. We all are.

But at the same time, all of them, individually, were amazing people. Patriotic. Selfless. They were in "the Teams"—what we

SEALs call our community of Naval Special Warfare SEAL Teams—for the same reasons: to serve, to do their duty, and to offer everything they had for the task unit, the team, and our great nation.

And I was in charge of them.

But being "in charge" fell short of explaining the way I felt about these men. All of them. They were my friends, because I joked and laughed and carried on with them. They were my brothers, because we shared the common bond of our fraternal order. They were also like my children, because I was responsible for what they did—good and bad—and it was my job to protect them to the best of my ability: I had to overwatch them as they overwatched the city from rooftops and moved through the violent streets.

They gave me everything they had. At work, in training, and now on the battlefield. In turn, they were everything to me. In many ways I was closer to them than I was to my own parents, my siblings, even my wife and actual children. Of course I loved my family. But the men in this task unit were also my family, and I wanted nothing more than to take care of them.

But as much as I wanted to protect them, we had a job to do. A job that was violent and dangerous and unforgiving. A job that required me to put them at risk—tremendous risk—over and over and over again. This was an example of the Dichotomy of Leadership, perhaps the ultimate Dichotomy of Leadership that a combat leader must face: it is a combat leader's duty to care about his troops more than anything else in the world—and yet, at the same time, a leader must accomplish the mission. That means the leader must make decisions and execute plans and strategies that might cost the men he loves so much their very lives.

And this was incredibly difficult for me. Because in Ramadi, it wasn't a matter of *if* we would lose someone. It was a matter of *when*.

This is not to say I was fatalistic. I wasn't. It doesn't mean I thought we had to take casualties. I prayed we would not. We did everything we could to mitigate the risks we could control in order to prevent casualties.

But it did mean that I was facing reality. The reality was that U.S. Army Soldiers and Marines were being wounded and killed every day in Ramadi. *Every day.*

We continually attended memorial services for these fallen heroes.

I recognized that this deployment to Ramadi was completely different from my first deployment to Iraq in 2003–2004, where things had been much more controlled and much less kinetic. In Ramadi in 2006, the violent, sustained urban combat held risks that were beyond our control. And every day that my men were in the field, which was almost every day, I knew it could be *The Day.*

That was the heaviest burden of command.

And then *The Day* came.

On August 2, 2006, Leif and his Charlie Platoon SEALs, along with the Iraqi Army platoon for whom they were combat advisors, teamed up with our U.S. Army brethren from Team Bulldog* for a large clearance operation in South-Central Ramadi. The operation kicked off in the early morning hours, and for the first hour or so, all was quiet.

Suddenly, a single shot rang out, quickly followed by a frantic "man down" call over the radio. Ryan Job, an outstanding young Charlie Platoon SEAL machine gunner, had been hit in the face by an enemy sniper's bullet. He was gravely wounded. All hell broke loose in South-Central as insurgents started shooting from multiple directions. Leif and Charlie Platoon fought to get Ryan evacuated, and Team Bulldog M2 Bradley Fighting Vehicles and M1A2 Abrams tanks came to their rescue with heavy firepower. Charlie Platoon loaded Ryan into a medevac vehicle and sent him off the battlefield to proper medical care. Then Leif and the rest of Charlie Platoon and their Iraqi soldiers patrolled back

---

* Team Bulldog: Bravo Company, 1st Battalion, 37th Armored Regiment, 1st Armored Division.

to Combat Outpost Falcon (or COP Falcon), a fortified U.S. Army position several dangerous blocks away. But the fighting in South-Central Ramadi only escalated as enemy fighters flooded the area. Charlie Platoon could hear the gunfire as their U.S. Army brethren from Team Bulldog—Main Gun Mike and his Soldiers—were still engaged in a vicious gunfight that spread across multiple city blocks. Leif and the leadership of his platoon discussed it briefly, and finally Leif called me on the radio and requested permission to go back out and take down some buildings where suspected enemy fighters were holed up. "Do it," I told him.

Leif and his platoon did everything they could to mitigate risk. They rode to the suspected buildings in heavily armored Bradley Fighting Vehicles. They had the Bradleys soften the target buildings with fire from their powerful 25mm chain guns. They even had the Bradleys ram through the walls of the compounds so that the platoon could get off the open street and have some protection from enemy bullets as they moved toward the buildings to breach the entryways. But even that couldn't mitigate all the risk. And it didn't.

I watched on a live video feed from a drone overhead as Charlie Platoon dismounted from the Bradleys and entered a building. I could tell the gunfire was heavy. Once my SEALs entered the building, I could no longer see what was happening.

A few long minutes after they entered, I saw a group of SEALs carrying a casualty out of the building and back to a waiting Bradley nearby. It was one of ours. A lifeless body.

As I watched from the TOC, a horrible pit opened up in my stomach. I wanted to cry and scream and throw up and shake my fists at the sky.

But I had to stifle those emotions—I had a job to do. So I simply stood by the radio and waited for Leif to call me. I did not call him, because I knew he had work to do and I did not want to interfere with what he was doing.

A few minutes later, he called. I could tell he was forcing himself to sound calm, but I heard a flood of emotions in his voice.

He gave the report: as Charlie Platoon entered the building, they were engaged by enemy fighters from an adjacent building. As SEAL machine gunner Marc Lee courageously stepped into a doorway to engage the enemy fighters and protect the rest of his SEAL teammates entering the hallway behind him, he was struck by enemy fire and killed. It was over instantly.

Marc Alan Lee, an amazing warrior, friend, brother, son, husband, uncle, man of faith, comedian, and truly incredible spirit of a human being, was gone. This was on top of the fact that Ryan Job, another Charlie Platoon machine gunner and saint of a human being, had already been severely wounded and was in a medically induced coma and en route to surgical facilities in Germany. Ryan's fate was yet unknown.

The burden of such loss settled heavily on my soul.

When Leif got back to base, I could see his heart was heavy with grief. His eyes were filled not only with tears but with doubt and questions and the solemn weight of responsibility. Leif never even mentioned that he had also been wounded: a bullet fragment had entered his back, just missing the protection provided by his body armor. He didn't care about his wounded flesh. It was his heart that was broken.

A day passed.

Leif came to my office. I could see his soul was in absolute turmoil.

As the leader on the ground, Leif had made the decision to go back into the firestorm. I had approved that decision. But it was Leif who carried the burden that he had survived and Marc had not.

"I feel like I made the wrong decision," Leif said quietly. "I just wish I could take it back. I wish I would have done something—anything—differently so Marc would still be here with us."

I could see that this was tearing Leif apart. He felt that in all that chaos and all that madness, he could have made a different decision, chosen a different path.

But he was wrong.

"No, Leif," I told him slowly, "there was no decision to make. Those Army Soldiers were in a vicious battle—a massive fight— and they needed our help, they needed our support. You gave it to them. The only other option would have been to sit back and let the Army fight it out by themselves. You couldn't let Charlie Platoon sit inside the protected compound and let Team Bulldog take the risk and take the casualties. That's not what we do. We are a team. We take care of each other. There was no other choice— there was no decision to make."

Leif was quiet. He looked at me and slowly nodded. As hard as it was to hear, he knew I was right. He knew he couldn't have sat on the sidelines while other Americans were in harm's way and needed help, in what was probably the largest single engagement in the months-long campaign of the Battle of Ramadi. If he had, everyone in the platoon would have known it was the wrong decision. Leif would have known it was wrong, too. But with the weight of such a burden on his soul, he needed more reassurance.

So, I continued: "We are Frogmen. We are SEALs. We are American fighting men. If there is something we can do to help our brothers-in-arms, we help. That is what we do. You know that. Marc knew that. We all know that. That is who we are."

"I just wish I could trade places with Marc," Leif said, his eyes teared up with emotion. "I'd do anything to bring him back."

"Look," I said. "We don't have a crystal ball. We don't know when guys are going to get wounded or killed. If we could know that, then we wouldn't go out on those particular operations. But we don't know. We can't know. The only way we can guarantee everyone will be safe is to do nothing at all and let other troops do the fighting. But that is wrong—and you know it. We must do our utmost to win. Of course, we have to mitigate whatever risks we can, but in the end, we cannot eliminate every risk. We still have to do our duty."

Leif nodded again. He knew I was right. He believed it because it was the truth.

But it did not take away the punishing torment of losing Marc. Marc's death was something Leif would carry with him forever. I already knew that. And so did Leif.

It was difficult to grasp, the hardest and most painful of all the dichotomies of leadership: to care about your men more than anything in the world—so much so that you'd even willingly trade your life for theirs—and yet, at the same time, to lead those men on missions that could result in their deaths.

Even back in the States in a non-hostile environment, SEAL training in preparation for deployment was dangerous. To mitigate every danger would mean that trainees could never conduct parachute jumps, fast rope from helicopters, board ships from small boats, drive vehicles in high-speed convoys at night using only night vision, or conduct live-fire training drills. Unfortunately, every few years, despite strong safety measures and controls, a SEAL is killed or seriously injured during this high-risk training. And yet to not take the risks inherent in conducting realistic training would put more SEALs in even greater danger when they deployed to combat zones not fully prepared for missions they would be called upon to execute. So even though a leader must care deeply for his troops—a leader must also put those troops at risk, in training and even more so in combat. Of course, it is incumbent upon the leader to mitigate the risks that can be controlled. But there will always be risks beyond the leader's control, and the potential consequences can be deadly.

That dichotomy, of caring for your men's welfare while simultaneously putting them at risk to accomplish the mission, is something felt by every combat leader—and was felt to the core by the leaders on the ground in Ramadi. Because while we were determined to do our utmost to close with and destroy the enemy to help secure Ramadi, we also knew that victory would be paid for in the blood of our most promising young American men and women.

And the blood continued to be shed by Task Unit Bruiser. After Ryan was wounded and Marc was killed, we took other minor casualties—small flesh wounds and little injuries—but nothing serious. Then, on September 29, only weeks from the end of our deployment, Leif and I were in our tactical operations center listening to the radio traffic while the other SEAL platoon of Task Unit Bruiser, Delta Platoon, was outside the wire on a combat operation. We listened as Delta Platoon reported enemy movement and passed updates on enemy fighters killed, all of which were part of an ordinary day in Ramadi. Then we heard Delta Platoon's request for casualty evacuation. From the radio traffic it was clear that several SEALs were wounded. It sounded severe.

My heart sank. Immediate support from a U.S. Army Quick Reaction Force rapidly launched and headed to Delta Platoon's position. A few minutes later, the U.S. Army tactical operations radioed that multiple SEALs were wounded, with one SEAL described as "urgent surgical," meaning he needed immediate medical attention and was at risk of dying. We continued to listen to the radio calls solemnly, with hopes that our wounded brothers, especially the critically wounded ones, would be okay.

A call from the battalion commander of the 1/506th* shattered those hopes. He gave me the grave news. Three of the men were wounded, but each had injuries that would heal—they were not at risk of losing life or limb. But then this bold and professional battalion commander grew quiet for a moment. He told me a fourth man was also wounded: Mikey Monsoor was hurt very badly. His voice trembled slightly. He told me he didn't think Mikey was going to make it.

For what seemed like an eternity, Leif and I waited for an update. Finally, we got word from the field hospital that crushed our souls. Michael Anthony Monsoor, an exceptional young SEAL, beloved by everyone in the platoon and task unit, another saint of a human being—an unbelievably strong, determined, kind,

---

* 1/506th: 1st Battalion, 506th Parachute Infantry Regiment of the U.S. Army's 101st Airborne Division. 506th was the legendary "Band of Brothers" unit whose World War II exploits were detailed in the book *Band of Brothers* by Stephen Ambrose and the HBO series of the same name based on the book.

compassionate, and inspiring young man—had died from his wounds.

Once the rest of Delta Platoon had been extracted from the field, I received a call from my friend Seth Stone, the Delta Platoon Commander, who gave me the details of what had occurred on the operation. He told me that an enemy fighter had tossed a hand grenade onto the rooftop of one of Delta Platoon's sniper overwatch positions. In the most completely selfless act possible, Mikey Monsoor heroically dove on top of that grenade, shielding three of his teammates from the blast. He sacrificed himself to save them. The operation would likely have been Mikey's last mission in Ramadi, just days before he was scheduled to fly home.

Just as Leif struggled with the loss of Marc, Seth bore the crushing weight of losing Mikey. Seth continued to lead missions and completed his turnover with the SEALs who had arrived to replace us, but I could tell his soul was tormented by the loss of Mikey. When we got back to America, only a few short weeks after Mikey's death, Seth told me his feelings as we sat in our task unit office after work.

"I feel like it is my fault that Mikey died. I feel responsible," Seth told me with tears in his eyes.

I thought about it for a moment and then told him the truth: "We are responsible."

I paused for a moment. Seth didn't say a word. He was surprised by what I had said.

"We *are* responsible," I said again. "It was our strategy. We came up with it. We knew the risks. You planned the missions. I approved them. We were the leaders. And we are responsible for everything that happened during that deployment. Everything. That's the way it is. We can't escape that. That is what being a leader is."

I looked at Seth. It was clear that his heart was broken. Both Leif and Seth—as tough as they were on the battlefield, as determined as they were to accomplish their missions, as aggressive as they were in pursuit of the enemy—cared for and loved their guys more than anything else in the world. They would have given anything to trade places with their fallen men. Anything. But that wasn't an option. That isn't the way the world works.

And now here they both were, dealing with the aftermath of the ultimate Dichotomy of Leadership: as much as you care for your men, as a leader you have to do your duty—you have to accomplish the mission. And that involves risk, and it could very well cost people's lives.

My last statement was sinking into Seth's mind. Finally he spoke. "I keep replaying the mission in my mind—trying to figure out what I could have done differently. Maybe I should have put that overwatch in a different building? Maybe I should have told them to set up on the second floor instead of the rooftop? Maybe we shouldn't have even done this mission?" His voice got more and more emotional as he listed these thoughts.

"Seth," I told him calmly. "Hindsight is twenty-twenty. There are a million things that could have been done differently if we knew exactly what was going to unfold that day. But we didn't. You picked that building because it was the best tactical position in the area. You had guys on the roof because that gave them the best visibility—and thereby the best protection. And you did this mission because that is what we do: we take the fight to the enemy. You had done countless operations like this. You mitigated every risk possible. But you couldn't know the outcome."

Seth nodded. Like Leif, he knew this was true. But it did not alleviate the pain of losing Mikey.

Over the next few weeks, as we stood down from deployment, turned in gear, and completed administrative requirements, Seth and I talked about his future. Leif and I had orders to report to training commands so we could pass on the leadership lessons we had learned in Ramadi to the next generation of SEALs who would go forward into the fray in Iraq and Afghanistan. Seth was undecided on what to do next with his life. He wasn't sure if he was going to stay in the Navy. It had been a hard deployment. Under constant pressure for six straight months, Seth had suffered several of his men wounded and one killed. He had faced fear and death on an almost daily basis.

At the same time, SEAL Team Three needed someone to take over my job as commander of Task Unit Bruiser. They had offered the job to Seth.

"I don't know," he told me. "I don't know if I can do it again."

"I know," I told him, understanding his mentality. He had been through hell. "You don't have to take the job. You can do whatever you want. You can get out of the Teams. Travel. Surf. Go get your MBA. Make a bunch of money. You can go do all that. And that is cool if you want to. You've done more for me and for the Teams than I ever could have asked of you. But I'll tell you something else. There are two SEAL platoons that need a leader. They need someone to look out for them and take care of them on and off the battlefield. You have more combat experience than anyone on this team. No one could do a better job leading this task unit than you can. You can do whatever you want—but these guys, they need you. They need a leader. And that isn't going to change."

Seth sat quietly for a few seconds. He had given everything in Ramadi. He had so many opportunities waiting if he got out of the Navy—he was extremely intelligent, creative, and industrious, and he already had an incredible résumé. I knew Seth had aspirations beyond the military, to pursue other, different challenges as a civilian. I would understand if he walked away from the Navy. He had done his share. I sat and watched Seth ponder silently. Then I saw his expression change and a look of confidence come across his face.

"Alright," Seth said as he stood up from his chair.

"Alright, what?" I asked.

"I'm going," he said as he moved toward the door.

"Going where?" I asked.

"I'm going to tell the executive officer that I'm taking this task unit. I'm taking command of Task Unit Bruiser. I have to," he said. "There is no decision to make."

Seth smiled and walked out the door.

*There is no decision to make,* I thought to myself. Even with all those other options in life, there was no other option for Seth. He knew what the right thing was. He knew his duty. And he did it.

Just as he had in Ramadi, time and time again, Seth stepped forward—he stepped up. He shouldered the heavy burden of command once more, to struggle with the opposing forces that make up the countless dichotomies of leadership. To balance being a leader and being a follower. Being confident, but not cocky. To be aggressive, but still cautious. To be bold, but at the same time thoughtful.

And most significant, he chose to face the ultimate dichotomy: to train, work with, and develop a team of friends and brothers, to care about those men more than anything in the world and then lead those men on missions that could get them killed.

That is the burden. That is the challenge. That is the dichotomy.

*That is leadership.*

## Principle

There are limitless dichotomies in leadership, and a leader must carefully balance between these opposite forces. But none are as difficult as this: to care deeply for each individual member of the team, while at the same time accepting the risks necessary to accomplish the mission. A good leader builds powerful, strong relationships with his or her subordinates. But while that leader would do anything for those team members, the leader must recognize there is a job to do. And that job might put the very people the leader cares so much about at risk.

In war, this is the ultimate dichotomy: a leader may have to send his most treasured asset—his people—into a situation that gets them wounded or killed. If his relationships are too close and he can't detach from his emotions, he might not be able to make tough choices that involve risk to his men. With that attitude, the team will get nothing done—that team fails the mission. At the other end of the spectrum, if a leader cares too much about accomplishing the mission, he may sacrifice the health and safety of his men without gaining any significant advantage. Beyond the horrible impact it has on the men, it also impacts the team, who recognize the leader as callous and no longer respect and follow him. The team will fall apart.

While not as extreme, this dichotomy reveals itself in the civilian sector as well. This is one of the most difficult dichotomies to balance, and it can be easy to go too far in either direction. If leaders develop overly close relationships with their people, they may not be willing to make those people do what is necessary to complete a project or a task. They may not have the wherewithal to lay off individuals with whom they have relationships, even if it is the right move for the good of the company. And some leaders get so close to their people that they don't want to have hard conversations with them—they don't want to tell them that they need to improve.

On the other hand, if a leader is too detached from the team, he or she may overwork, overexpose, or otherwise harm its members while achieving no significant value from that sacrifice. The leader may be too quick to fire people to save a buck, thereby developing the reputation of not caring about the team beyond its ability to support the strategic goals.

So leaders must find the balance. They must push hard without pushing too hard. They must drive their team to accomplish the mission without driving them off a cliff.

### Application to Business

"These people work hard!" the regional manager told me emphatically. He oversaw five mining operations, which pulled raw materials out of the ground and sold them on the market as commodities. It was a straightforward business: the cheaper the cost of production, the more money the business made. But even with commodities, human beings' lives and livelihoods come into play.

"I know they do, I've seen them out there in the field," I replied.

"You've seen them for a few hours. That's nothing compared to the days, weeks, months, and years on end these folks work to make this place function," the regional manager replied in an aggressive tone.

The regional manager clearly didn't think I got it. I looked at it from his perspective—he was right, I couldn't fully appreciate what these men and women did every day in the mines. But his aggressiveness also came from the fact that he thought I was one of "them," one of the corporate know-it-alls who had been sent down from the ivory tower to help him try to "fix his problem." He was, of course, right: I had been sent from corporate to help him fix his problem.

Eight months ago, corporate shut down one of his mines, moving the number of mines he oversaw from six down to five. The cost to produce had become too high, and the mine simply wasn't making enough money. When they shut it down, the regional manager kept about a quarter of the employees on board, spreading them around his other mines. Corporate fought this, but he fought harder, assuring his chain of command that with the additional manpower at each of the remaining mines, production would increase across the board. But it seemed evident that what really drove the regional manager's decision was the fact that he cared about his workforce—truly and deeply cared. He was a third-generation miner. He knew the hardships of the job.

My conversation with him was not going well. I had to de-escalate.

"I know that I don't fully understand how hard they work," I told him, admitting I didn't completely know the level of effort his people put in. "I'm definitely no expert. But it is certainly obvious how hard they work, even from only a couple of hours' worth of observation."

That wasn't good enough for the regional manager.

"They aren't just hard workers," he responded. "They have

skills. They are some of the best operators in the world. Take Miguel, over there on the backhoe. He is one of the best I've ever seen." He pointed out the window at a massive backhoe busily moving earth into a giant dump truck.

"Yeah. He runs that thing like it was part of his body. He is good," I told the regional manager.

"And you know what?" the regional manager continued. "He isn't just a good equipment operator—he's a good man. He's got a wife and four kids. Good kids."

"Family man," I confirmed.

"Damn right," the regional manager told me. "Damn right."

"Well, let's go to the office and talk through some of these numbers," I said, not wanting to put off the inevitable conversation any longer. The regional manager knew the numbers better than I did. The surplus of personnel from the mine that had closed had increased production at each of his remaining mines, but not by nearly enough to make up for the added expenses. He had too many employees now, and he knew it. The remaining five mining operations for which he was responsible were not making enough money.

We went into his office and sat down.

"I know what you are going to say," he told me. From the tone of his voice, I could tell he wanted to pick a fight—he wanted to be mad at me. I had to tread carefully.

"Well. I guess I don't need to say much, then," I said. "The numbers speak for themselves."

"The numbers don't tell the whole story," the regional manager declared.

"Of course they don't," I responded. "But the numbers tell the part of the story that pays the bills."

"There's more to it than that!" he replied, clearly frustrated.

"I know there is," I told him, trying to be empathetic.

"Do you?" he responded aggressively.

I decided I needed to put him in check.

"Yes," I told him firmly. "Yes, I absolutely do know."

The regional manager sat there looking at me, slightly surprised at my tone as I now claimed to understand his business. But it wasn't his business I was claiming to know. It was the situation he was facing as a leader.

"I know there are lots of people out there," I said. "Lots of people who depend on you to make the right decisions—decisions that determine if they will continue to have a job or not; decisions that determine if they can pay their mortgage and put food on the table for their families. Those are heavy decisions and those are hard decisions. I've been there. I have had people's lives hinging upon decisions that I made. On what missions we did. On what areas we went into. On who I assigned to do what. I sent my men— my friends, my brothers—into harm's way over and over and over again. And the outcome was not always good."

The regional manager was now listening—really listening to me for the first time. I had finally connected with him.

"Look," I continued, "you are the leader. And that comes with a heavy burden. In the military, we call it the 'burden of command.' It is the responsibility you feel for the lives of the people who work for you. In the SEAL Teams, I was dealing with lives— here you deal with people's livelihoods. It isn't the exact same thing, but it is close. People are counting on you to keep their paychecks coming so they can feed their families. And you care about these people, just as you should. Just like I cared about my men—they were everything to me. They still are. That is one of the most difficult dichotomies of leadership."

"What is?" the regional manager asked.

"The fact that you care about your people more than anything—but at the same time you have to lead them. And as a leader, you might have to make decisions that hurt individuals on your team. But you also have to make decisions that will allow you to continue the mission for the greater good of everyone on the team. If military leaders decided that they were simply going to shield their troops from every risk at all costs, what would they get accomplished?"

"Well, they wouldn't accomplish anything," he admitted.

"That's exactly right," I said. "Where would our country be without the military doing its job? I'll tell you: we wouldn't even have a country. That's why military leaders have to do what they do. And you are sitting in a very similar position. You've done everything you can to save jobs. But the work isn't there. It just isn't. You've been struggling for eight months. How many employees did you transfer from the mine that closed?" I asked him.

"One hundred and forty-seven people," the regional manager answered.

"And how many people did you employ at your other five mines prior to their transfer?" I asked.

"About six hundred," he said.

"So, in an effort to try to save the jobs of a hundred and forty-seven employees," I noted, "you are putting at risk the other five mines and six hundred jobs—the entire mission. If you don't make some hard decisions, that is exactly what will happen."

The regional manager sat quietly. It was sinking in. I could see it in his eyes.

"But . . . I don't know . . . I don't know if I can do it," he said soberly. "Some of these folks are like family to me."

"Well—let me tell you this," I replied. "If you don't step up and lead, what do you think corporate will do?"

"They'll either shut us down . . . or . . ." He trailed off, not wanting to admit the other obvious possibility.

"Or what?" I asked.

"Or get rid of me," he replied.

"Exactly," I agreed. "Now what would be better for everyone here? To get shut down completely? Or to have someone else who doesn't care as much for the team as you do come in, take over, and drive down costs by chopping the staff to the extreme? I know it's hard. I know. But if you don't do what you need to do—what you know you need to do—you aren't helping anyone. And you definitely aren't leading. In fact, just the opposite. If you don't make the hard decision, you will be hurting the people you care about, not helping them. That's another dichotomy: in order to help your team, sometimes you have to hurt them. Just like a doctor performing a surgery. Surgery is a brutal thing: cutting open a body and removing parts of it, then sewing it back together. But in order to save a life, a surgeon has to do just that. What you have to do here is also brutal—I get it. But failure to do it is going to have far more brutal consequences."

The regional manager was nodding. He understood. He was a good-hearted leader who cared for his people, an admirable and important quality in a leader. But he had strayed too far and unbalanced the dichotomy by caring more about his people than he did about the mission. He lost sight of what was most important strategically. To protect some employees, he had placed his entire mission and every other employee at risk. Now, he understood that doing so was a failure of leadership. Once he acknowledged this, he could then course correct and rebalance the dichotomy. He had to make the tough decisions. He didn't like it, but he understood.

Over the next two weeks, the regional manager let go of almost eighty people. He didn't like it. But he had to do it. He had to lead. That cost savings moved the mines from the red into the black. They were profitable once again and on a sustainable path for the foreseeable future. The regional manager now understood this most difficult dichotomy of leadership: a leader must care about the troops, but at the same time the leader must complete the mission, and in doing so there will be risks and sometimes unavoidable consequences to the troops. The regional manager now realized that he had to balance caring for his people with accomplishing the mission and that failing to balance those two opposing goals would result in his failure to do either.

SEAL Team Seven Echo Platoon rolling out on a nighttime direct action mission to capture or kill suspected terrorists in Baghdad, 2003. Note: the Humvees had no armor and doors were removed so that the SEAL operators inside could face outward, enabling them to both return fire with their rifles as well as present their body armor ballistic plates to threats for at least some level of protection.

(Photo courtesy of Jocko Willink)

# CHAPTER 2

## Own It All, but Empower Others

*Jocko Willink*

### FALLUJAH, IRAQ: 2003

There was blood all over the floor and smoke in the air. I heard shots fired outside, but I wasn't quite sure who was shooting or what they were shooting at. I moved down the hallway, confirming that all the rooms had been cleared. I soon found the source of the blood: a wounded Iraqi civilian, on whom my SEAL hospital corpsman—a highly trained combat medic—was working to apply medical care.

"What happened?" I asked.

"He was by the door on the breach," the SEAL corpsman answered. "He must have been close. Lost an eye and part of his hand. Hit an artery. That's why there's so much blood."

The explosive breaching charge our SEAL platoon had used to enter was designed with enough power to open the door but minimize any potential collateral damage to civilians inside the house. This man was apparently just on the other side of the door and hit by shrapnel.

"Is he going to make it?" I asked.

"Yeah. I've got the bleeding stopped," the corpsman answered.

He motioned to a tourniquet he had on the Iraqi's arm. He was now working on the man's eye.

"Roger," I said, and continued on. The hallway was a loop that circled the whole floor of the building. It ran back into itself near the stairwell that we had ascended to start the clearance. Checking the last room, I saw that it had been cleared.

I keyed up my radio and announced: "Target secure. Set security and start the search."

It was the fall of 2003 and my SEAL platoon had launched on this operation to capture or kill a terrorist leader in the Iraqi city of Fallujah. It was one of the most dangerous areas in Iraq, with high probability of an enemy attack. I was the platoon commander, but my senior enlisted leaders knew what to do. They took charge, ensured security was set, and initiated the search of each room. We detained thirteen military-age males, any one of whom could have been the terrorist we were after. We zip-tied their hands, searched them, and prepared to walk them out of the building to our vehicles for transport from the target.

A voice crackled over the radio headset on my ear: "Might want to hurry up a little in there, Jocko. The natives are getting restless out here."

It was my task unit commander on the radio. He was outside, controlling the Humvees* and the dismounted SEALs on external security, as well as coordinating with the U.S. Army units in the area. As the ground force commander, he was in charge of the entire operation, including me and my assault force. My assault force had entered the building where the terrorist was believed to be located, cleared and secured it, and now it sounded as though we needed to hurry up our search.

"Roger that," I replied.

There was some confusion on target for my assault force—even more than we might have expected. Clearing a building can

---

* High Mobility Multipurpose Wheeled Vehicle, or HMMWV, spoken as "Humvee."

be complicated, but the layout of this building was particularly unorthodox: lots of small, adjoining rooms and nooks to be cleared. To further complicate matters, the multiple explosive breaching charges and crash grenades* we deployed left a cloud of thick smoke in the air that obscured our vision and added to the confusion. There were also a number of prisoners and the wounded Iraqi requiring medical attention, so it was no surprise: we were bogged down and had lost our momentum. It seemed no one was quite sure what the next step should be. I told a couple of my guys to start wrapping it up.

"We need to leave," I said. They nodded their heads and kept doing what they were doing. No progress was made. On top of everything else, I had heard shots fired outside, which could have been anything from warning shots to an escalating firefight. The shots were what had prompted the warning from my task unit commander. I had to get the platoon moving.

"Listen up!" I yelled loudly. Suddenly, the whole building was quiet. "If you aren't on rear security, start moving back here to me. Check out, grab a prisoner, and escort them out back to the Humvees. We are taking all military-age males. *Go!*"

Almost instantly, the platoon was back on track. Guys moved toward the exit, checked out with me, grabbed a prisoner, and took them down the stairs to the street. A minute later, my leading petty officer (LPO)—a key leader in the platoon—came up to me, tapped me on the shoulder, and reported that all prisoners had been escorted out. Only the two of us and the last two guys on rear security were still in the building.

"Alright then, let's roll," I said. The LPO told the rear security team to collapse—to move toward the exit—and once they reached us, we made our way out of the building. We waited at the doorway to the street, and when the rear security element reached us, we all moved to our assigned Humvees.

---

* Crash grenade, or "flash bang" grenade, a nonlethal device that creates a bright flash and loud explosion meant to stun but not injure.

Once we were in, the lead navigator made the call: "Up count from the rear."

The vehicle commanders in each Humvee sounded off.

"Six is up."

"Five is up."

"Four is up."

"Three is up."

"Two is up."

"One is up—we're rolling."

And with that, the convoy moved out, down the darkened streets of Fallujah, guns pointed outward, eyes peering through our night-vision goggles, scanning for threats. Traveling at a fast pace and completely blacked out proved effective in avoiding an enemy ambush. Half an hour later, we were safe inside the perimeter of an Army forward operating base. We turned over our prisoners to the Army detention facility and the intelligence personnel with whom we had been working.

Once that turnover was complete, we got back on the main road that connected Fallujah and Baghdad. The roads in the vicinity of Fallujah were rough—damaged from continuous violence. But once outside of Fallujah, the road became a highway not unlike many found in America. An hour or so later, we were back at our base adjacent to Baghdad International Airport. A few short months earlier, before the war kicked off, the airport had been named Saddam Hussein International Airport.

Once on the base, we followed our standard operating procedures (SOPs). First, we refueled the Humvees in case we got another call to go out. We wanted to be ready. Next, we parked the Humvees, dismounted, and mustered in our platoon planning area to debrief the mission. Still wearing our op gear just in case we needed to relaunch on short notice, we went through each detail of the operation: where mistakes were made, what we could have done better, and what we did well. Once the debrief was complete, we went back to the vehicles to perform the maintenance of the platoon gear: in this case, the Humvees, heavy weapons, navigation systems, and communications gear. When that was complete, we moved to our weapons-cleaning area and cleaned our personal weapons. Only after the team and platoon gear had been taken care of did the SEALs clean and perform maintenance on their personal gear and then, finally, themselves—a shower and perhaps a quick bite to eat. As soon as that was complete, the assistant platoon commander and I began looking at possible operations for the next night, preparing approval documents to run up the chain of command, and building operations briefs to give to the platoon. By six or seven o'clock in the morning, we would go to sleep for a few hours and be up in time for lunch at eleven.

That quickly became the cycle for running these operations—conducting largely nighttime direct action raids targeting suspected terrorists or Saddam Hussein regime loyalists. It might seem hard to believe, but like most SEAL platoons at the time, we had no previous real combat experience. Everyone in my platoon had missed the first Gulf War, which had lasted only seventy-two hours with limited ground combat. We were too young to have fought in Grenada or Panama. SEALs who saw action in Somalia were few and far between, and there weren't any with us. The closest most of us had come to combat before the Iraq War kicked off had been anti-smuggling operations in the Northern Arabian Gulf, enforcing UN sanctions against Saddam's government. We boarded ships and smaller wooden vessels called dhows that were suspected of smuggling oil or other contraband out of Iraq. We shadowed the vessels from our small boats or by helicopter, and once we were confident they had entered international waters, we boarded the vessels, quickly made our way to the bridge of the ship, and took control of the vessel and crew. Once we had them secured, we would call in a U.S. Navy or Coast Guard boarding team to take over for us.

While the anti-smuggling operations during the late 1990s and early 2000s were better than nothing, they were hardly challenging missions. I conducted a number of them while I was an assistant platoon commander, but we never fired a shot—and to be frank, there was never even a real, legitimate threat. But it was our mission and we did it professionally.

Those missions were a far cry from being on the ground in Iraq hunting down terrorists. In Iraq, the threat level was infinitely higher and the operations infinitely more aggressive. Because we were all so inexperienced in combat, I got down in the weeds on much of the planning and execution of the operations. With my first time in real combat, I subconsciously felt I had something to prove—to myself and to those around me. In order to ensure we did the best job possible, I got very granular in the entire mission process. As soon as we received a target from our intelligence group, I was all over it, looking at the routes into and out of the target, poring over the intel, helping plan the breach team sequence, task organizing the assault force, building the load-out plan for the Humvees, running rehearsals. In short, I owned everything in my world. All of it.

Of course, I wanted my junior personnel to step up, take ownership, and lead some of the missions themselves. But they didn't. And this was a little surprising, because I had solid senior and junior enlisted personnel who I knew could handle much more. But they weren't taking ownership the way I needed them to. So I continued to oversee everything in close detail. I micromanaged.

But there was only so much I could do—and so much I could own. Very quickly, our operational tempo picked up. On top of the direct action missions we conducted to capture or kill enemy insurgents, we began to conduct numerous additional operations, including airborne and vehicle-borne reconnaissance missions and other intelligence-gathering operations.

One morning we were tasked with multiple reconnaissance missions and we received information for two simultaneous potential direct action capture/kill missions that evening. I knew there was no way to own all of those operations myself. I assigned responsibility for each of the missions to four of my junior leaders and told them to come up with a plan, deconflict* with each other for assets and personnel, and check in with me after they came up with their plans. Then I stood back and let them go.

The results were beyond anything I'd expected. They took ownership. Not only did they come up with solid, tactically sound plans, they also got creative and developed new and innovative ideas to make our execution of those plans more effective. Most important, *they* took full ownership of the operations and worked with all the confidence and aggressive leadership we needed to be successful in combat. It was everything I had wished for them to do from the start. Of course, I still took Extreme Ownership—this is the underlying philosophy that guides everything I did, and still do, as a leader. I was still 100 percent responsible for their operations, their plans, the manner they executed missions, and the success or failure of those missions. But my ownership had to be balanced with Decentralized Command; I needed to allow them to own the missions at their level so they were fully empowered and could execute with conviction and lead from their positions with certitude.

The more our operational tempo picked up, the less time I had to spend in the weeds and the more ownership they demonstrated. Soon, I was doing nothing more than a cursory check of their mission plans before sending them out to conduct operations on their own without me, my assistant platoon commander, or my platoon chief—in other words, without senior SEAL supervision.

Yet my junior leaders performed tremendously well. And I learned a valuable lesson: the reason they hadn't stepped up prior to this was that I hadn't allowed it. My attitude of taking Extreme Ownership of everything had left them with nothing to own. They didn't realize it—nor did I—but my micromanagement was so controlling that they had shut down mentally. Not that they gave

---

* Deconflict: a U.S. military term for detailed coordination between units to integrate timelines, ensure maximum support to each other, and prevent friendly fire or "blue-on-blue" incidents.

up or had a bad attitude; they didn't at all. But as the leader, I had set the precedent that I would do everything myself. And when I ran everything, they just sat back and waited for me to dictate the plan and make the calls. As soon as I backed off and let them start to run things, they ran with *every*thing and they ran hard. It was beautiful to behold. I watched them delve into their missions with total intensity and dedication.

The benefits to this approach were multifaceted. First, since I was no longer in the weeds, I saw much more of the big picture. I was able to start focusing on coordination with other elements in the area, gaining a better picture of the intelligence, and making sure I fully understood the terrain and the targets in the area.

Second, since I was not focused on one specific operation, I was able to see how the different operations might support or conflict with each other. From this perspective, I was able to better allocate resources to the right places and at the right times without burning out our people or equipment.

Finally, with my subordinate leadership running the tactical operations, I had the chance to look at operations at a little higher level. I could now piece together the intelligence picture and understand how we could capture or kill the most terrorists possible. It allowed me to start looking up and out at the next level instead of down and in at my own team.

While I had known that ownership—Extreme Ownership—was critical for a leader, this situation made me realize that I had taken it too far. True Extreme Ownership meant that all responsibility rested with me, as the leader. It didn't mean that I, as the leader, personally *did* everything myself. My misunderstanding of Extreme Ownership had overrun the Decentralized Command that was integral for our platoon to execute most effectively. I had to find the right balance between taking all ownership myself and allowing my team to take ownership.

But there were other times when I hadn't taken enough ownership—when I had let the dichotomy slide too far in the other direction and been too hands-off. Prior to arriving in Iraq, my platoon was preparing and rehearsing for an important and sensitive mission. It was a maritime operation that required us to create some new techniques for rendezvousing with a vessel at sea and then transferring people under extreme conditions.

As a leader trying to practice Decentralized Command, I strove to empower my subordinate leaders and let them lead, so I tasked one of my senior SEAL petty officers to lead the operation. This included creating the new techniques and running the training and rehearsals to ensure we were prepared to execute. He was an experienced, mature SEAL with a great operational reputation, and I trusted him and knew he would get the job done. The mission called for us to work closely with a Naval Special Warfare (NSW) boat unit, the crews who operated high-speed watercraft designed to support SEAL missions. We needed to collaborate with them to understand how to best utilize their assets. The senior petty officer set up some meetings with the boat unit, and we began initial pierside dry runs, where we practiced the techniques on land, and rehearsals at sea to develop and test the procedures we were going to use. The new procedures utilized gear and equipment we were already familiar with: maritime radios, night-vision goggles, radar, one-inch tubular nylon, and some other maritime rigging. Once we had the concept figured out, it was straightforward and relatively easy.

As we continued the meetings and pierside rehearsals, I noticed my senior SEAL petty officer was running things relatively loosely compared with the approach I would normally have taken. And because I wasn't breathing down his neck, he didn't provide much oversight on the rest of the platoon either. The more slack he gave the platoon, the more they took advantage of it.

When we met the boat crew at 0700,* some of our guys would arrive at 0659. When the platoon had planned to do six

---

* 0700 military time, based on the twenty-four-hour clock, equivalent to 7:00 a.m. civilian time, based on the twelve-hour clock.

rehearsals, we would only execute three rehearsals. Guys were showing up in incomplete uniforms, even mixing in some civilian clothes. They looked unprofessional. And while the platoon was rehearsing the mission the way they predicted it would happen, they weren't rehearsing any unexpected contingencies.

This went on for a couple of weeks as we got closer and closer to executing the actual mission. I maintained my lofty attitude and allowed the senior petty officer to continue to lead with a relative amount of slack. I didn't feel comfortable with it, but I wanted him to have ownership and know that I trusted him. My gut was telling me it had gone too far; I had allowed things to get too loose. But I never addressed it with my senior petty officer or the platoon. I figured that since I had put him in charge, he had to own it.

That changed the first day we were to rehearse at sea. We had an underway time of 0600—meaning the NSW boats would launch from the pier at 0600 sharp. I showed up, in uniform, prepared and ready to go at 0530, and boarded one of the two vessels to which I had been assigned. I checked and rechecked my gear and made sure I was ready to execute.

As 0600 approached, the rest of the platoon straggled in. Two or three guys at a time, in sloppy uniforms, rushing around, running late.

By 0600, two of our guys were still missing.

The special boat unit chief approached our senior petty officer and told him it was time to get under way. The senior petty officer explained that he had just talked to the last two guys and they were running a few minutes late and that we needed to wait for them.

They arrived and crossed the brow—the gangway from the pier—onto the boat at 0607.

Seven minutes late.

I was embarrassed. Embarrassed for myself, embarrassed for the platoon, and embarrassed for the SEAL Teams. Normally a Navy ship would leave stragglers behind—and those stragglers would "miss movement," as it is called in the Navy, a substantial violation that incurs severe punishment. But since this mission revolved around our participation, the boat chief agreed we would wait for the two SEALs. But it was still inexcusable.

Finally, with all our platoon onboard, the two NSW boats got under way and moved out over the horizon, out of visibility of the shore. Once we were on station at sea in the area we had designated for rehearsal, the senior petty officer gave the order to commence. The platoon members moved into their positions and started to work, setting up rigging, breaking out our communications gear, and preparing to execute the actions at the objective. Since I was letting the senior petty officer run this mission, I carried out my assigned tasks as if I were one of the SEAL shooters—one of the frontline troopers.

Then I sensed some distress, and then panic, among the platoon.

From the conversations among the SEALs in the platoon, it was clear something was missing:

"I don't have it."

"I thought you brought it?"

"Where did you put it last time?"

"That wasn't my job."

"No one told me to get it."

I watched quietly for a few minutes as the the platoon panicked. Then, I walked over to the senior petty officer.

"What's the issue?" I asked him.

"We forgot the one-inch tubular nylon," he said dejectedly, knowing that this simple item was a mission-critical piece of equipment.

Once again I was disappointed, embarrassed, and angry. It was clear that, as the leader, I had been too hands-off.

"Roger," I told him. "Well, you better figure something out. Quick. Start with the boat chief. They might have some somewhere."

The senior petty officer asked various people if they had any extra one-inch tubular nylon. Eventually, the boat crew guys came up with enough half-inch tubular nylon that we could tie together and use to execute the mission. It was not pretty, not ideal, and not as safe as we would have liked it, but we made it work. Worse, we were now running even further behind schedule—all of which was nobody's fault but our own.

We continued with the rehearsal, completed the mock mission, and then headed back to the pier. There, we off-loaded our gear and made our way back across the base to our platoon planning space.

Back in our platoon space, I had the platoon debrief the training operation. They mentioned the missing gear and some other things that we needed to do better. But the criticism was light compared to what it should have been. I didn't say anything. As the debrief wound down, I asked, "Does anyone have anything else?" No one did. I sat for a moment to be sure. No one addressed our subpar performance. This was not good. I had to take Extreme Ownership.

I called the platoon leadership into my office. They could tell I was not happy. When the last man came in, I shut the door.

"I want to do every one of your jobs—all of them," I told them bluntly. "I know how to do them. And I know how to do them right. I know how to make sure no one is ever late. I know how to make sure we never forget anything for a mission, ever. I know exactly how to do that. And I want to do that. I want to run this platoon. I want to run every facet of this platoon to the exacting and unwavering standards that I know cannot be questioned. But I also know that isn't the right way to run a platoon. I know that will stifle your growth as SEALs and as leaders. So. I am going to give you one more chance. One more chance to ensure that nothing like this ever happens again. No one will ever be late again. No one will ever forget gear again. Everyone will be early. You will inspect all gear. You will conduct every mission, every operation, every training event, as if it is the most important thing in your life. If we drop the ball one more time, you are done. I am taking over. That will be it. Do you understand?"

The senior SEAL petty officer, a friend of mine and a solid SEAL, knew exactly where I was coming from. He knew I was right and that I meant what I said.

"We got it, sir," he replied. "This won't happen again. I will make sure of it. We all will."

And that was that. The platoon never did let me down again. A few weeks later, we deployed to Iraq and conducted combat mission after mission, aggressively pursuing the enemy throughout the country. The threat I had made of micromanagement after the maritime operation had been enough to change their attitudes, their actions, and their ownership. They never slacked off again; instead, I was the one who had to slack off a little once we got to Iraq. I had to let them take charge. I had to let them take ownership. I had to let them lead. I had to balance the dichotomy between taking too much ownership and not taking enough.

## Principle

Micromanagement and hands-off leadership styles are obviously opposites.

The micromanager tries to control every thought and action of each individual on the team. Micromanagement fails because no one person can control multiple people executing a vast number of actions in a dynamic environment, where changes in the situation occur rapidly and with unpredictability. It also inhibits the growth of subordinates: when people become accustomed to being told what to do, they begin to await direction. Initiative fades and eventually dies. Creativity and bold thought and action soon die as well. The team becomes a bunch of simple and thoughtless automatons, following orders without understanding, moving forward only when told to do so. A team like that will never achieve greatness.

The hands-off leader with a laissez-faire attitude is on the opposite end of the spectrum. Such a leader fails to provide specific direction—in some cases almost no clear direction whatsoever. Instead of a lack of thought like a team that is micromanaged, a team with a hands-off leader thinks too much. Its members have grand ideas and plans, they come up with new tactics and procedures—they even start to develop their own broad strategies beyond the boundaries of their responsibilities and competence. Such grandiose ideas and thoughts become a major problem when they are not aligned with the greater vision and goals of the company. So the troops, instead of pushing the team toward its strategic goals, move in random directions. They not only fail to provide each other with simple support but often work on projects or efforts that directly conflict with what other members of the team are doing.

In order to correctly balance these two leadership styles, a leader must find the middle ground and pay attention to the team, ensuring that the leader doesn't push too far in one direction or the other. There are some clear warning signs that indicate when a leader has leaned too far in the direction of one of these leadership styles. Here are the commons symptoms that result from micromanagement:

1. The team shows a lack of initiative. Members will not take action unless directed.
2. The team does not seek solutions to problems; instead, its members sit and wait to be told about a solution.
3. Even in an emergency, a team that is being micromanaged will not mobilize and take action.
4. Bold and aggressive action becomes rare.
5. Creativity grinds to a halt.
6. The team tends to stay inside their own silo; not stepping out to coordinate efforts with other departments or divisions for fear of overstepping their bounds.
7. An overall sense of passivity and failure to react.

Once a leader sees these behaviors in the team, corrective action must be taken. The leader must pull back from giving detailed direction; instead of explaining what the mission is and how to accomplish it, the leader should explain the broad goal of the mission, the end state that is desired, and why the mission is important and then allow the team to plan how to execute the mission. The leader should continue to monitor what is happening and check the progress of the team but refrain from giving specific guidance on the execution, unless the plan that is being formulated by the team will have extremely negative results. Finally, if there is an opportunity when time and risk levels permit, a leader can step away from the team completely and allow it to plan and execute a mission on its own. In Task Unit Bruiser, this was done regularly during our pre-deployment training cycle. Senior leadership, including Leif, the Delta Platoon commander, Seth Stone, and the senior enlisted personnel, would step back and allow junior leaders to step up, plan, and execute training missions. We saw the junior leaders quickly transform from passively waiting to be told what to do into proactive leaders who assessed problems and implemented solutions.

Here are common symptoms that indicate when a leader is too hands-off with his team:

1. Lack of vision in what the team is trying to do and how to do it.
2. Lack of coordination between individuals on the team and efforts that often compete or interfere with each other.
3. Initiative oversteps the bounds of authority, and both individuals and teams carry out actions that are beyond what they have the authorization to do.
4. Failure to coordinate. While a micromanaged team might not coordinate with other teams because it doesn't want to overstep its bounds, a team without good guidance may also fail to coordinate not out of

fear but out of ignorance. In its efforts to solve problems and accomplish the mission, the team forgets that other teams might also be maneuvering and end up interfering with their efforts.

5. The team is focused on the wrong priority mission or pursuit of solutions that are not in keeping with the strategic direction of the team or the commander's intent.

6. There are too many people trying to lead. Since everyone is trying to lead, there won't be enough people to execute. Instead of progress, the leader will see discussion; instead of action, the leader will see prolonged debate; instead of unified movement, the leader will see fractured elements pursuing individual efforts.

When these behaviors are observed by a leader, there are some basic actions to take to get the team back on course. First and foremost, clear guidance must be given. The mission, the goal, and the end state must be explained in a simple, clear, and concise manner. The team must also understand the boundaries that are in place and what actions to take should it bump up against those boundaries. If multiple, simultaneous, overlapping efforts are being pursued, the leader must decide on and clearly implement the chosen course of action. The team must also be educated on efforts being executed by other teams so that deconfliction can occur. Finally, if a team is paralyzed by too many people trying to lead—the classic case of "too many coaches, not enough players"—then the leader must assign and clearly delineate the chain of command, roles, and responsibilities of the team leaders and give them proper authority.

I saw this manifest itself in SEAL task units, including Task Unit Bruiser, when a mission tasking would be given to the platoons without a clearly assigned lead. A SEAL task unit consists of two platoons, each with its own leadership: a platoon commander, a platoon chief, an assistant platoon commander, and a leading petty officer. If a mission was given to the platoons without assigning a platoon as the lead, they would both begin to come up with their own separate and distinct plans and courses of action. The longer the platoons were left without guidance as to which one had the lead on the operation, the further they would head down the paths of their own plans, wasting time and effort. This is easily solved by delineating one platoon as the lead element on the operation and the other as the supporting element. With that clear direction, efforts were coordinated and the team could work together toward a unified plan.

But once again, the key is balance, maintaining an equilibrium where the troops have the guidance to execute but at the same time the freedom to make decisions and lead.

### Application to Business

The finished product had been sold. The problem was, the finished product wasn't finished yet. Sure, there were some functional beta models that had been manufactured one at a time by hand, but no final version had been solidified. Furthermore, no standard manufacturing process had been established for a large production run.

What made this even harder was the industry. The product was to be utilized in cars, which added some significant difficulties. First, the software to integrate it had to be interoperable with several different manufacturers and their car models. Second, the product had to fit into pre-designed spaces that allowed no significant change in shape or volume of the equipment. Finally, given the safety regulations in vehicle production, there was very little leeway with regard to material that could be used in manufacturing.

When I showed up to run leadership training aimed at developing new leaders at this growing company, things seemed to be on track. While the company was well established with many years in the industry, it was in a growth phase and needed training for newly promoted and hired leaders. The attitude at the company was excellent, and the employees were abuzz with the opportunities ahead and the promising progress on the horizon.

There was also a great deal of confidence. Much of the company's growth was geared toward supporting a high-demand signal for a new product that the company planned to release. When I first showed up to work with the company, it was in the final stages of the new product rollout. They had completed the bulk of the design, done preliminary testing on the software, and initiated the rollout of a manufacturing process for adaptation to the final design. Sales had already started, and they were strong. Overall, I was impressed with the situation and how things were going. I spent most of my time training the newly promoted and hired leaders. The rest of the time I spent in familiarization with the company's leadership and the state of the business.

When the three-day leadership development program I ran for the company's new leaders was complete, I departed with a plan to return in six weeks. At that time, I would host follow-on training for those leaders from the first course and run a new course for the next round of new hires and recently promoted leaders.

But when I returned six weeks later, the atmosphere at the company had completely changed. Gone was the enthusiasm and the confidence. Gone was the vision of opportunity and success. There was a new attitude: fear and uncertainty.

The CEO was blunt with me. "I don't think we are going to make it," he said, referring to the scheduled release of the new product. "Since the last time you were here, we have barely moved. Our progress has ground to a halt. The teams just aren't getting anything done."

"Are these the team leaders that I just trained?" I asked him, referring to the group of midlevel managers who had been through Echelon Front's basic leadership course.

"No. Not at all," the CEO answered. "They are the least of my problems. I'm not getting performance from my senior leaders."

"What seems to be the issue?" I asked.

"I don't know," he replied. "But we need to get it fixed. Can we postpone your next block of training for the midlevel managers so you can spend a few days with my senior leadership team to figure out what is wrong?"

"I think so," I answered. "Let me confirm my schedule."

I called Jamie, our director of operations at Echelon Front, who quickly shifted some events in my schedule and freed up the time so I could adapt to the CEO's request and engage with the company's senior leadership team.

"Do you want to talk to the team?" the CEO asked.

I had already put his senior leadership team through a course on Extreme Ownership and the fundamental principles of combat leadership. They seemed to have grasped it pretty well. I didn't need to say more—I needed to get in and see what was happening and where the issue was.

"No," I replied, "I have talked enough. I need to see the team in action. When is the next meeting where the whole group will be together?"

"Well, actually we have a meeting in a few minutes with everyone and then another one just after lunch," the CEO replied. "And in between those two and throughout the afternoon, I meet with the leaders and their team lead."

"Busy schedule. How many times a week do you hold those meetings?" I asked.

"We actually have them every day. There is a lot going on right now and I have to take ownership—Extreme Ownership—to keep things in check and on track."

"Got it," I replied slowly, as I wondered if I'd just gotten my first indication of the problem.

We walked down the hallway and into the first meeting. The entire leadership team was present. I thought the meeting would be a quick, broad update of what was happening. I was wrong. Each leader gave a full update of what was happening in his or her department. Minute details were covered that should have been outside the scope of the executive-level team. As courses of action were discussed, virtually indistinguishable options were presented and drawn-out arguments made, and finally, the CEO made decisions on how the various teams would execute. The meeting lasted nearly two full hours. If that wasn't bad enough, as soon as the meeting concluded, it was followed by another meeting, this time with the engineering team, which wanted guidance on what manufacturer to use for several parts of the product. That meeting, which also got bogged down in the details, lasted another forty-five minutes. Before we knew it, it was lunchtime.

I walked with the CEO back to his office. While we ate, he answered a plethora of questions that had come through e-mail and made two phone calls—not to his direct reports but to front-line engineers who explained some minute elements of the electronic components to be embedded in the new product.

After these e-mail conversations and phone calls, we went into the afternoon leadership huddle. I again hoped the meeting would be a quick confirmation of progress made and any necessary troubleshooting. Once again, I was wrong.

Like the others before it, this meeting quickly devolved into a detailed discussion of the minutiae involved in every aspect of the engineering, manufacturing, marketing, and sale of the product. The CEO drilled down on each aspect of the planning and execution and made decisions at every level. As I looked around at the others in the meeting, I expected to see frustration. But most of the faces didn't look frustrated. They sat and stared and waited for their turn to talk and get questions answered by the CEO. There was no emotion, no frustration or sense of urgency—there was no initiative in the group.

Two more days went by with much of the same: meetings, meetings, meetings. Decisions were made, almost every single one of them by the CEO. Finally, after one meeting ended, the CEO and I walked back to his office.

"Now do you see what I am talking about?" he asked.

"I do indeed," I responded.

"They aren't taking any initiative; they aren't pushing things to happen—they aren't taking ownership!" he lamented.

"That was very evident in every one of those meetings," I noted.

"So. What do I do?" the CEO asked. "How can I get them to take Extreme Ownership?"

"The answer is simple, but it isn't easy," I answered. "*You* have to *give* them ownership."

"I'm trying to—and I'm taking ownership to set the example—but they aren't taking any ownership at all!" the CEO complained.

"Yes. That is exactly what is happening: you are taking ownership—but you are taking *too much* ownership," I told the CEO.

"Too much ownership?" he asked, confused. "You didn't even tell me that was possible."

"It is. And yes, I should have explained that more clearly to you," I said. "Leaders can actually take too much ownership. Yes, with Extreme Ownership you are responsible for everything in your world. But you can't make every decision. You have to empower your team to lead, to take ownership. So you have to give them ownership.

"When a leader tries to own everything—to run every single move their team makes," I continued, "it doesn't work. Maybe it is the desire to make sure everything goes right. Maybe it is a lack of trust that subordinate leaders know what to do. Maybe it is ego—leaders want to feel they are the person who is critical for every little decision. But when a leader takes too much ownership, there is no ownership left for the team or subordinate leaders to take. So the team loses initiative. They lose momentum. They won't make any decisions. They just sit around and wait to be told what to do."

Although this was a lot to absorb, I could see it was making complete sense to the CEO.

"I've smothered them, haven't I?" he said.

"Well, that's a strong word—that implies death," I joked. "But metaphorically, yes. That is a good description of what has happened."

"So what do I do now?" the CEO asked.

"Give them space. Give them air," I instructed. "Let them breathe again. You have to let them make decisions. You have to let them plot the course. You need to tell them the destination, but you need to let them figure out how to get there. You have to let them take ownership—real ownership—of their piece of the mission. Then you will have a team with a culture of true, effective Extreme Ownership and your performance will skyrocket."

"That sounds good. But how do I actually make that happen from a tactical perspective?" the CEO inquired.

"First—let's cut down all the meetings. That is one of the reasons things aren't moving. Instead of finding solutions, right now they just ask you for the solution. When you do have meetings, stop being the 'Easy Button,'" I told him.

"The Easy Button? How am I an Easy Button?" the CEO asked.

"By answering every question, solving every problem, and making every single decision," I answered. "Why should your leaders think for themselves when they can just press the Easy Button and have you think for them and make the decisions for them as well? And they can blame you if something goes wrong because you made the decision. When you do all that for them, they don't need to think or act, and then they won't think or act. That's where these guys are at."

"But if I don't answer their questions—" the CEO began.

I cut him off: "Then they will answer the questions themselves. They will find solutions for themselves. They will work together to solve problems at the source, instead of running them up to you."

"So Decentralized Command is what you are talking about, right?" the CEO asked.

"Exactly," I said. "And that is the balance you need to find, the balance between Decentralized Command and Extreme

Ownership. When your team is too decentralized, no one knows in what direction to go. Too much ownership, and people won't act with any level of initiative."

"And I've gone too far in that direction. I've taken too much ownership," the CEO recognized.

"Yeah," I replied, "but it's okay. You are recognizing the dichotomy. Now, swing the pendulum back—but make sure you don't go too far. I see people make that mistake all the time: they overcorrect themselves. So. Make the move. Cancel some of the meetings. Let the teams and the leaders make decisions. But don't completely check out. You don't need to row the boat—or even steer it. You just have to make sure it is heading in the right direction."

Over the next few weeks, the CEO adjusted his level of control. I had to restrain him a few times and ease him away from his tendency to run everything himself. But he did check himself, and the change from his subordinate leadership—and the rest of the team—came about fairly quickly. Within a few weeks, their attitude shifted. Leaders at every level of the team began to lead. They took ownership. Progress picked up and the team got the product back on target for launch.

"Frogman on the Roof" was the radio call that let others know that SEALs were on the high ground. Here, Task Unit Bruiser SEALs, from a combined force of Charlie and Delta platoons, maneuver on the rooftop, keeping as low as possible to minimize exposure to incoming enemy bullets. Marc Lee, at left, carries his Mark 48 machine gun. At right, in the foreground, is the SEAL operator who was later gravely wounded, as described in Chapter 1.

(Photo courtesy of Todd Pitman)

# CHAPTER 3
Resolute, but Not Overbearing

*Leif Babin*

**SOUTH RAMADI, IRAQ: 2006**

Bright orange tracers streaked like laser beams just a few feet over our heads, each supersonic bullet zipping past with a thunderous crack.

*Holy shit,* I thought as we quickly ducked down behind the roof wall. *Those are friendlies shooting at us.*

I looked over at Dave Berke, who crouched down nearby. Like the other SEALs on the roof with us, we tried to stay low enough to not get our heads shot off.

Dave looked back at me and shook his head with a smile that mixed humor and concern.

"That's not cool," Dave said—the understatement of the year.

Dave Berke was a U.S. Marine Corps major. A fighter pilot by trade, he had been the lead instructor at the legendary U.S. Navy Fighter Weapons School, better known as TOPGUN. Dave had left the cockpit behind and volunteered to serve on the ground as a forward air controller in the most dangerous place in Iraq: Ramadi. He led a Supporting Arms Liaison Team (SALT) attached to the U.S. Marine Corps 5th Air-Naval Gunfire Liaison Company. Dave and his twelve Marines from SALT 6 accompanied Charlie Platoon to coordinate with the aircraft supporting this operation in the skies overhead. They patrolled in with us on foot to spearhead the operation ahead of the U.S. Army and Iraqi Army units.

A U.S. tank two hundred yards away had fired a burst from its heavy machine gun directly over our position. It was friendly fire, a blue-on-blue in U.S. military parlance. To be killed or horribly wounded by enemy fire was one thing. To be killed by our own American forces was something much worse.

*That was way too close for comfort,* I thought in the seconds following as I crouched as low as possible behind the low concrete wall that was our only means of cover. We had to shut that down immediately and alert the tank that we were friendly forces. To do so, I had to contact the specific tank commander directly via radio and tell them to "cease fire."

The tank's heavy machine gun was the .50-caliber M2 Browning. Known as "the Ma Deuce," it packed a hell of a punch. In U.S. military service since 1933, it had proven its deadly effectiveness in every American war since. Each massive round could take a man's head clean off or remove the bulk of his chest cavity. It could also punch right through concrete walls, like the one we were hiding behind. We had just received a fully automatic burst of probably a dozen rounds in a matter of seconds. If I didn't shut down that fire immediately and let the U.S. tank know we were friendlies, it could mean horrible wounds and death for a number of us.

Moments before, I stood with several Charlie Platoon SEALs on the rooftop of an Iraqi house deep in enemy territory. Dave stood next to me, communicating with a U.S. Air Force AC-130U "Spooky" gunship that circled high overhead, wielding both awesome firepower and extraordinary surveillance capability from thousands of feet in the night sky above. The first U.S. troops on the ground in this volatile neighborhood, we had patrolled in on foot several hours earlier in the night and set up a sniper overwatch position to disrupt any attacks from insurgents on the main force of the operation: some fifty U.S. tanks and armored vehicles, and nearly one thousand U.S. and Iraqi troops, led by Task Force Bandit, 1st Battalion, 37th Armored Regiment, 1st Armored Division. Our SEAL snipers were set up in shooting positions along with our machine guns and security teams. Dave and his Marine radioman were on the rooftop with us, relaying updates from the Spooky gunship overhead.

We watched as the heavy phalanx of American armor—M1A2 Abrams tanks and M2 Bradley Fighting Vehicles—rolled in our direction, crossing the railroad bridge over the canal and following the road that led to the village where we were positioned. To clear the field of view for our snipers, our explosive ordnance disposal (EOD) bomb technicians and SEAL breachers put explosive charges in place to knock down several palm trees. We'd taken great steps to alert Task Force Bandit—the battalion, companies, and platoons—to the exact location of our sniper overwatch so they wouldn't mistake us for enemy forces. We had also marked our position with a pre-determined signal device. But I hadn't considered how dangerous it was for us to set off the explosions to take out the trees.

This was one of the first major operations of the "Seize, Clear, Hold, Build" strategy to take back Ramadi from the deadly insurgents who controlled the city, and it was a historic and massive undertaking. It had been meticulously planned for weeks, examining every realistic contingency we could imagine. Heavy fighting was expected, as were major U.S. casualties. The Soldiers manning the tanks were already on edge, expecting attack as they maneuvered into enemy territory. Though the key leaders had been briefed on the specific building where we planned to set up our overwatch position, that information didn't always make it down to the forward troops on the front lines of the operation. And even if the word was passed to the frontline troops, understanding locations on the battle map and correlating this with the actual street and buildings seen from the ground level proved difficult at best. I had radioed to Jocko, who was co-located with the Army battalion at the U.S. staging point across the bridge, that we would be conducting a "controlled detonation": a non-combat explosion of demolition charges that we'd set ourselves. The battalion acknowledged via radio they understood. But again, that didn't guarantee that the word was passed to the tank crews or that they fully processed what that meant. The tankers had their own challenges and risks to confront: significant threats from massive IEDs buried in the road and enemy attacks with machine guns and RPG-7 rockets.

When our controlled detonations shattered the quiet and the blasts of fire momentarily lit up the dark, one of the Abrams tank commanders must have thought it was an enemy attack. Seeing our silhouettes on the rooftop and thinking we were insurgent fighters, he lit us up with a burst from his heavy machine gun. We had been casually peering over the roof wall, watching the armored vehicles crawl toward us on their tracks, when the burst of .50-caliber rounds cracked just over our heads. That sent us all diving to the deck to seek cover.

Every nanosecond counted as I reached into my gear for my radio.

Our typical radio procedures were for me to communicate directly to Jocko, who would then pass the word to the battalion staff he was standing next to, who would relay to their company, who would relay to the platoon in whose unit the tank belonged. But there was no time for that now. Every moment was crucial. I needed to speak directly to that tank immediately, or the next burst of .50-caliber machine gun rounds might chew us to bits—though the .50-cal was preferable to a massive main gun round from the tank's 120mm smoothbore cannon, which could be next.

Quickly, I switched my radio channel dial to the tank's company net and keyed up. "Cease fire, cease fire," I said. "You are shooting at friendlies."

Receipt of the radio transmission was acknowledged. The shooting stopped.

*That was a close one,* I thought. I wasn't angry, but more

concerned with the recognition of how easily friendly fire could happen, despite our extensive efforts to mitigate the risk of blue-on-blue.

The ability to switch my radio to a different net and talk directly to the tank from which we were taking fire may well have saved us. It was a mission-critical skill upon which I depended during nearly every combat operation, as did the other leaders in Charlie Platoon and Task Unit Bruiser. Yet, when we had first arrived in Ramadi, as SEALs, we didn't understand the U.S. Army and Marine Corps radio networks and were unable to directly communicate with them via radio.

In the SEAL Teams, we had a different culture, different tactics, and different gear from our U.S. Army and Marine Corps brethren. Nowhere was that more apparent than in our radio communications equipment. They used an entirely different system. In order for us to talk to them, we needed to learn how to use their system. Typically, in a SEAL platoon, the radioman is the communications expert who programs the radios and troubleshoots any issues for everyone else in the platoon. We came to depend on our SEAL radioman for everything involving radios. On previous deployments, if you had a problem with a radio, you just popped it out of your gear and tossed it to the radioman to fix or swap out for a new one. Additionally, the leader depended upon the SEAL radioman for all communications back to the tactical operations center and all units outside of the SEAL squad or platoon. But in Ramadi, we often broke up into small units and there weren't enough SEAL radiomen to go around. You might very well find yourself serving as the radioman of an element when the actual SEAL radiomen were in a different element or squad in a separate building or on a different operation altogether.

As task unit commander and a prior SEAL radioman in his enlisted days, Jocko understood that each member of Task Unit Bruiser had to be competent with our radios. He knew we all individually needed to learn how to program our radios so any one of us could talk directly to the Soldiers and Marines we fought alongside and depended on for help when we found ourselves in a jam. It was a skill critical to saving lives on the battlefield.

"Everybody make sure you know how to program your radios," Jocko commanded during an early brief in the Charlie Platoon mission planning space. Even among SEALs, Jocko was a big, mean-looking, and intimidating guy. You might think that whatever Jocko said, we were going to do it. If not because we feared his wrath, because we respected his leadership and experience.

But we didn't learn how to program our radios. At least, most of us didn't. It wasn't that we didn't think it was important or that we didn't respect Jocko. We did. But we simply were overtasked, and in the hectic schedule, other pressing issues always took precedence. Jocko's order to learn how to program our radios slipped to the back burner. Most of us never got around to it.

A few days after Jocko's decree that we had to learn to program our radios, Task Unit Bruiser put together a plan and received approval to launch on a nighttime raid to capture or kill the leaders of an Iraqi insurgent terrorist cell responsible for multiple deadly attacks on U.S. and Iraqi troops in Ramadi. Charlie Platoon had the lead and came up with a plan. Just as we did prior to every operation, we gathered the troops for the mission brief, known as an "operation order," or OPORD. The key leaders stood up and presented their respective parts of the plan. We talked through the details and answered remaining questions.

As we were wrapping up the OPORD, Jocko stood up and made some final strategic comments. Finally, he asked a question that caught us red-handed.

"Does everyone know how to program their radios?" Jocko asked. There were blank stares. But nobody had the courage to say, "No."

I thought: *We didn't have time. We didn't make the time.*

But Jocko didn't need to hear an answer. No doubt he could tell from the blank stares and lack of response that most of the

SEAL operators in the room, about to launch on this combat operation, didn't know how to program their radios themselves.

Jocko looked at one of the SEAL operators, a new guy in the platoon, whom we called "Biff" after the character from the movie *Back to the Future*.

"Biff, let me see your radio," Jocko said bluntly. Biff quickly complied, unscrewed the connector to his headset, unclipped the fast-tech fastener, pulled the radio from his gear, and handed it to Jocko. There was a function on the radio that would clear its memory, requiring it to be reprogrammed. Jocko cleared the radio and handed it back to Biff.

"Reprogram that," Jocko directed.

Biff stared back blankly. He didn't know how to reprogram his radio. It was an uncomfortable place to be, called out in front of everyone in our SEAL platoon and task unit, having failed to comply with Jocko's order. But he wasn't alone, as most of us were in the same boat.

Jocko wasn't angry. He understood that many of us in the room hadn't learned to program our radios, not through willful disobedience but because we hadn't fully understood its importance. Since we didn't clearly understand the importance, we didn't make the time to learn. Yet Jocko wasn't backing down. He didn't let it go. Jocko held the line, enforced the standard. Jocko knew that when we were out on the battlefield, in smaller elements beyond the reach of help or support, we had to be able to operate the radios ourselves. With Decentralized Command, it was crucial that leaders at every level be fully self-reliant, ready to step up and execute to accomplish the mission.

Turning to the Charlie Platoon's senior SEAL radioman, he said: "Teach Biff how to reprogram his radio."

To the rest of us in the platoon, Jocko added: "Everybody else make sure you know how to program your radios. It could save your life. And if you don't know how to program them by the next mission, you're not going outside the wire."

By the next combat operation, everyone in the platoon—every

SEAL in Task Unit Bruiser—knew how to program their radios; we had practiced it multiple times. The boss had called us all out and made it clear that he fully expected his order to be carried out, no exceptions.

For leaders, it is often a struggle to know when and where to hold the line. In the SEAL Teams, just as in any organization, leaders who constantly crack the whip on their team and verbally berate their people over trivial issues are despised, not respected. Those leaders are ineffective and few will follow them when it matters. A leader cannot be overbearing. But the dichotomy here is that a leader cannot be too lenient and let things slide when the safety, mission success, and long-term good of the team are at stake.

Had Jocko not called us out to prove we could program our own radios, we would never have done it. It is quite likely that our inability to do so would have cost lives. I certainly would never have been fully competent in talking directly to Soldiers and Marines on their company and platoon radio nets. Had Jocko not done this, would he truly have been taking care of the SEAL operators in the task unit? The answer is most certainly not. But Jocko understood that taking care of your people means looking out for their long-term good and the long-term good of the strategic mission. There are some standards that simply cannot be compromised.

Going forward, everyone in Task Unit Bruiser was competent in programming and utilizing their personal radios. As non-radiomen, we also practiced utilizing the larger radios that the radiomen carried, in the event we needed them—which happened frequently. As other SEALs visited Camp Ramadi and joined our platoon and task unit as "strap hangers" on combat operations, one of the very first things we taught them was how to program their own radios and communicate directly with Army and Marine Corps units. Jocko had held the line. As a result, we were prepared for the realities of the battlefield, able to mitigate risk and operate most effectively to accomplish our mission.

As I reflected upon Jocko's demonstration of a leader's responsibility to ensure standards are maintained, I thought about the times in my career when I failed to do so. As a young leader, I knew there were times we needed to improve our performance, do another run-through in the kill house (where we practiced close-quarters combat), or add an additional rehearsal to ensure we were fully prepared. Yet in those moments, I sometimes hadn't held the line; I hadn't pushed the team hard enough. Any additional work assigned to the team was going to get pushback and generate complaints. And there were times when I let things slide, confusing the idea of "taking care of your people" with allowing them not to work as hard. But in the end, that resulted in mediocre performance. And the team never got better, never held each other accountable. This was a failure of leadership—my leadership.

I also recognized the dichotomy: there were other times when I was overbearing. I insisted on doing things a certain way, because it was my way, or harped on trivial matters that were strategically unimportant, thinking I was doing right by holding the line. It caused unnecessary friction, stifled growth, and inhibited junior leaders on the team from stepping up. It prevented us from functioning properly with effective Decentralized Command.

I had seen and worked for numerous leaders throughout my Navy career who had been overbearing, and it wasn't the way I wanted to lead. Some of them imposed harsh discipline, screamed at their people, and crushed the morale of the team. No one wanted to follow them. They might accomplish an immediate task, but in the long run, the team's growth was smothered. Often, their negative example stood starkly in my mind: *I never want to be a leader like that.*

But there are times when every leader must give a little and allow the team some room to maneuver. In 2005, when we formed up Task Unit Bruiser and started training, we were determined to get to Iraq and get in the fight. We knew we would be working with large numbers of U.S. Soldiers and Marines—infantry, armor, and airborne units. They all had strict protocols for their uniforms and combat gear. Soldiers wore their official unit patch and the American flag. Marines wore the American flag and their eagle, globe, and anchor emblem, the symbol of the Marine Corps. But in the SEAL Teams, SEAL operators generally wore whatever the hell they wanted. Often, this was a mix of different uniforms and gear. Early SEALs in Vietnam had worn blue jeans and civilian "duck hunter" camouflage on combat operations. And a lot of SEALs carried on the tradition of dressing "unconventionally." Beyond the uniform styles that made us look different from other military units, many SEALs had custom Velcro patches made for our gear. Each SEAL platoon would design a logo and have a patch made for the platoon. In Task Unit Bruiser, Delta Platoon had a "bone frog" design with a Delta triangle and frog skeleton. Charlie Platoon had utilized the Cadillac logo with a "3" and a "C" for "SEAL Team 3" and "Charlie Platoon." Beyond unit patches, some of us wore other patches such as the traditional first U.S. Navy jack—a flag flown for the jack staff of U.S. Navy vessels—with thirteen stripes, a rattlesnake, and the words "Don't Tread on Me," adopted from the Gadsden flag of the American Revolution. SEALs would often design their own patches with whatever logo they thought was cool, a line or a movie quote they found funny. As we kicked off our training cycle in Task Unit Bruiser, one popular patch was a "Fun Meter," with the meter arrow buried in the red, meaning: "The fun meter was pegged." Several SEALs had patches that read, "More Cowbell," inspired by the popular *Saturday Night Live* Will Ferrell skit of the band, Blue Oyster Cult. Other patches were even less professional and far more crude.

I knew all the patches were unprofessional. I knew that some of the patches were pretty offensive and that as the platoon commander, I should probably order my guys to get rid of their patches. But I also thought they were funny, and I didn't fully understand the problems something as simple as patches could cause for us once deployed alongside Army and Marine Corps units. I believed that removing the patches would hurt morale and make me look overly harsh. So I let it go.

Jocko recognized that someone who saw these crude and unprofessional patches and took them out of context might take offense, which would cause frictions that might escalate into something serious. Not that Jocko was some virtue-signaling angel. I knew he thought many of the patches were funny. But he also knew that if there was even a chance that the patches might cause issues for us, it wasn't worth the risk. It could harm our task unit's chances of being selected to deploy to Iraq. When we did deploy to Iraq, as we hoped to do, the U.S. Army and Marine units we worked alongside would initially judge us by our appearance. They took pride in squared-away uniforms as a testament to good order and discipline. With our random, unprofessional patches, the first impression the Soldiers and Marines would have of Task Unit Bruiser wouldn't be good. Jocko knew it was important and had no problem dropping the hammer on patches.

"Get rid of the patches," Jocko told me. I told him I would make it happen.

Then he addressed the issue to all Task Unit Bruiser personnel.

Jocko declared: "No more patches in Task Unit Bruiser. The patches many of you have been wearing are unprofessional. I get that they are funny. But funny patches won't help us build strong relationships with the conventional forces we will be serving alongside. They will inhibit our ability to operate in Army and Marine battlespace. They will prevent us from getting after it to close with and destroy the enemy.

"No patches," he repeated. "None. Everybody clear?" The only exception was the standard American flag patch we were authorized to wear. Jocko's senior enlisted advisor, our task unit senior chief, ensured the boss's order was enforced without exception.

"Roger," we acknowledged, in the military lingo for "understood." The task unit—particularly Charlie Platoon—wasn't happy about it, but everyone understood and would comply. The new standard had been set, the line in the sand drawn. All patches were removed.

But as the months wore on and Task Unit Bruiser was selected to deploy to Iraq, I privately felt that Task Unit Bruiser was a historic unit destined for great things on the battlefield, and we needed to have an official unit patch. On liberty one day, when we were out surfing and on a rare occasion away from Jocko, I talked it over with my close friend, the Delta Platoon commander, Seth Stone.

"Bro, we need a unit patch for Task Unit Bruiser," I said. "I know Jocko said no patches. But I think we should design one and have it made for everybody."

"Agreed," Seth replied. We both loved and admired Jocko. We respected his leadership. We rarely disagreed with him on anything, large or small. But we knew that having a task unit patch was important for unit cohesion. We knew there was a line between patches that were offensive and a unit patch with a logo that would represent the task unit.

"We will have to do it in secret," I said. "And make sure that Jocko doesn't see them."

"Let's do it," Seth agreed.

Later, back at my house, Seth and I designed two different patches to be worn on the shoulder of each operator. Both patches were circular and desert tan with "Task Unit Bruiser" printed across the top. Seth decorated one patch with a cow skull with downturned horns, and the words "Big Balls in Cowtown" across the bottom. Being from Texas, Seth and I were big fans of the classic country-western song by Bob Wills and His Texas Playboys, "Big Ball's in Cowtown." The pun seemed most appropriate, as we had just learned we were deploying to Ramadi. I designed another patch with Lord Humungus, the muscle-bound leader of the postapocalyptic antagonists from the *Mad Max* movie sequel *The Road Warrior*, wearing a hockey mask and wielding a large-caliber handgun. At the base of the patch, I used the phrase "The Ayatollahs of Rock N Rolla," borrowing the title bestowed upon Lord Humungus in the movie.

With only a couple of weeks left prior to deployment, I hurriedly found a shop that could sew our designs, create the patches, and add the Velcro backing necessary for easy application and removal from our working combat uniforms. The patches arrived only days before we departed for Iraq. I threw the box, unopened, into one of my kit bags and packed them on the pallet just before it was loaded on the aircraft that would take us overseas. Once we arrived in Ramadi, I discreetly removed the box without Jocko's knowledge and pulled Seth aside. We opened the box and pulled out enough patches for each of the members of our platoons. In secret, we distributed the patches to everyone in Task Unit Bruiser, except for Jocko and his immediate headquarters staff.

While on base, or on combat operations within visual range of Jocko and his senior enlisted advisor, no one wore patches other than our standard American flag patch. But each of the SEAL operators in Charlie and Delta Platoons, along with our EOD bomb technicians, kept the patches hidden inside the cargo pocket on the shoulder of our combat uniforms. For the operations where Jocko stayed back to man the TOC, as our convoy of Humvees departed the base, we gave a call over the intersquad radio: "Patches on." Each operator pulled his Task Unit Bruiser patch out of his cargo pocket and slapped it onto the Velcro on the outside of his uniform. We were now ready to do battle as Task Unit Bruiser and close with and destroy the enemy.

But as with any blatant violation of the rules, it was only a matter of time before we were busted. That fateful day happened on one of the first major operations that Task Unit Bruiser participated in. An embedded civilian journalist with the U.S. Army unit we were working alongside took some photos of Task Unit Bruiser SEALs in action. The photos were shared with their higher headquarters staff and eventually shared with Jocko and his senior enlisted advisor. In the photos the Task Unit Bruiser patch could clearly be seen on the shoulders of several of our SEALs.

The senior enlisted advisor blew up about it and prepared to drop the hammer on us. He was just trying to do his job and enforce Jocko's order. I expected to feel the wrath of Jocko, and since I had orchestrated the violation, I planned to fully own the brunt of the punishment.

But a day passed. And then another day. Jocko didn't mention it. I was surprised. Jocko knew we had violated his order—willful disobedience. But in this case, Jocko didn't hold the line and enforce the standard he had set. He let it go.

As I thought about why he hadn't confronted me, his reason became clear, and later, when we came home from deployment, he confirmed my thoughts. Jocko had recognized that the task unit patches strengthened our unit cohesion—they were a source of pride. He also knew that we had gotten rid of all the other patches; no one was still wearing the assortment of offensive and unprofessional patches he had seen stateside. Instead, everyone wore the same uniformed Task Unit Bruiser patch, all desert tan that matched our uniforms. He knew that if we were hiding the patches from him, we would hide the patches from other U.S. units on the base.

While Jocko never told us we were cleared to wear the patches, he allowed us to bend the rules. And since the patches were unique and matched our reputation on the battlefield, rather than alienate us from the Soldiers and Marines, it cemented in their minds that we were a cohesive unit. At the end of our deployment, we gave several Task Unit Bruiser patches to key Army and Marine leaders with whom we worked closely, including the U.S. Army colonel in charge of the entire brigade combat team.

Witnessing how Jocko held the line and enforced the standard to ensure we knew how to program our radios, yet allowed some slack when it came to us wearing patches, set a powerful example of how to balance the dichotomy. There is a time to stand firm and enforce rules and there is a time to give ground and allow the rules to bend. Finding that balance is critical for leaders to get maximum effectiveness from their team.

### Principle

Leaders, on the one hand, cannot be too lenient. But on the other hand, they cannot become overbearing. They must set high standards and drive the team to achieve those standards, but they cannot be domineering or inflexible on matters of little strategic importance. To find this balance, leaders must carefully evaluate when and where to hold the line and when to allow some slack. They must determine when to listen to subordinate leaders and allow them ownership, making adjustments for their concerns and needs.

Some have used the term "leadership capital" as a means to understand the careful analysis required for a leader to balance this dichotomy. Leadership capital is the recognition that there is a finite amount of power that any leader possesses. It can be expended foolishly, by leaders who harp on matters that are trivial and strategically unimportant. Such capital is acquired slowly over time through building trust and confidence with the team by demonstrating that the leader has the long-term good of the team and the mission in mind. Prioritizing those areas where standards cannot be compromised and holding the line there while allowing for some slack in other, less critical areas is a wise use of leadership capital.

Just as we wrote in *Extreme Ownership*, chapter 8, "Decentralized Command," the most important explanation a leader can give to the team is "why?" Particularly when a leader must hold the line and enforce standards, it must always be done with the explanation of why it is important, why it will help accomplish the mission, and what the consequences are for failing to do so. It must never be done with the attitude of "because I said so." To do so will result in far more pushback and more difficulty in getting the team to achieve the standards you are trying to enforce. As a leader, you have to balance the dichotomy, to be resolute where it matters but never overbearing; never inflexible and uncompromising on matters of little importance to the overall good of the team and the strategic mission.

## Application to Business

"I've read a lot about Patton," the executive vice president said with pride, referring to General George S. Patton Jr., the famous U.S. Army general whose exploits in World World II were legendary. "I love that you referenced Patton in your presentation. I want exactly the kind of disciplined organization around here that Patton expected. We need people who carry out orders, not question them."

I could tell right away that the executive vice president (EVP) had no previous military experience. He clearly misunderstood how effective leaders in the military lead their teams. It was not through rigid authoritarianism: *Do this because I said so, or you'll be punished.* Sure, there were those in the military who tried to lead like this. But it was never effective.

I sat in a conference room with the EVP to learn more about him and his role in the company. As part of our Echelon Front leadership assessment for the company's Leadership Development and Alignment Program, such one-on-one meetings were integral to understanding the true challenges and frictions within the organization among leaders, departments, teams, and strategies. For our Echelon Front team, this was critical knowledge that allowed us to tailor our leadership program to address these challenges and implement leadership solutions to get the problems solved.

The EVP's company had a long history of quality and service. But recently the company's executive team had set its horizons for expansion beyond the regionally focused area that had traditionally been their market. To do this, the company, which had previously relied on the extensive experience and on-the-job training of its frontline leaders, now had to lay down standard operating procedures to try to get each of its teams and each of its divisions operating on the same page.

The EVP had sat through the opening leadership presentation I delivered. During the question-and-answer session following my brief, I had referenced General Patton. That had clearly resonated with the EVP.

"Discipline equals freedom," the EVP said, quoting Jocko's mantra, which we had just covered in the training session. "I've been trying to instill discipline in our team here. We need a lot more of it."

"In what way?" I asked, interested to hear more.

"Cell phones," the EVP declared. "It burns me up every time we call a meeting, somebody will inevitably be on their phone. Here I am, up in front of the room trying to put out some critical information, and I see somebody on their phone answering an e-mail. Or somebody steps out of the room to take a phone call as I'm trying to impart key information."

"They even do it to our CEO," the EVP added, incredulous at such behavior.

"That can be frustrating," I replied. "We see it all the time with our work at Echelon Front. But obviously there are important things that come up that need immediate attention for the good of the company."

"Not in my meetings," the EVP boasted. "I've made it clear to every one of our department leaders and supervisors: there are no cell phones in my meetings whatsoever."

"How do you enforce that?" I asked.

"Easy," the EVP said. "Before every meeting, I make each of them pull their cell phones out of their pockets and physically turn them off. Then, they have to hold up their phone and show me it is fully powered down. I won't start the meeting until I see that everyone has complied."

The EVP was smug, clearly proud that he was holding the line, uncompromising in this effort, and enforcing a strict standard on the team.

"What has the team's reaction to this been?" I inquired.

"They gripe about it, of course," he answered. "But I'm going to keep holding the line, just like Patton would do."

"How important are these meetings?" I asked.

"Oh, they're important," the EVP insisted. "I'm putting out the new standard operating procedures that everyone should now be following. That direction came straight from the CEO, and I'm going to get this implemented no matter how much they resist. Besides, what could be so important that they can't shut off their phones for an hour or two to focus on what I need to discuss with them?"

"Well, I can think of a few things that may take precedence," I said. "How about an immediate pressing issue with a major customer that needs quick resolution to preserve the relationship so you don't lose a huge contract? Or a serious quality issue that might result in angry clients and bad press coverage that impacts your market growth? Or a major safety incident that results in serious injury or death?"

The EVP nodded, agreeing that any of those would take precedence over his meeting. "Look," he said. "I'm just trying to enforce discipline on the team. Like Patton would do—like you and Jocko talk about. If we are disciplined in the small things, won't that translate to discipline in the bigger things?"

"Discipline even in the small things is important," I said. "But as a leader, you need to carefully balance the dichotomy between these two opposing forces: understanding where to stand firm and where to bend. You need to carefully prioritize where you hold the line and enforce standards.

"I'm sure you've heard the term 'leadership capital' before," I continued. "As a leader, you only have so much authority that you can spend, and you need to choose wisely where you apply it. It seems to me you are expending a great deal of your leadership capital on cell phones when it might be much better utilized elsewhere.

"You mentioned there is resistance to the new standard operating procedures," I observed. "Can you tell me more about that?"

"I'm meeting a lot of resistance," he admitted. "A lot of our leaders have their own particular way of doing things. And they don't want to change."

"Well, that's a pretty standard human response," I said. "People want to keep doing what they have always done. It's up to you to help them understand why they need to change—why they need to implement standardized procedures. If they understand how it will benefit them personally, how it will benefit their team, and benefit the overall mission, they are far more likely to embrace the change."

"Why is it up to me?" the EVP inquired. "It's *their* problem. *They* need to get on board. I've told them over and over again why we need to do this. Frankly, I'm sick and tired of trying to explain it to them. We just need to start holding the line and enforcing standards: implement the new procedures, or else."

To me, it was perfectly clear. The EVP's attitude was the major reason most of the company's leaders were pushing back and refusing to implement the new standardized procedures. He had unwisely expended his leadership capital enforcing things such as the "no cell phone" policy in his meetings, with no strategic impact. Meanwhile, he had little leadership capital left to implement the new standardized procedures, which would have major strategic impact on the company's success or failure.

"It's great that you've read some military history," I said. "But I think you might have a misunderstanding of how leadership in the military actually works. That stuff you have seen in movies and television shows about military personnel who blindly carry out orders—that isn't true. Military personnel are not terminator robots that just mindlessly follow instruction, regardless of the outcome. They are thinking individuals who need to understand why they are doing what they are doing."

"But in the military, don't you have to follow orders?" the EVP asked.

"Even in the military, if you give someone an order that they disagree with, or don't believe in, where the risk of death or horrible injury to the team is high, you don't think you'll get any pushback on that?" I asked. "Of course the team will push back. They may even defy orders or refuse to execute, even if it means a court-martial.

"The best military leaders," I continued, "like the best business leaders, take the time to explain 'why' so that the team understands it. They don't force things down the throats of their subordinates. And they also don't sweat the small stuff. That way, when they explain the importance of something that really matters, it doesn't get lost on the troops. Then, the troops are far more likely to execute what the leader puts forth."

The EVP nodded, beginning to understand that in order to get the team on board with the new standardized process, he needed to adjust his tactics.

"In terms of strategic importance to the company," I asked the EVP, "what is more important? That your leaders not access their cell phones during meetings? Or that your leaders get on board with the new standardized process and implement it within their teams?"

"The standardized procedures, of course," the EVP admitted. "It's far more important strategically that our leaders implement the new process."

"Roger that," I said. "Then you need to be more discerning in expending your leadership capital. Don't waste it on the 'no cell phone' policy. That's hurting your ability to implement the important stuff.

"This too is a dichotomy," I explained. "You can't have everyone on their cell phones throughout an important meeting. So make it clear that cell phones are allowed, but only for the most crucially important matters."

"But won't that make me look weak?" the EVP asked. I could tell he was probably thinking of Patton again.

"Actually," I said, "it will make you look stronger. It shows that you understand what is strategically important—where to hold the line, and where to be flexible and give some leeway to your leaders. That will *increase* your leadership capital with the department leaders you are relying on to implement the new procedures."

Now, the EVP began to see how carefully he needed to evaluate when and where to hold firm on standards and where to give. He began to understand that it was his job as a leader not to say "Do it my way or suffer the consequences" but to explain. Most importantly, he now saw the value of balancing the dichotomy, to be resolute but not overbearing.

"REDBULL SIX," the call sign for Naval Special Warfare Task Unit Ramadi Commander Jocko Willink, provides command and control for his SEALs and the Iraqi soldiers for whom they served as combat advisors during a large-scale cordon and search operation with Task Force Red Currahee (1st Battalion, 506th Parachute Infantry Regiment of the U.S. Army's 101st Airborne Division) in the Malaab District of eastern Ramadi. Such combat operations were vastly different than what SEALs had trained for, but were essential operations to the counterinsurgency mission in Ramadi.

(Photo courtesy of Todd Pitman)

# CHAPTER 4
## When to Mentor, When to Fire

*Jocko Willink*

### THE MALAAB DISTRICT, EAST RAMADI: 2006

I heard gunfire in the distance. It wasn't effective fire—no rounds were impacting in our immediate vicinity. But it was a reminder that at any moment we could find ourselves in serious trouble. Threats were everywhere. Every footstep could potentially trigger an IED. Every window might be a sniper-firing position. Even the sky itself could rain down deadly mortar fire at any moment.

All these threats, and even the thought of such dangers, produced fear. But while we were on patrol, fear was not our focus. The focus was the job—the task immediately at hand. Cover a corner. Sprint across the street. Hold security on a door or a window. Check your field of fire. Maintain visual contact with the SEAL in front of you and the SEAL behind you. Note the buildings and streets as you pass by, to keep aware of your position on the battlefield. Listen to the radio in your ear with updates of friendly locations and suspected enemy movements, while also listening for threats in the streets and surroundings.

With all that going on, fear couldn't occupy much mental real estate—there wasn't time to dwell on it. But occasionally, on patrol, I detached and observed not just my surroundings but also my teammates. In those moments, our Task Unit Bruiser SEALs were an amazing sight to behold—like a single organism, functioning as one. When one weapon moved away from a threat, another picked it up. When one man stepped into a danger zone, he was covered by his shooting partner. Movement took place without any verbal communication—no voice or radio calls—just subtle head nods, the way a weapon was pointed, occasional hand gestures, and well-understood body language that directed the team in a manner that others could barely detect. I was proud to be a part of this team. We functioned so well together, we seemed to operate with one mind. And I had complete trust and confidence in the skills and competence of everyone in the task unit.

But it was not always like that. Before our deployment to Ramadi in the spring of 2006, through twelve months of difficult training, we had worked hard to achieve that level of teamwork. Although we all shared a common baseline, having been through Basic Underwater Demolition/SEAL Training (known as BUD/S)—the SEAL basic training program—that was where the similarities ended. SEALs come from every imaginable socioeconomic background, from every part of the country, every ethnicity, and creed. Contrary to popular belief and the common depictions in movies and television shows, SEALs, like all other members of the U.S. military, are not robots. Even through the indoctrination of the different military services' boot camps, the continued training, lifestyle, and culture that permeated the minds of military servicemen and women, the people in the military are just that: people. They had different drives and motivations, unique senses of humor, varied backgrounds, different religions, and different personalities. They also have different strengths and weaknesses in their capabilities. The SEALs in Task Unit Bruiser contained a wide variety of athletic abilities: some were like endurance athletes, lean and svelte; some were like weight lifters, bulky and powerful. They also had different cognitive abilities, different intelligence levels; each handled stress differently and exercised different abilities to process complex problems. With such variation in individuals on the team, the challenge for any leader was to raise the level of every member of the team so that they could perform at their absolute best. In order to do that, a leader must make it his or her personal mission to train, coach, and mentor members of the team so they perform to the highest standards—or at least the minimum standard. But there is a dichotomy in that goal: while a leader must do everything possible to help develop and improve the performance of individuals on the team, a leader must also understand when someone does not have what it takes to get the job done. When all avenues to help an individual get better are exhausted without success, then it is the leader's responsibility to fire that individual so he or she does not negatively impact the team.

Of course, firing people is one of the most difficult things a leader must do. In Task Unit Bruiser, where a strong esprit de corps* quickly developed, this was especially difficult. People often wondered how to develop unit camaraderie. We learned one of the best ways is "simple, but not easy:" hard work. In any organization, and especially in the military, the harder a unit trained, the more its members were pushed, the tighter they became. That is true in the broader military, and certainly within the special operations community. Task Unit Bruiser was no exception. Of course, we developed powerful relationships through living, working, eating, partying, working out, and being around each other almost twenty-four hours a day for weeks at a time. But the most important factor in our becoming a tight-knit group was the way we pushed hard during training. We wanted to be the best; we didn't want to be second place in anything. So we pushed each other hard and held the line, and we also protected one another, like a family. Unfortunately, not every member of

---

* Esprit de corps: the common spirit existing in the members of a group inspiring enthusiasm, devotion, and a strong regard for the honor of the group (Merriam-Webster dictionary).

the family had the capabilities to perform to the Task Unit Bruiser standard.

The six-month pre-deployment training "workup" in the SEAL Teams is mentally and physically challenging, especially for those going through it for the first time—the new guys, or "FNGs" for short. Live fire and maneuver, weapons handling, patrolling on night vision, the weight of the gear, the heat and the cold, the lack of sleep—none of it is easy, and when combined, it can be too much for some individuals.

In Task Unit Bruiser, when our workup kicked off, our first block of training was out in the hot desert of Southern California, where we conducted land warfare training. It was mountainous, rocky, and rugged terrain. We always said that land warfare training in this environment was where men became "Frogmen." The high-stress, dynamic environment posed challenges for all, but particularly for some of the new guys. As task unit commander, I paid attention to who struggled and watched how each leadership team of my two platoons handled its underperforming members. As I watched Leif, Seth, and their SEAL platoon chiefs interact with the members who were subpar, they led just as I expected them to: they tried to help less stellar performers get up to speed. There were a couple of new guys in each platoon who didn't quite get it. They seemed unable to keep up with the progression of skills required to do the job.

But I saw the platoon leadership work with them, tirelessly counsel them, coach them, assign more experienced SEALs to mentor them, train, and retrain them. And I knew why. The new guys they were helping might be struggling, but they were still part of the platoon. They were SEALs, they'd graduated from BUD/S and SQT (SEAL Qualification Training). They were members of the gang—and the leadership wanted to protect them and see them succeed.

Fortunately, the time invested in the struggling new guys seemed to pay off. Everyone successfully completed the multiweek land warfare block of training and then the next multiweek block, mobility training, where we learned to shoot, move, and communicate from Humvees instead of on foot. During that block, I again saw some of the new guys struggling—making mistakes with the heavy weapons, not reacting properly to tactical commands, or hesitating to take action at critical moments. But once again, I saw the platoon leadership and other experienced SEALs in the platoons take ownership and rally around their young teammates, relentlessly working with them to get them up to speed.

After mobility training, I talked to Leif about the SEALs who were floundering.

"What do you think?" I asked. "A couple of those guys seem like they are having a hard time."

"They are," he replied. "But we'll get them where they need to be." That was exactly the answer I thought he would give—he was protective of every member of his platoon. After all, they were *his* men, he was responsible for them, and he and his platoon would make sure they got up to speed. I was happy to hear Leif taking ownership of the performance of his men and confident in the ability of his platoon to get every member to perform to standard. It was exactly what a leader should do.

The next block of training was close-quarters combat (CQC), where we learned to clear hallways and rooms in an urban environment. In the CQC training block, the pressure increased even more as the platoons executed dynamic, live-fire drills in confusing, complex buildings. "Live fire" meant SEALs were shooting lethal ammunition just inches apart from each other as they moved through the house and engaged targets. It was challenging and fun for most. But for some SEALs who struggled, the pressure was overwhelming. It was here that Leif first voiced a concern that perhaps one of the new guys in his platoon—Charlie Platoon—might not have what it takes to conduct such missions in actual combat.

He approached me to talk about one of his men, a young enlisted SEAL whom we called "Rock." Rock was a new guy, fresh out of BUD/S training, and Charlie Platoon was his first SEAL platoon. He had never been through the training cycle before. And he seemed to be having some trouble.

"He tries hard," Leif said, "and everybody likes him. We have been working with him—you've seen us. But he is struggling even more here at CQC. It seems like he might be in over his head. Frankly, I'm just not sure he is ever going to be capable of deploying to combat with us."

"What do you mean?" I asked. "He is in good shape and a hard worker, right?"

I knew Rock was physically capable and he had a great work ethic.

"It's not that," Leif replied. "He's got heart, and he is physically tough. But he is having some real problems. We got him through land warfare, where he had a little more time to think. But here, he gets completely overwhelmed when the pressure is on to make split-second decisions. And he panics and freezes up. Or makes really bad decisions in the house."

I knew neither one of those was good.

"The house" is what SEALs commonly call a "kill house," a building with a complex floor plan of rooms and hallways with ballistic walls that allow for live-fire training and room clearances in close quarters. In the house, dynamic tactical situations unfolded quickly, demanding that split-second decisions be made at the individual level by the shooters in the rooms. Because buildings were divided by walls that blocked visual and verbal communications, there were times when junior SEAL operators had to make decisions that impacted the direction of the entire operation. So every individual operator needed the tactical and operational savvy to make important decisions quickly and confidently. On top of the stress of decision-making, because of the high-risk nature of live-fire training in close quarters, there were very strict safety protocols in place to ensure no one got hurt or killed. If any of us violated the rules, the SEAL instructors issued a safety violation—a citation that documented the discrepancy. Getting a

safety violation or two was problematic. But if a SEAL went beyond two safety violations, it was a major red flag that might get
him ejected from the platoon and could cost him his career as a
SEAL.

"What kind of problems is he having?" I asked.

"He's had some major safety violations," Leif replied. "And
he doesn't seem to be learning from them. He's not making improvements. Rock tries, but when there is any pressure applied to
him, he quickly gets task saturated."

"Task saturated" was a term we used in the SEAL Teams to
describe how an individual, or a team, would get overwhelmed
when multiple problems were encountered simultaneously. They
couldn't properly Prioritize and Execute. Trying to process too
much information at once, they broke down and either failed to
take any action or made a bad decision that put them at risk, along
with the team or the mission.

I understood this was a major problem. But I also wanted to
be absolutely sure that everything possible had been done to help
Rock improve before consideration was given to firing him. Leif
and his platoon chief, Tony, were strong leaders—both high performers who expected the individuals on their team to perform.
And most of their SEALs in Charlie Platoon were outstanding. But
with strong leaders, I knew there could sometimes be a tendency to
fire someone who underperformed before he fully had a chance
to improve. I knew Leif and Tony and the rest of Charlie Platoon
were doing what they could, but I wanted to ensure they completely understood: *Most underperformers don't need to be fired,
they need to be led.*

"Have you talked it through with him? Helped him out?" I
asked. "What about Tony?" In order to ensure Rock received the
full benefit of the coaching and mentoring he needed to get up to
speed, I wanted to make sure my good friend and tactical expert,
Tony Eafrati (Charlie Platoon's chief), who was a highly experienced
SEAL with multiple deployments overseas, had been working
with him. As a training instructor, Tony had taught just about

every block of advanced training, and I knew he would have the best chance of getting through to Rock.

"Absolutely," Leif replied. "Chief is doing everything he can. So am I. So is our leading petty officer. We've tried hard to get him up to speed. We had some guys working with him through the weekend, when everybody else was out partying. But Rock just doesn't seem able to cut it. I don't know how much more we can do."

The consternation in Leif's face made it clear: he was trying to balance the dichotomy of leadership between coaching and mentoring—and making a decision to get rid of someone.

"You think we need to let him go?" I asked.

"I think it might be best," Leif said somberly. It wasn't an easy thing.

"Look, he's a great guy," Leif continued. "He works hard. And I'd like nothing more than to see him succeed. But in real combat scenarios, he'd be at serious risk—to himself, to the other guys in Charlie Platoon—if we put him in a position where he has to act decisively."

I understood exactly where Leif was coming from, and he was right. When we deployed, Rock would have to face situations where his life, the lives of his SEAL teammates, and innocent civilians' lives were at stake. He would have to make split-second decisions and make the right calls. On the battlefield, if Rock froze up and failed to engage an enemy fighter, he might get himself or others killed. If he made a bad decision and misidentified an unarmed civilian as an enemy combatant, it might cost the life of an innocent person. That could also get Rock sent to prison. We simply could not have someone who wasn't ready to step up and make things happen, to execute in high-pressure situations, as a member of the platoon or the task unit. But there was another angle to this that I wasn't sure Leif fully understood—and another thing that made this dichotomy a challenge to balance.

"You know if we get rid of him, we won't get a replacement,"

I said. "You will be a man short for the rest of workup—and probably for our deployment as well."

"You don't think we could get a replacement for him?" Leif asked.

"Not likely. As you know, there aren't enough SEALs," I said. "That's the way it is. Every platoon at every team is scrounging for guys. If you let Rock go, don't count on getting another guy. So you need to ask yourself: Do you want Charlie Platoon to be a man short?"

Leif stood quietly shaking his head, grappling with how to proceed.

"Think about it," I said. "Are there other jobs he could do? Maybe keep him out of the assault train. How about using him as a driver or a turret gunner in one of your vehicles? Maybe he could be in charge of marshaling prisoners. There are a lot more jobs we need filled besides door kickers."

"But even in those roles, we'd need Rock to make decisions," Leif commented. "Even in those roles, he will still be put in situations that I don't think he can handle."

"True," I agreed. "But maybe he's just a little slow on the uptake. Maybe he just needs more time to get a grasp on all this. Even if he only works in the rear, in the camp, for this platoon rotation, maybe next time he'll get up to speed. Work with him some more. Have Tony and the boys work with him. Let's see if he can fulfill some kind of role that helps the platoon."

"Roger that," Leif said. "Makes sense. We'll do everything we can."

With that, Leif walked away, clearly with the intent to figure out a way to succeed with Rock. If they couldn't get him fully up to speed, perhaps they could at least get him to a point where he would have the skill set to handle some of the less dynamic jobs, where there was a lower probability of his being overwhelmed by tasks and getting himself or somebody else killed.

Our CQC training continued on, and with each day the

intensity picked up. We graduated to clearing larger buildings with more rooms and more complex hallways and more threats. We moved on to even more difficult problems: simultaneous entries into the kill house by two separate assault forces, live explosive breaching charges, and dealing with even greater numbers of prisoners and unarmed civilians. I observed Rock closely on some of the runs to see how he was doing. Leif was right: he was really straining to stay on track. Because I had to keep an eye on forty more SEALs in the task unit, especially the platoon leadership, I couldn't focus my attention solely on Rock. But I saw enough to understand that his performance was well below that of his peers—the other new guys in Charlie and Delta Platoons. Still, I didn't see him commit one single blunder so egregious that we'd be forced to fire him. But he did acquire more safety violations, and I constantly heard the instructor cadre counseling him.

Even still, Charlie Platoon continued to keep Rock as part of the team. Leif, Tony, and the rest of the platoon kept working with him to try to help him improve. Task Unit Bruiser wrapped up our CQC training and went on the next multiweek training block, then the next. Finally, we arrived at our last training block, called "special reconnaissance," or SR. SR was where the platoons would spend extensive periods of time in the field—off base, on the training battlefield, to observe and pass reports from clandestine observation positions. The point of this training was to "sneak and peek" and get out of the area before the enemy even knew you were there, so there wouldn't be any shooting or quick decisions to be made. The stress level was a lot lower, and I figured Rock would be able to handle it.

I touched base with Leif and Tony. "How's Rock doing?" I asked Tony.

"Not too good. Even here, he can't seem to get it together," Tony responded.

"Yeah, he is still making mistakes. Simple stuff. I don't know.

I see a little glimmer of hope now and then. But he is definitely struggling," Leif added.

"Well, we are almost done with workup," I said. "We need to make a decision. If you guys have done everything you can and he is still not able—we might have to let him go."

"Got it, boss," Tony said.

"Check," Leif responded.

This was going to be one of the hardest decisions that we were forced to make as a task unit up until this point. The challenge of balancing when to keep working with someone to improve and deciding when it was time to let that person go isn't easy.

Leif and Charlie Platoon headed out on another operation in the field for a couple of days. When they came back, Leif came straight to me.

"I think we crossed the line on this last operation, Jocko," he said. "Rock had some simple tasks out there. No pressure. No stress. But he failed at all of them. We had to pull him off those tasks and give his job to others. Luckily, they picked up the slack and we accomplished our mission. But it made it a lot tougher with Rock along. Not only did he not contribute, his deficiencies dragged the rest of the team down. It's clear to me—there is nothing else we can do."

Leif shook his head. "I hate this," he continued. "Rock's a good man. But he just gets overwhelmed. He's a danger to himself and everybody else. He just can't get to where we need him to be. I think we need to let him go."

"It is a hard decision. Especially because I know you like him," I told Leif.

"We all like Rock," Leif replied. "He tries. He's got heart. But he's proven over and over again that he just can't do the job. I'm afraid Rock is going to hurt himself, hurt someone else, or get someone hurt—especially once we get into combat. I feel I owe it to Rock to not put him in a situation so far beyond his capability. If he makes a bad decision and someone gets hurt or killed, Rock will have to carry that guilt for the rest of his life. I can't, in good conscience, let that happen."

"You're right, Leif. And I know you've done everything you can to get him up to speed," I assured him.

"I have, Jocko, I really have. We all have," Leif replied.

I sat quiet for a minute, thinking about it. It was a hard decision—the hardest. When you fire someone in the SEAL Teams, you are ripping out their heart, smashing their dreams, taking them from their friends, ruining their career, and taking away their livelihood. It is not to be taken lightly. But at the same time, there is an even heavier burden: the lives of all the other men in the platoon—men who count on every SEAL being able to do his job and do it well. We all had to be capable of watching each other's backs. And that's all there was to it.

Another factor that weighed on my decision was equally important: Charlie Platoon was Leif's platoon. He was the leader. I needed to trust his judgment. This was his toughest leadership decision yet as a platoon commander. Sure, he had made decisions during training operations and directed the day-to-day function of the platoon. But none of those decisions would have the same repercussions on one of his men as firing Rock. This would permanently impact Rock's life. But Leif had thought long and hard about it—and so had I. We had done our utmost to find balance in the dichotomy: on the one hand, we wanted to be loyal to Rock; we wanted Rock to succeed and have a great career as a SEAL. But on the other hand, we had to be loyal to the greater team—to Charlie Platoon, to Task Unit Bruiser, and, above all, to our mission. We had to ensure everyone on the team could pull their weight. Rock couldn't. We needed to do the right thing—the hard thing.

"Alright then," I said. "We will pull him out of the platoon and send him back to the team for a Trident Review Board."

With that, Leif and Tony called a meeting with Rock. They explained the situation to him, why they had made the decision, and what would happen next. Rock would have to await the results of the Trident Review Board.

The "Trident" was what we called the SEAL warfare insignia pin—a large golden eagle, flintlock pistol, anchor, and trident—we wore on our uniforms. A Trident Review Board consisted of the most experienced SEALs at the team, the noncommissioned officers: SEAL chiefs, senior chiefs, and master chiefs. They would review Rock's case to decide whether he would continue as a SEAL and get another chance in a SEAL platoon down the road—or whether to pull his Trident and send him away to a non-SEAL command in the U.S. Navy surface fleet. The board reviewed Rock's case, examined his safety violations, and heard testimony about his performance from Tony and Charlie Platoon's leading petty officer. The decision was clear: the board ruled that Rock's Trident be removed and that he be sent to the fleet. He would no longer be a SEAL, no longer be a part of the SEAL Teams.

Rock wasn't happy about it. Yet, while he was upset to no longer be in the SEAL Teams, at the same time he showed some signs of relief—relief from the stress of trying to do a job he wasn't capable of performing well. Although he was disappointed, he maintained a positive attitude and went on to have a successful career in the Navy.

In Ramadi, in the toughest combat situations I could have envisioned for us, Task Unit Bruiser performed as an exceptional team. The extensive training, mentorship, and guidance that had been passed on was critical to this. But our exceptional performance was also a function of making the tough decisions to let underperformers go. But resorting to the extreme of firing someone was the exception. On the other side of this dichotomy were the other four new guys in Charlie Platoon who excelled under the mentorship, coaching, and special effort made by the platoon leadership and experienced SEALs. While each new guy struggled at times, all of them, with the exception of Rock, got up to speed. Charlie Platoon's veteran SEALs worked with them, trained with them, counseled them, and drove them to become upstanding members of Charlie Platoon and of the SEAL Teams. And that attitude—of doing everything you can to help your subordinates, peers, and leaders be the best they can possibly be—was critical to the success of Charlie Platoon and Task Unit Bruiser.

But that attitude had to be balanced by knowing when we as leaders had done everything we could to help an individual get up to speed, but the individual still fell short and the decision had to be made to let him go.

### Principle

Most underperformers don't need to be fired, they need to be led. But once every effort has been made to help an underperformer improve and all efforts have failed, a leader has to make the tough call to let that person go. This is the duty and responsibility of every leader.

Leaders are responsible for the output of the individuals on their team. The goal of any leader is to get the most out of every individual—to push each individual to reach his or her maximum potential so that the team itself can reach its maximum potential. Conversely, leaders must also understand that human beings have limitations; not every person on a team will be suited for a particular job. Some people might need a less technical position. Some people can't handle stress. Some might not work well with others. Some might lack the creativity to come up with new ideas or solve problems. This doesn't mean they are worthless—it just means that the leader needs to utilize them in a position where their strengths are fully capitalized. Once again, the leader is still trying to maximize the potential of every individual.

Occasionally, there are people who simply cannot perform to the required level in any capacity. Once a leader has exhausted remedial measures through coaching, mentoring, and counseling, the leader then must make the tough call: remove that individual from the team. The dichotomy in this situation is balancing between taking care of individuals by keeping them around even if they lack the skill set to do the job properly and protecting the team by removing people from positions where they negatively impact the team and the mission. A leader must be loyal to his individual team members and take care of them, but at the same time he must be loyal to the team itself and ensure that every member of the team has a net positive impact and doesn't detract from mission execution.

One thing that causes problems with this dichotomy is the idea of Extreme Ownership. With Extreme Ownership we say, "No bad teams, only bad leaders." When leaders try to live by that mantra, it usually has a positive outcome. When a leader has a substandard individual on the team, that leader takes ownership of the individual and ensures that the individual gets the training, coaching, and mentoring needed to get up to speed. That personal investment usually pays dividends: the substandard individual improves and becomes a solid contributor to the team.

But sometimes the substandard individual doesn't improve; sometimes he or she can't improve. Sometimes the individual simply lacks the necessary skills, capacity, or attitude to do a job. So the leader takes ownership of it and continues to invest time, energy, and money into the individual—but the individual's capabilities still don't improve. As the leader continues investing time and resources into one individual, other members of the team and other priorities are neglected and the team can begin to falter. Also, as other team members see a leader pouring resources into one nonperforming individual, the team might question the leader's judgment.

This is when leaders must bring their efforts into balance. Instead of focusing on one individual, leaders must remember that there is a team—and that the performance of the team trumps the performance of a single individual. Instead of continuing to invest in one subpar performer, once a concerted effort has been made to coach and train that individual to no avail, the leader must remove the individual. It can be one of the hardest decisions a leader has to make, but it is the right one.

We are often asked, "When is the right time to fire someone?" Some leaders are too quick to pull the trigger and fire people without giving them the right guidance and enough opportunity to gain competency. Other leaders wait to let someone go even after the individual has shown no potential at becoming competent and is negatively impacting the team. The answer is this: When a leader has done everything possible to get an individual up to speed without seeing results, the time has come to let that individual go. Don't be too quick to fire—but don't wait too long. Find the balance and hold the line.

### Application to Business

"The Tower Two super just doesn't seem to know how to get things done. They are lagging behind Tower One by six days right now," the project manager told me and the regional vice president, referring to the superintendent in charge of one of two condominium towers they were building.

"Six days behind?" the VP asked. "Doesn't that throw everything off track?"

"It absolutely does," the project manager answered. "We are having to repeat the same events instead of getting them done at once; things like concrete pours and crane movements—it costs us time and money!"

"That isn't good," the VP said. "This is the *only* project I'm a part of that is off schedule."

"Well . . . I'm doing the best I can with what I've got," said the project manager. "The Tower Two super just isn't getting it done."

I looked at the VP and gave him a nod. I could tell he was thinking what I was thinking. We had already put this whole team through a course on Extreme Ownership, yet this project manager was casting blame and making excuses. The VP wasn't having any of that.

"Whose fault is it that the Tower Two super isn't getting it done?" the VP asked.

Immediately, the project manager recognized what was being

implied. The look on his face changed and he started shaking his head.

"How can it be my fault?" he asked. "He's the one running Tower Two, not me."

"Well, what are you getting paid for, then?" the VP asked, going strong—maybe a little too strong—at the project manager. The project manager didn't answer. The VP backed off.

"I mean, seriously, you are the project manager," the VP continued. "Tower Two is part of this project. If the Tower Two super isn't doing his job, who is supposed to fix him?"

"I've been trying to fix him," the project manager countered. "But like I said, he just doesn't seem to get it."

"Okay then," I interjected. "If he truly doesn't get it, then why is he still in that position? If I had a platoon commander or a squad leader who was failing repeatedly, they would be out of a job."

"That's easier said than done," the project manager insisted. "This job has a lot of baggage behind it. We have had to clean up a lot of stuff from the architects and the engineers. This isn't an easy job—and he has a lot of knowledge that any other super wouldn't have if we brought someone new on board. That knowledge is critical to this project."

"Well, this clearly isn't working," said the VP.

"Alright, alright," the project manager protested. "Let me talk to him some more."

"While you are talking, you better prepare for action," I said, thinking that this might require the removal of the superintendent from Tower Two.

"I'm prepared," the project manager said.

"No. Beyond you being prepared. We need to be legally prepared," the VP said.

"What do you mean?" he asked.

"Well, let's look at the situation," I told him. "You say you have talked to him already. That obviously isn't working. Now, maybe you need to be more direct with him. Tell him exactly where he is failing and what he needs to do to improve. You also need to give him warning that the next time you talk to him about this, you are putting it in writing. And then if he doesn't fix himself, you need to *actually* put it in writing. The company must prepare to take action—to terminate him—if he doesn't improve. And all indicators are that he won't improve. So you need to prepare the situation so that he can be terminated without legal blowback."

"But what if he does improve?" the project manager asked, clearly fearful of my guidance.

"If he does improve, that's great," I said. "Problem solved. We can move on. No factor. But if he doesn't, then you'll be ready."

"But won't it ruin his attitude if I write him up?" the project manager asked.

"It might. But think about where we're at," I countered. "You and I had this discussion early on—you put him through an escalation of counseling. You started with a friendly conversation. He didn't change. You asked how you could help him change. He didn't change. You told him directly what he needed to change. He didn't change. You gave him plenty of opportunity, and so far, he has made no improvement.

"It's clear you've made an effort not to put too much pressure on him or be too negative," I continued. "It simply hasn't been effective. The next step in the escalation is to tell him he is going to be written up, which is a final plea for him to fix himself. But if he doesn't, you have to move further up the escalation of counseling—you will need to write him up. And of course, there is a chance that it will help him. It might make him finally realize how serious you are and how serious the situation is. You owe it to him to make clear where his deficiencies are and to help him improve. If that happens and he gets his act together, great. But if that doesn't happen, you need to be ready to act accordingly. Having a documented formal counseling will make termination easier. Plus, the work you have done to help him, to coach him, to mentor him, and to make clear that his performance is substandard and must improve, is ultimately to his benefit."

I explained that one of the things that makes it so hard to fire someone is the leader's knowledge that they have not done everything to actually lead a poor performer. As leaders, we feel bad when we haven't done enough: We haven't trained. We haven't mentored. We haven't led. And that makes us feel guilty—and rightly so.

"If you have done all you can as a leader," I said, "if you have given him direct feedback on his deficiencies, coached and mentored him, and given him ample opportunity to correct himself, then getting rid of a subpar performer isn't just the right thing to do, it's the only thing to do. Anything less is letting down the team. Does that make sense?"

"It does make sense, but it doesn't solve the other problem at all," the project manager said.

"What problem is that?" the VP interjected.

"The problem of replacing him. This is a complex job. And like I said, there are all kinds of issues," answered the project manager. "If I have to fire him, who else could I bring in that could get a grip on this job?"

"Who said you would have to bring someone in?" I asked. "Why not just bring someone *up*?"

"Bring someone up?" the project manager asked.

"Absolutely," I replied. "You've got a whole job site's—really two job sites'—worth of people out there. Are there no capable leaders among them? Do you not think there is anyone who could step into the role of superintendent and lead?"

"Maybe," he replied without much enthusiasm.

With that, the project manager walked back into his trailer, and the VP and I made the rounds, talking to the troops and leaders on the job site. Overall, they had great crews of experienced workers making steady progress on both towers. In fact, many of the crews were actually bouncing back and forth between towers, doing work on both.

"The two teams are basically equivalent," the VP said to me.

"Yeah, they are. Isn't it amazing how one tower is doing so well and the other isn't?" I said with a hint of sarcasm in my voice. We both knew exactly what was happening here.

"'No bad teams, only bad leaders,'" the VP said, quoting the chapter from *Extreme Ownership* that explained how when a team is failing it is the leader's fault. "The Tower Two super isn't working out. And the project manager won't do anything about it."

"Indeed," I replied. "That is some bad leadership, isn't it?"

"It sure is . . . ," the VP replied, fading off at the end as he realized what I was *really* saying. He gave me an inquisitive yet knowing look. I simply nodded.

"This is on me, isn't it," the VP said.

"You are the leader," I replied.

He stood for a moment looking across the construction site. Then he looked at me and said, "I get it."

"You get what?" I replied.

"I get it. I get that everything you just said to the project manager you might as well have been saying to me," the VP observed. "If the Tower Two super isn't working out, and the project manager isn't doing anything about it, that is actually my fault . . . and I need to fix it."

"That is Extreme Ownership," I acknowledged.

The VP was quiet for a few moments. Then he said, "Okay. I get that too. But here is the problem: The Tower Two super, he's a good guy. He's worked other jobs for us before and done just fine. And the project manager—he can get it done. Look at Tower One. I want to take care of these guys."

"Sure. The project manager can get it done, but he is not," I noted. "And are you really taking care of these guys by letting the project fall behind? Letting them fail? This is one of the dichotomies of leadership: balancing between when to keep people, to coach them and mentor them until they get up to speed, and when to make the call that they are hurting the team and get rid of them. Of course, when you coach and mentor and try to help them, you are going to develop a relationship with them—you are going to build trust. But as a leader, if you are investing too much time into one person, that means others are being ignored. Also, if a member of the team isn't able to perform effectively, it is likely impacting the mission as a whole. I think that is where you are with this situation. You are letting the project manager deal with the super, but he isn't doing it well and the whole job is suffering. You need to get in there and get it fixed."

"I do," the VP agreed. "I'll make it happen."

He asked for some time alone with the project manager. I went and talked to some of the contractors on the job and learned more about how the leadership interacted with them as contractors. An hour or so later, the VP texted me and told me he was in his trailer and wanted to debrief the conversation with the project manager, so I headed to his trailer.

"That was easier than I thought," he said.

"That's good. What did you tell him?" I asked.

"First, I told him that I liked him and thought he was very capable," the VP said. "But then I told him he was failing—and that if he was failing, I was failing. Then I explained that if I was failing, I needed to take ownership of the situation and fix it."

"How did he like that?" I asked, expecting that the project manager would get defensive and ask him to back off a little and let him do his job.

"Surprisingly, he didn't mind," answered the VP.

"Really?" I asked, surprised.

"I think he needs some help with the hard decisions," the VP said. "And I think he knows that. So I told him to give an extremely firm written counseling to the super of Tower Two. And at the same time, I told him to find someone who could step up and take over Tower Two. That was his biggest concern: he didn't think anyone in Tower Two was ready to step up. But I told him to look at some of the guys from Tower One. They have the same information. And they have the benefit of having followed a good leader on Tower One for the last six months. They know what they are supposed to do and they have already seen it done right. He liked that idea—and immediately offered a couple of names that could potentially pull it off. I think this is going to work out pretty well."

"That's great, at least the talk went great," I said. "Now comes the hard part: execution. The project manager has to have some tough conversations with the superintendent. Those conversations are hard. And if the conversations don't work, he may have to terminate the superintendent. It's tough to go from trying to coach and help someone to firing them. But, as a leader, it is unfortunately a dichotomy you have to deal with," I told him.

Over the next few weeks, I was not on the job site, but I received regular updates from the VP. He and the project manager executed the plan. The project manager wrote up the Tower Two superintendent. The VP and project manager worked together to identify and speak with the best possible candidate from Tower One to step up and become the superintendent of Tower Two. After three weeks and three written counseling sessions, the super from Tower Two made no improvement. So they let him go. The project manager elevated a new superintendent into the position and pressed on with this new leadership in place. Because of the relationship between the Tower One super and the new Tower Two super, the Tower One super went out of his way to get the new Tower Two super up to speed—even giving him manpower and resources to get them caught up, in an excellent example of Cover and Move. And although Tower One did finish ahead of Tower Two, Tower Two team's performance radically improved once the proper balance was found between continuing to coach the underperforming superintendent and deciding it was time to remove and replace him with good leadership.

# PART II

## BALANCING THE MISSION

A combined force of SEALs from Task Unit Bruiser's Charlie and Delta platoons lay down cover fire from the rooftop for their fellow SEALs, Iraqi soldiers, and U.S. Army Soldiers of Task Force Red Currahee (1st Battalion, 506th Parachute Infantry Regiment, 101st Airborne) in the streets below. The urban landscape of closely packed buildings and cramped city streets in Ramadi was inherently difficult terrain in which to fight. Extensive and challenging training in urban environments prior to deployment was crucial to Task Unit Bruiser's success, and lessons learned from Ramadi were passed on to future SEAL task units and platoons during training.

(Photo courtesy of Todd Pitman)

# CHAPTER 5
## Train Hard, but Train Smart

*Leif Babin*

### HOSTILE TERRITORY: 2009

"Big Walt is down," came the call over the intersquad radio net. Every SEAL in the platoon monitored this via the headset and radio they carried. Explosions burst all around with ear-shattering booms and incoming rounds impacted from multiple directions. In the whirlwind of an epic gun battle, the bitter news of the loss was devastating to the other SEALs in the platoon. They were in a hell of a bad spot, pinned down by enemy fire in the middle of a hostile city. One of the Humvees from their convoy had been hit and was inoperable, stranded helplessly on the street. And now their beloved platoon chief, "Big Walt"—the key leader on whom they depended to make the tough calls and rally the troops in the thick of the fight—was gone. *Who would they turn to now?*

In the chain of command, the leading petty officer (or LPO) was next in line. He knew it was his place to step up and lead. But from the look on his face, he was clearly bewildered and overwhelmed. To the rest of the SEAL platoon, who needed a leader for encouragement and direction to get disaggregated elements back on the same page, the LPO projected little confidence. The other SEAL shooters took cover from a wicked barrage of incoming rounds and returned fire as best they could. They waited for the LPO's direction. What was the next move? Consolidate forces? Attack? Retreat? The direction never came.

"WHERE IS EVERYONE?!" the LPO screamed into the radio as rounds smacked the wall inches from his face. There was no answer. How could they answer? They were scattered among a series of buildings that stretched nearly the full city block, and all of them were heavily engrossed in their immediate tasks—returning fire, dealing with casualties, and trying to figure out their own dire situation. To most of the other SEALs in the platoon, the radio query in their headset was mere background noise. Besides, trying to describe their exact location over the radio in this nondescript urban environment was difficult. Answers via radio such as "I'm over here by the wall," "I'm in the backyard of a house," or "I'm in the street halfway down the block" would provide no clarity on exact locations or action steps to take next. It would just crowd the radio net and prevent critical commands from being passed.

Only a handful of SEALs were located in the immediate room with the LPO. He didn't know where the rest were. Enemy fire was pouring in from all directions. A few SEAL shooters did what they could, returning fire from the windows and doorway. Pinned down, none of them could see the other scattered elements of the platoon taking cover in additional buildings, separated by concrete walls and the buildings between them. In reality they were all only a few yards apart, but without this knowledge it might as well have been miles.

*Boom! Boom! Boom!*

Explosions rocked the street just outside the building. Machine gun fire echoed from the walls. The LPO was rattled. His troops were hunkered down, waiting for someone—anyone—to step up and make a call.

"What are we doing?" shouted one SEAL operator. Another yelled, "WE NEED TO GET THE HELL OUT OF HERE!"

It was total mayhem and growing worse by the second as

enemy fighters converged from the surrounding city blocks and closed in on the SEALs' position. But while the enemy maneuvered to envelop the SEALs, nobody in the SEAL platoon moved. Nobody gave a command. No one took ownership to solve the problem and make things happen. Instead, they all waited while the LPO ran around frantically and tried in vain to get a head count of the SEALs in his immediate vicinity.

Meanwhile, another SEAL was hit. Then another.

*MAN DOWN.*

They had already lost Big Walt. And without his leadership, they were paralyzed, unable to extract themselves from this horrific situation. With every passing moment, their casualties grew. The LPO didn't make a call. And neither did anyone else.

The platoon's SEAL hospital corpsman, a highly trained combat medic, moved to where the casualties closest to him lay, but there were already too many for him to treat simultaneously. He would have to triage only the teammates he could save.

As casualties mounted, the chaos crescendoed and the frustrations of the SEALs in the platoon boiled over. All the while, enemy fighters crept closer and closer from multiple directions.

"SOMEBODY MAKE A CALL HERE!" one of the younger SEALs yelled in frustration.

*SOMEBODY MAKE A CALL.*

It was heartbreaking to watch. As an observer, from a position of detachment, I could clearly see what needed to happen: someone—anyone in the platoon—needed to step up and lead, consolidate the forces into one central location, establish a head count, and then get them all moving in one direction. For the SEALs immersed in this scenario, in the midst of the storm, it was much more difficult to see the way out. Staying put, not maneuvering, was the worst thing they could do.

Luckily for the SEAL platoon, the enemy fighters in this scenario weren't real. They were SEAL instructors and civilian volunteers serving as role-players simulating enemy fighters. The bullets flying around were paintball rounds; while they stung, they weren't lethal. And the explosions weren't RPG-7 rockets but grenade simulators that exploded with a loud *bang,* but without the deadly shrapnel that would rip through flesh and bone. The hostile city was a cinder-block town, constructed with walls and streets and multistory buildings with windows, stairwells, and doorways to mimic the urban environment the SEAL platoon might encounter in Iraq or elsewhere. We called it a MOUT (military operations, urban terrain) town. This was a training operation, a realistic scenario that tried to capture the chaos and difficulties of urban combat, the most complex and challenging terrain in which to fight. While it was only preparation for the rigors of combat and not actual combat itself, the lessons learned were very real. Knowing how to manage, and even thrive, in such chaos would save lives on the real battlefield and ensure a far higher probability of mission success.

The SEAL training program to prepare deploying combat units for the battlefield was legendary for both its difficulty and its superior results—not to be confused with BUD/S (Basic Underwater Demolition/SEAL training), the seven-month program that was our initial screening process, designed to weed out those who didn't possess the characteristics deemed most important for SEALs on the battlefield. The SEAL training that was actually responsible for preparing SEAL units to take on the most challenging missions and succeed in combat was called Unit Level Training. That was where SEAL platoons and task units learned to work together as a team to overcome challenges and accomplish the mission in a multitude of environments.

As detailed in chapter 8 of *Extreme Ownership,* "Decentralized Command," our success in Task Unit Bruiser in the Battle of Ramadi in 2006 was a testament to the outstanding realistic and challenging training that we had been through prior to deployment. When we returned home from Ramadi, I sought out several of the SEAL training instructors who had put us through rigorous urban combat training. I told them just how much their training had helped us: it no doubt saved lives. Jocko also recognized how critical our pre-deployment training was, so for his next assignment after Task Unit Bruiser, he chose to become the officer in charge of Training Detachment, Naval Special Warfare Group One, known as TRADET. The mission of TRADET was to train and prepare all West Coast–based SEAL Teams for combat deployments. Jocko brought back the lessons that we had learned from Ramadi and used them to improve and build upon the existing training. Having learned that leadership—at every level of the team—is the most important thing on the battlefield, Jocko orchestrated particular focus on leadership development. The goal of training was to rigorously test leaders at every level of the team: the fire team leader in charge of four SEALs, the squad leader in charge of eight, the platoon chiefs and platoon commander in charge of sixteen, and the task unit commander in charge of it all. Training was never better or more challenging than when Jocko was in command at TRADET. The training scenarios were designed to create the chaos and mayhem inherent in combat, put significant pressure on leaders, challenge their decision-making and that of their junior leaders, and humble them. Every combat leader must be humble or get humbled. We knew that being humbled in training was infinitely better than being humbled on the battlefield, where lives could be lost. It was critical that leaders understand just how easily things could spin out of control, how quickly the enemy could maneuver and get the upper hand, how communication could break down, how easily a blue-on-blue or friendly fire incident could happen, and how easy it was in the chaos of a firefight to miss a head count and leave a man behind. If they learned and understood this in training, they were far better prepared to prevent such things from happening in real combat. Jocko's mantra for training detachment was this: "Hard training is the solemn duty of trainers and leaders every day."

For two years, I had run the Junior Officer Training Course—the basic leadership training program for all officers who graduated from BUD/S—passing on these same lessons to the soon-to-be

SEAL officers before they joined their SEAL Teams as assistant platoon commanders. I then transferred back to a SEAL Team where I served as the operations officer. In addition to my primary role there, a key part of my job (as with the job of any leader) was to train, mentor, and pass on lessons learned to the tactical leaders on my team. At our SEAL Team, that meant in particular the SEAL platoon commanders and SEAL task unit commanders who would soon deploy to combat zones around the globe.

During the months of our team's unit level training in preparation for deployment, I visited the training sites alongside Jocko to observe our platoons and task unit leaders in action during their field training exercises (FTXs). These were the latter portion of weeks-long training blocks, when full-scale scenarios combined mission tasking, planning, and execution, often with supporting assets such as helicopters, tanks, and armored vehicles, against role-players serving as the enemy forces. FTXs were challenging, designed to test leadership in simulated combat situations. Together, Jocko and I evaluated the SEAL leaders, providing feedback, guidance, and mentorship in order to better prepare those leaders for the battlefield.

In the scenario above, Jocko and I had traveled to a MOUT training site to observe one of my SEAL task units with its two platoons during the FTX portions of their training in urban combat. We had spent the last two days watching their runs. It was clear that the dominant leadership force in the task unit was one of the platoon chiefs, Big Walt. He was highly experienced and a natural-born leader. No matter how great the pressure, he was resolute and unflinching. In every scenario, he stepped up and made things happen. His platoon had excelled in previous scenarios based largely upon his leadership ability. The rest of his platoon, and even the other platoon in the task unit, leaned heavily on Big Walt to make decisions. While such an effective leader brings great value, the team is seriously hamstrung if its performance relies solely on a single leader. If that leader is wounded or killed, or is not immediately present to make a call, the team's performance suffers when others are reluctant to step up, having never done so.

Jocko knew there was only one way to address the issue. "Big Walt is dominating," he said. "I think we need to put him down to see if others will step up and lead."

"I agree," I said. "I've been thinking the very same thing."

As usual, Jocko and I were on the same page. He directed his training instructor staff to put Big Walt down on the next FTX run, meaning he would be "killed" in simulation.

For the next FTX scenario, the SEAL platoon had been tasked with a mission to enter the cinder-block MOUT town and capture or kill a terrorist leader—in this case, a role-player. We observed their planning process and operation order, the mission brief to the team. Then they launched on the operation. Jocko and I followed along, shadowing the leaders and observing.

To simulate the realities of urban combat, the TRADET cadre burned tires in the streets and set off grenade simulators. The smoke and noise built tension. Unarmed "civilians," role-players without visible weapons who might or might not be enemy fighters, approached the SEALs in the patrol to harass and delay them. Then SEAL training instructors ordered other, hostile role-players to attack. Soon "enemy" role-players began shooting at the SEAL platoon with paintball or Simunition* rounds. Despite the mounting chaos, Big Walt kept things under control. He was solid as a rock.

It was time for other leaders to stop leaning on Big Walt for everything and make the calls themselves. They needed to confront the challenge of leading in difficult situations, under pressure and outside of their comfort zone, so they could learn. As we often said: *There is no growth in the comfort zone.*

Unfortunately for Big Walt, his number was up. As the pressure

---

* Simunition: nonlethal training ammunition used by military and law enforcement that provides realistic training. It consists of paint rounds fired through the modified barrels of actual weapons systems.

and intensity of the battle increased with the SEAL platoon, Big Walt was out in the street directing the team. A SEAL training instructor ran over to him and said: "Chief, you're down."

Big Walt looked back at him in disbelief. He wasn't happy. After letting fly a few expletives, he very reluctantly sat down in the street. But he couldn't help himself: he continued to try to rally the SEAL shooters around him and organize them.

"Chief, you're dead. You're out of the scenario. You can't speak," the SEAL instructor insisted.

Big Walt reluctantly complied. Two SEALs picked him up and loaded him into the back of their Humvee, which unfortunately had also been put down by the instructor cadre and was now marked as inoperable and stranded in the street. Then the two SEALs moved to cover inside a nearby building.

That's when the call came out over the intersquad radio: "Big Walt is down."

With their trusted platoon chief out of the picture, the rest of the platoon and task unit broke down. No one stepped up, no one rallied the troops or gave them direction. The LPO knew he was expected to lead, but he wasn't making things happen. Meanwhile, "enemy" role-players continued to maneuver and pick off additional SEALs, who went down as simulated casualties.

After several minutes of this, it was apparent to Jocko and me—and the rest of the SEAL training cadre—that without Big Walt, the SEAL platoon was overwhelmed to the point where learning had greatly diminished. Hard training was crucial. No matter how difficult training could be, combat was infinitely harder. Therefore training must be hard to simulate the immense challenges of real combat and apply pressure to decision-makers. But we also knew that in training, as in everything else, finding balance was key.

If training is too easy and doesn't stretch the capabilities of the participants, their improvement will be minimal. But if training overwhelms the team to a point where its participants can no longer function, it greatly diminishes the lessons they will learn from it. While training must make the team, and especially leaders, uncomfortable, it cannot be so overwhelming that it destroys morale, stifles growth, and implants a defeatist attitude.

With this in mind, we knew we needed to reinsert Big Walt into the scenario. Jocko and I discussed it and were once again in complete agreement. Big Walt needed to be resurrected.

"Big Walt," Jocko yelled over the noise of gunfire and explosions. "You're alive."

"What?" Big Walt yelled from the back of the Humvee, where he was seated and clearly exasperated that his platoon was pinned down and he was unable to help them.

"You're alive," Jocko repeated. "You're back in the scenario."

Immediately, like the mythical phoenix rising from the ashes, Big Walt stood up, and from the back of the Humvee, his weapon pointed to the sky at high port, barked simple, clear, and concise orders:

"Everyone consolidate here in this building!" he yelled, pointing out a nearby concrete structure. "Fall back to my position now!"

He didn't use his radio, as the LPO had tried to do. He used simple verbal commands shouted so those within earshot could hear and understand.

Within seconds the platoon started moving. Even the SEAL operators who couldn't see him directly could hear his voice and moved in that direction. They passed the word to others via verbal command. Within only a few seconds, the platoon consolidated into a single building. Once secure in the building, Big Walt ordered security set and called for a quick head count. The word came back within a few moments—all SEALs were accounted for. Next, Big Walt ordered the team to "break out" of the building and head to the remaining Humvees that were still operable so they could mount up, depart the city, and move out of harm's way and back to the mock base. With Big Walt's leadership and clear direction, all of this took place rapidly and with relative ease.

Once back at the base, it was onto the most important part of the training: the debrief. Leaders from the platoon and task unit stepped up to analyze what went right, what went wrong, and how they could do it better. The SEAL training instructors piled on with their critiques. Jocko debriefed the leaders. And I passed my thoughts on as well.

There were always lessons to be learned. The best platoons and task units embraced those lessons with Extreme Ownership, acknowledged the problems, and figured out ways to solve them. They constantly improved. The worst units rejected the criticism and complained about how training was too hard.

For the FTX scenario, the biggest lessons learned were for the LPO. He had been pinned down and unable to get the team moving, thinking it was an impossible situation. Yet, Big Walt was able to immediately get the team engaged and moving with a single verbal command. The LPO now understood what he had to do in such circumstances. As failure is often the best teacher, he was determined to learn from this experience and do better. We had brought Big Walt back to life to ensure that such learning took place. The reincarnated Big Walt set the example and demonstrated clearly what good leadership can accomplish—even in the direst of situations. It was a lesson the LPO and other junior leaders in the platoon were not likely to forget.

Of all the lessons we learned in combat in Ramadi, the most valuable one was this: Leadership is the most important thing on the battlefield. Leadership—at every level—is the critical factor in whether a team succeeds or fails. I witnessed this many times, under the most dreadful real-world circumstances imaginable. When a leader stepped up and took charge, got the team focused and moving together, the results were incredible. This training scenario proved yet again how when all seemed lost, just one person stepping up and making the call meant the difference between victory or defeat. Had we left Big Walt "dead" and out of the scenario, the task unit would have been completely destroyed by the enemy role-players. They would not have seen the importance of battlefield leadership. They would have thought that when things got too bad, nothing could be done to save them. But that is wrong. And as much as we wanted the scenarios to be hard, they also had to educate. It was crucial that the other SEALs in the platoon and task unit personally witnessed how a decisive call from a bold leader made all the difference, even in the most chaotic situations. Seeing this, many of those junior leaders would emulate that leader and step up to lead their teams. The whole point of training was to demonstrate this fundamental truth and build a culture of Decentralized Command where everyone leads, where leaders at every level take charge, act decisively to overcome obstacles and accomplish the mission. In order to achieve this, training had to be challenging; it had to be difficult. It had to push the team members far beyond their comfort zone so they understood what it was like to be overwhelmed, outmaneuvered, and on the defensive. But training could not be so challenging that it overwhelmed the team to a point where no learning took place.

Finding the balance between training that was too easy, where the trainees weren't truly challenged, and training so hard that the trainees were crushed was a dichotomy that leaders and instructors had to balance during every training event. Often, we didn't recognize that the dichotomy had become unbalanced until we had strayed too far in one direction.

In Task Unit Bruiser, during our training workup—before we had deployed to Ramadi—I had experienced this firsthand during our own MOUT FTXs. The instructors had sent us out on a suicide mission. They had dragged the fuselage of an old UH-1 Huey helicopter into the center of the MOUT town, surrounded by streets and cinder-block buildings. It was a *Black Hawk Down*\* scenario: our mission was to "rescue" the crew from a downed

---

\* *Black Hawk Down*, a book by Mark Bowden (also a Hollywood film based on the book), depicting the story of the Battle of Mogadishu between U.S. special operations forces and local Somali militants in October 1993.

helicopter, which the Huey hulk would represent, in the midst of a hostile city. The TRADET instructors had bolted a quarter-inch-thick steel plate to one side. In the scenario, our SEAL platoon would have to use a "quickie saw"—a heavy-duty power tool—to cut through the steel plate and access the cockpit and passenger compartment of the Huey fuselage, the simulated "wreckage." In Charlie Platoon, we knew it was going to be a tough mission, but we were determined to do our utmost to get it done as quickly and efficiently as possible.

We launched on the nighttime operation in Humvees that stopped three blocks away and dropped off the main force of SEALs who would go in for the rescue. Quickly and quietly, we patrolled on foot through the dark streets. All was quiet until we arrived at the downed helicopter—the Huey fuselage resting ominously in the MOUT town's main intersection.

Our SEAL fire teams moved into position and set up a defensive perimeter. Meanwhile, the SEAL breacher started his quickie saw and revved the engine, going to work on the steel plate as the saw bit into the metal with a loud *screech,* sending sparks flying.

Within seconds, all hell broke loose. Role-players—the "enemy" fighters we were up against—unleashed a vicious barrage of paintball rounds from every direction. The SEAL fire teams on security returned fire, but it was of little use. We were stuck in the middle of the street sawing through the steel plate while the enemy had the high ground from the second-story windows and rooftops all around us. There was nothing we could do except abandon the mission. And with our mentality in Task Unit Bruiser, that was not an option. We were determined to get into the helicopter and "rescue" the two crew members inside, as per the scenario we had been given. So we were stuck, out in the street with no cover, taking fire from all directions. It was a total bloodbath. The instructors tossed grenade simulators that exploded with loud *booms* and blinding flashes.

I moved around, checking on the guys under the ridiculous

onslaught. Our breacher running the quickie saw was taking the worst of it. I moved up to him to see how he was doing.

"How we looking?" I yelled over the din.

"Almost there," he answered, gritting his teeth as multiple paintball rounds impacted his gear at high speed, splattering his load-bearing equipment and leaving nasty welts on his neck, arms, and legs. His back was turned to the enemy, and because he was operating the heavy saw with both hands, he couldn't even shoot back. But he stood there and took it like a man—a "Big Tough Frogman." I knelt next to him and returned fire on his behalf to try and suppress the enemy onslaught, to no avail. I got hit from every direction as dozens of paintball rounds slammed into me, stinging my hands, arms, legs, and neck. Pretty soon, the face mask and goggles I wore to protect my eyes were so covered in greasy paint from the paintball rounds, I could barely see. The TRADET instructors wore ChemLights that glowed to mark their position at night and let us know not to shoot them. They were supposed to be off-limits and treated as if they weren't there. I couldn't make out much, but I knew where they were located just a few yards away. Knowing they were controlling the situation, I unleashed several paint rounds of my own in their direction, sending the instructors scurrying for cover. Finally, the breacher cut through the steel plate and we rescued the two role-players acting as "pilots." We then beat a hasty retreat out of the city, cringing at the welts we had received and laughing about how much that evolution had sucked.

Of all the challenging FTX scenarios we'd been through at MOUT, that was the craziest—and also the least educational. It had gone beyond a difficult scenario that challenged us and turned into nothing more than a huge suckfest that we just had to grit our teeth and bear until it was over. When we got back, I counted at least thirty-seven different paintball impacts on my uniform and op gear, and probably even more that I couldn't distinguish. That didn't count the dozen or so that had hit my face mask and goggles. Had they been real bullets, I would have died many times over. When Jocko saw me covered head to toe in colorful paint splotches, he just shook his head and laughed.

"I guess you guys GOT SOME," he said with a smile.

"Yeah," I said. "We got some alright. We got the 'full benefit' of that evolution."

The "enemy" attack by the role-players had been so overwhelming, there'd been nothing we could do to counter it. Cutting through the steel plate on the Huey had taken several agonizing minutes—much longer than the TRADET instructors had anticipated. It would have been better training and more educational for us had they eased back the attacks once they realized we were overwhelmed and pinned down, unable to move until the saw cut through the steel. The biggest thing I did learn from the scenario was that in such a situation, we would need a much larger force to clear all the buildings on the entire block and put SEALs on the high ground, to ensure we had tactically superior positions on the enemy and not the other way around. The other thing I learned was that at some point, I had to be willing to cancel a mission. I would have to make the tough call to pull back and abort the mission so we could regroup and re-attack rather than pointlessly sacrifice my entire team.

In Task Unit Bruiser, we embraced hard training. We took on difficult challenges and physically demanding scenarios with eagerness. But I realized that there was a line. Training had to be hard, but it couldn't be so hard that it crushed the team and diminished the learning that is supposed to take place. It was a dichotomy that had to be carefully balanced.

On the other side of the dichotomy, good leaders must ensure that training incorporates the most difficult, realistic challenges of the real-world battlefield. There were some SEALs who didn't want to train hard. They constantly complained at being challenged and driven beyond their comfort zone. They said training was unrealistic, too basic, or that they wanted to work on what they referred to as "advanced tactics." In truth, most of this was just a euphemism for "I don't want to train hard; I don't want to be challenged." It was weak and frankly shocking to see such attitudes in a few SEALs, but particularly so in experienced SEAL leaders.

"This training is ridiculous," one SEAL chief said of the challenges in the training scenarios that TRADET built under Jocko's leadership. "I've deployed multiple times and nothing that bad has ever happened on any of my deployments."

But just because someone hasn't experienced the worst-case scenario in real life doesn't mean it couldn't happen. It doesn't mean the team shouldn't be prepared for the harshest realities of combat. In fact, quite the opposite is true. The team must be prepared for those worst-case scenarios—multiple downed men at the same time, a vehicle that hits an IED, or a "low-risk" mission that goes horribly wrong.

Often, one of the biggest points of pushback from such complainers in the SEAL platoon or task unit was that the "enemy" role-players—the SEAL TRADET instructors and other volunteers—were too "good" at their job. They were more skilled and better equipped than any of the enemy fighters we faced overseas. But that should have been embraced as a good thing, challenging the team so it would be more prepared. Besides, many of the enemy fighters we were up against in Ramadi were pretty damned skilled. They had years of real-world combat experience from which they had learned, innovated, and adapted. You could never take them for granted, never get complacent, or they would overrun your position and wipe you out.

Along with this, another common criticism of why training was too hard was that the training instructors "cheated."

"They know our plan," some SEALs would complain about the role-players. "And we have to follow the rules, while they do not."

Jocko countered this with logic: "The enemy fighters you are going up against overseas, they don't follow rules either: they have no rules of engagement like we do. They use treachery, to conceal their attack or lure you into an ambush. They use women and children as human shields. They use suicide bombers. They set up opposing ambushes where they might shoot each other to try to kill more of us. They don't care. But we do. We play by different rules than they do. So if my training instructors—our role-players—are breaking the rules: GOOD. That is realistic training. Instead of complaining about it, embrace it and figure out a way to overcome it."

*Hard training is the solemn duty of trainers and leaders every day.*

It was the mantra that Jocko and his TRADET instructors lived by. And it was incumbent upon them to ensure that training was difficult, that standards were held high so that SEAL platoons and task units were ready to survive and thrive in the toughest environments they might be thrust into on distant battlefields.

Some leaders strove to make sure their people were happy, which might include overlooking performance deficiencies, allowing the team to cut corners, and not holding the line to train hard, maintain discipline, follow standard operating procedures, and overcome obstacles. Some leaders thought they were encouraging their team through false cheerleading, telling their people they're doing better than they truly were. And perhaps that's what the SEAL leaders who complained were seeking. But leaders who never pushed the team outside its comfort zone in training, who didn't push the standards and drive their team toward exceptional performance, and who didn't provide a direct and honest critique ended up with less productive, less effective teams that failed when truly tested under the rigors of real-world challenges.

The best leaders—often those who learned through experience what worked and what didn't—looked out for the long-term success of the team and the mission. They didn't shy away from tough conversations to correct underperformance. They held the standards high and ensured the team was fully prepared for the worst-case scenario. Leaders who pushed their people to excel, to continuously learn and grow, enabled their teams to become comfortable in situations where they were previously uncomfortable. By challenging frontline leaders and junior or less experienced personnel to take on greater roles and responsibilities, the team implements proper Decentralized Command so that leaders at every level of the team step up to lead. The team then becomes far more effective and able to accomplish its mission. When the team succeeds and outperforms all others, that opens up the biggest opportunities for its people's long-term success.

The strategic goal of training must always be to build capable leaders at every level of the team. For this, hard training is essential. But if training is too hard, it will break the team and minimize learning and growth. So there must be balance: train hard, but train smart.

### Principle

Hard training is critical to the performance of any team; this is clearly the case with SEAL platoons and task units deploying to combat zones, where we say: "You train how you fight and you fight how you train." The best training programs push their teams hard, far beyond their comfort zone, so that the team can learn from mistakes in training. Hopefully, this prevents the team from making those or similar mistakes in real life.

In *About Face: The Odyssey of an American Warrior,* Colonel David H. Hackworth (U.S. Army, Ret.),\* quoted a mentor of his, U.S. Army Colonel Glover Johns: "The harder the training, the more troops will brag." Ask any SEAL: "What was the hardest BUD/S class?" and you'll get your answer: their class number. Everyone wants to say that they had it the toughest, that their training was harder than everyone else's—after the fact, at least.

---

\* *About Face: The Odyssey of an American Warrior,* by Colonel David H. Hackworth (U.S. Army, Ret.) and Julie Sherman (New York: Simon & Schuster, 1989).

But sometimes in the midst of training some teams want to stay in their comfort zone. Leaders can't allow that.

Training must be hard. Training must simulate realistic challenges and apply pressure to decision-makers. *There is no growth in the comfort zone.* If training doesn't push the team beyond the limits of what is easy, the team, and particularly leaders within the team, will never develop the capacity to take on greater challenges. But training is designed to make the team better, to enable its members to function in realistic conditions they might face. It can't be so difficult that it crushes the team, demoralizes it, or overwhelms participants to the point where they fail to learn. As in everything, leaders must find the balance in training and focus on three critical aspects: realism, fundamentals, and repetition.

Training must be realistic. Every training scenario should be based upon something that is likely to (or could potentially) be encountered in a real scenario. The takeaways must be immediately applicable to the team's mission. For those who haven't experienced it, the chaos and uncertainty of the battlefield can be overwhelming. That's why it was critical to create that chaos as much as we could in training. Training should push the team, and particularly leaders, into realistic, uncomfortable situations where they aren't sure what to do. In the business world, training must do the same. Role-play scenarios dealing with a problem client or customer, or a high-pressure decision that must be made immediately, when the outcome isn't certain and the picture not 100 percent clear. Rehearse the contingencies for a serious accident and run the procedures that must be followed even under high stress.

Training must focus on the fundamentals. While units must adapt and innovate, some basic tactics do not change. Just as this is true in military tactics, it is true in any business or area of life. Often people want to skip through the basic fundamentals into what they call "advanced tactics." But advanced tactics are worthless if a team can't do the basics well. Leaders must ensure that a training program develops the foundation of basic fundamentals.

Training must be repetitive. It is not enough to have a training program for new hires in the first days or weeks that they join the team. Training must be continuous for everyone. Each person gets better with iterations, so it is important to plan repetitive training over time that challenges each member of the team—particularly leaders.

Take Extreme Ownership of training. Rather than wait for someone else to build a training program or make training more realistic and effective, seize the initiative on your own. The best training programs are not orchestrated from the top but driven from the bottom—the frontline leaders who are closest to the action and the lessons learned. Utilize the most accomplished members of the team to drive training programs and pass on lessons learned to others.

"We don't have the budget to train" isn't a valid excuse. It costs nothing to set up a role-playing scenario to put leaders in situations where they are unprepared, to make tough decisions and therefore make them better.

"We don't have time to train" isn't a valid excuse. Make time for the things that are important. And good training is essential to the success of any team. Building frequently recurring training into the schedule is the most effective way to improve the team's performance.

Again, the key to great training is finding balance. Hard training is essential, but smart training is crucial to maximize the use of time and enable optimal learning.

### Application to Business

"I don't trust my frontline leaders to execute the mission," said the senior project manager. "You're telling us that we need to use Decentralized Command, but I don't have faith that my junior leaders can properly execute."

"Training is how you develop your leaders and build that trust," I replied. "Let's take a look at your training program."

"We don't really have one," the senior project manager responded.

"Well, that could certainly be your problem," I observed. "Why don't you take ownership of building it?"

I had given a keynote presentation to the company's annual leadership off-site, and the combat principles we wrote about in *Extreme Ownership* had resonated powerfully with the team. The company brought me back to build a leadership development program for two dozen of the company's senior leaders—the department heads and senior project managers, just below the c-suite level, who executed the vision of the company's senior executive team.

It was a great company with solid leaders in place, some with substantial experience and others fairly new to the team. As a result of their success, the company had experienced rapid growth and expansion. But the dispersion of resources, particularly experienced leadership, on a vast number of projects happening concurrently was causing a problem.

While eager and aggressive to win, some of the company's senior leaders recognized that the speed of growth thrust very junior leaders with inadequate experience into critical management positions with little oversight. The senior leaders recognized the risk associated with this in the quality of service the company delivered and the ability of the frontline teams to effectively accomplish the mission on time and within budget.

As I worked with the company's senior leaders over the course of many months, I heard a consistent theme: "We don't have enough experienced leaders in the field to run these projects. We're piling too much on inexperienced leaders who are unprepared."

It was a genuine concern, and a risk that didn't seem to be fully comprehended by the company's executive team when brought to their attention.

I addressed the problem head-on during one of my meetings with the senior leaders in the class. "The point you bring up is a valid one," I said, "but the only way to prepare those inexperienced leaders is to train them. You need to place them in tough circumstances in training that will prepare them for the challenges of the real world."

Some on the team seemed skeptical.

"How is training ever going to replicate actual experience?" one leader inquired.

I could see others in the group nodding, agreeing with the premise of the question.

I explained that training could not replace actual experience. There was nothing better than real-world experience. But I emphasized that challenging training programs that focused on realism, fundamentals, and repetition would greatly improve the performance of their junior leaders. It would also go far to mitigate the risk of failure by inexperienced junior leaders operating with too little oversight.

I had talked extensively about the Battle of Ramadi and the lessons we had learned from it. We did this to give context to the group so they fully understood where the leadership principles we taught had come from.

"Do you know how much experience I had on the actual battlefield as a SEAL platoon commander before I deployed to Ramadi in 2006?" I asked the group.

Some shrugged. No one answered. They either didn't know, didn't want to guess, or perhaps didn't want to admit the answer.

"None," I said. "That was my first time. I had never been a platoon commander before. I had never led a platoon of SEALs in advance of a huge conventional U.S. military force of fifty tanks and thousands of Soldiers and Marines. I had never been in a real firefight before. No one in my platoon had done any of that before.

"Do you know how much experience Jocko had as a task unit commander, when we deployed to Ramadi?" I continued. "None.

And yet he showed exceptional strategic vision in counterinsurgency operations and led Task Unit Bruiser as a key supporting element to the U.S. victory there. The Delta Platoon commander, Seth Stone—he was deploying as a platoon commander for the first time and he proved himself an extraordinary combat leader in his very first firefight."

I relayed a story that Jocko had told me about Seth and Delta Platoon on their first operation in the dangerous and violent Malaab District of eastern Ramadi. Seth had led his platoon, including Delta Platoon's courageous and aggressive point man, machine gunner and sniper, J. P. Dinnell, on a patrol with a company of U.S. Soldiers from the legendary 1st Battalion, 506th Parachute Infantry Regiment, "Band of Brothers," of the U.S. Army's 101st Airborne Division and their Iraqi soldier counterparts, led by an Army major as their advisor. The 1/506th Soldiers had been on the ground in this volatile neighborhood for months. They'd seen daily, violent combat and scores of intense gun battles. Our Task Unit Bruiser SEALs had only just arrived. Not long after the combined patrol of SEALs, U.S. Soldiers, and Iraqi troops had moved out into the streets of the Malaab, they soon found themselves in what we called a "Big Mix-It-Up"—a significant firefight—as enemy fighters attacked them with machine guns and RPG rockets. The U.S. and Iraqi patrol was pinned down and unable to move. Seth made his way over to the Army major in charge of the Iraqi soldiers, crouching low as bullets zipped past.

"I'll take a section of my SEALs and flank the enemy fighters," Seth said calmly over the clamor of incoming and outgoing gunfire, pointing to the location on his map where they planned to maneuver. "We'll take the high ground from the rooftop of one of those buildings there," he added, pointing at a cluster of buildings.

"Sounds good," said the major. "Do it."

Seth gave the signal to move out, with J. P. Dinnell in the lead wielding his Mk46 machine gun and the squad of SEALs following behind. They aggressively maneuvered to flank the enemy, entered and cleared one of the buildings, then took the rooftop. From there, they engaged enemy fighters from the high ground, killing several and forcing the remainder to flee.

The patrol, no longer pinned down, was able to continue and soon made its way back to the safety of the base.

As Jocko listened to the debrief after the operation, the major said to Seth: "That was really impressive how you calmly maneuvered your element under fire and flanked the enemy. You must have been in a lot of urban combat—and a bunch of firefights."

"No, sir," Seth replied. "That was actually my very first firefight."

To the senior leaders in the classroom, I explained that the only reason Seth and Delta Platoon were able to perform so well in their first firefight was that they had participated in extraordinary, realistic training prior to deployment. It was the same for us in Charlie Platoon.

"We were all thrust into some incredibly difficult situations," I continued. "But we had spent months preparing in rigorous training scenarios. That training saved lives, enabled us to effectively execute, and played an integral role in Task Unit Bruiser's success."

"We could use a training program," one senior leader agreed. "It would be nice if the executive leadership would develop one."

"That's what you are going to do?" I asked. "Wait for the executive team to build the training program? Does that sound like Extreme Ownership? Look, they've already got a lot on their plates. Besides, all of you in this room are closer to this problem. You understand where the experience is lacking and you have the knowledge that your junior leaders need. So *you* need to develop it."

I explained that in the SEAL Teams, it isn't the senior leaders— the admirals and captains—who run the leadership programs.

It's the returning platoon commanders and platoon chiefs and leading petty officers.

"It's up to you to develop the training program," I said. "Then run it up the chain of command for their support and approval.

"Put your junior, inexperienced leaders in difficult scenarios," I continued. "Role-play with them. Force them to make decisions under pressure. Then debrief and analyze those decisions."

I reminded them of Jocko's mantra at training detachment: *Hard training is the solemn duty of trainers and leaders every day.*

"But you have to train smart," I reminded them. "Maximize the use of time and resources. Make training realistic to prepare your key leaders for their real-world challenges. I guarantee you that the return on investment from a good training program will be substantial."

Throughout the leadership development course, I grew to know many of the company's senior leaders well. There were several outstanding leaders in the group. Three of them recognized the pressing need for a training program and took ownership of the problem. They stepped up and took on the challenge of developing and implementing an effective training program, despite their busy schedules.

I followed up with the company's executive team and highlighted to them the need for an effective training program. Just as I suspected, the executive team was fully supportive. They welcomed the efforts of the department heads and senior project managers who took charge of the program.

It took significant effort and time to build the program. Finally, after months of preparation, they were ready to roll it out. I wasn't on-site to observe the initial training session, but the next week I followed up via phone with one of the senior department heads who had helped build the program.

"How did it go?" I asked him.

"It could have gone better," he said. "There was a lot of pushback."

I was surprised to hear this after the extensive efforts that had been made to build a solid training program.

"What happened?" I asked.

"It wasn't the content," the senior department head answered. "The content is good. The objectives are solid. It was the delivery.

"The leader who instructed this first course was probably not the right guy to lead this effort," he continued. "He put out too much information and constantly quizzed the participants, most of whom couldn't keep up. When it was clear they didn't understand, he yelled at them in front of the class. The class is normally an enthusiastic group, but no one was happy about that training. The feedback has been super-negative."

"Not good," I responded. "You know how important it is for the company to have an effective training program. First of all, training is only as good as the instructors who are teaching it. So you have to carefully select the right people for this.

"You have to push the standards and train hard," I said. "But you can't train so hard that it defeats the purpose of training in the first place: to educate and prepare your team to more effectively execute the company's mission.

"So, you need to rein that in," I continued. "Start over with a new instructor. In fact, you should instruct the next session. And make it clear to participants that this time will be different. Training should be challenging. But only as a means to make your team better, to prepare them for the challenges they face in the real world. You've got to train hard, but train smart."

A Task Unit Bruiser machine gunner holds security from inside a compound. The terrain in the battle of Ramadi was mostly urban, but some operations took place outside of the city in rural terrain. Yet, the fundamentals remained the same: Cover and Move. Notice the extra bandolier of ammunition slung over the shoulder. Bruiser SEALs carried as much ammo as possible, and still ran low on a regular basis.

(Courtesy of U.S. Navy. Photograph taken by Mate Second Class Sam Peterson.)

# CHAPTER 6
## Aggressive, Not Reckless

*Jocko Willink*

**"VIETRAM"—MC-1 AREA OF OPERATIONS, NORTHEAST OF RAMADI, IRAQ: 2006**

Suddenly, the sound of machine gun fire ripped through the quiet night air as beautiful but deadly red streaks of tracer fire arced across the sky. I wasn't exactly sure what was going on, but I knew that my sniper overwatch team out there in the darkness was in a gunfight. That was about all I knew for sure. I didn't know if they had been spotted by enemy fighters and fired upon. I wasn't sure what size enemy force they were engaged with. I definitely didn't know what support—if any—the SEALs in the overwatch element needed from me or our assault force, staged and ready to launch. But even without a clear picture of what was happening, I needed to make a call. And my default mind-set was aggressive— to take action to solve problems and accomplish the mission. With that in mind, I knew what we must do: EXECUTE.

We were poised and ready to launch on a major clearance operation in a particularly violent insurgent stronghold. Our objective was to clear a village and marketplace in that stronghold—a series of small buildings and market stalls—known to U.S. forces as "Mav Market." The name derived from a past combat operation nearby, when American forces under enemy attack had called for close air support, and U.S. war planes hit several enemy positions with AGM-65 Maverick missiles.

For the operation we were about to launch, I was the ground force commander, staged with the assault force of Charlie Platoon SEALs and a dozen Iraqi soldiers, at a U.S. Army combat outpost (COP) in a rural agricultural area outside the city. The area was known to U.S. forces as "MC-1." Although it shared a border with the northern edge of the city of Ramadi, MC-1 was physically separated by the Euphrates River that ran west to east through the area, demarcating the urban cityscape from a rural farming community. Beyond the river, the landscape opened into irrigated farm fields, levees, palm trees, and canals interspersed with small, scattered groups of houses. It did not look at all like the urban or desert terrain we had come to expect in Iraq; it was more like a scene from a Vietnam War movie. Task Unit Bruiser and other U.S. forces had nicknamed the area "VietRam," an ode to the place so many of us had grown up hearing about in stories passed down through oral history from the generations of SEALs who had fought in Vietnam and through the Hollywood celluloid depictions in movies we had all watched growing up.

Although the Euphrates River separated the urban zone of Ramadi proper and VietRam, the violence from the city spilled over and permeated the countryside. The roads contained massive IEDs, large enough to take out armored vehicles, with frequent attacks along the main thoroughfares. Coalition patrols, when crossing fields or open terrain, were a vulnerable target for enemy mortar teams that knew the area well. The U.S. Army's 1st Battalion, 109th Infantry Regiment (1/109th), was responsible for the area. They were an outstanding combat unit of experienced, professional, and courageous Soldiers. By the time Task Unit Bruiser arrived, the 1/109th had been on the ground for nearly a year fighting in this area. Because of the expansive rural terrain, with limited roads, troop concentrations were impossible—a single infantry platoon had to cover several square kilometers of battlespace. With so little combat power to affect such a large space, it was difficult to penetrate deep into enemy-held territory.

One of Leif's assistant platoon commanders (or AOIC, for assistant officer in charge) in Charlie Platoon had built a solid relationship with the Soldiers of the 1/109th Infantry. The AOIC had teamed up with the Army company and platoon leadership that patrolled the area. Together, they made aggressive plans, orchestrating a bold push into the enemy-controlled territory along the river. The AOIC, along with Charlie Platoon's leading petty officer (or LPO), and sniper Chris Kyle led their element of SEALs and the Iraqi soldiers they worked with on patrols and sniper overwatch missions deep into the contested areas, frequently receiving heavy enemy contact.

On one operation, the AOIC split his element of SEALs and Iraqi troops into two squads. One squad patrolled on foot across a muddy, open field when suddenly, insurgent fighters hiding in the tree line and nearby buildings opened up on them with machine guns. The patrol dropped to the ground for protection, pinned down by the enemy's effective fire. Once they were "sucking mud"—facedown in a prone position to avoid the hail of bullets—enemy mortar rounds rained down, impacting all around them. Miraculously, the muddy field saved the patrol, as the mortars penetrated deep into the mud before exploding; the ground absorbed the explosions and lethal shrapnel, leaving large holes in the mud but fortunately no holes in our teammates or their Iraqi soldiers. The other SEAL squad, which had maintained a covered position from the levee that bordered the field, quickly laid down suppressive fire and beat back the enemy attack. Their solid efforts and plan using Cover and Move enabled the SEAL squad stranded in the open to move to safety without any casualties.

Over time, the series of aggressive operations by the 1/109th Soldiers, Charlie Platoon SEALs, and Iraqi soldiers challenged the insurgents' control over the area. Together, the operations enabled the 1/109th to gain ground and set up a small COP in the midst of VietRam, from which a platoon of 1/109th Soldiers lived and worked. From that small outpost, 1/109th and the AOIC's SEAL element conducted patrols, gathered atmospherics, and acquired intelligence about enemy operations in the area. Eventually, they identified a small enclave of a dozen or so buildings that seemed to be the root of many enemy attacks: Mav Market.

With multiple intelligence sources indicating the area was a base of operations for insurgents, the AOIC had brought the intelligence to us—Leif and the rest of Charlie Platoon, and me at the task unit—with the recommendation that we conduct an aggressive operation in the area. We agreed and planned an assault to clear the village, capture any suspected enemy personnel, search the market, and destroy any weapons caches we found. The planning cycle commenced, mission approval given from our chain of command, and a few days later, we launched from Camp Ramadi to the 1/109th infantry's COP in MC-1.

Wanting to get "eyes on" the village and the market prior to the assault, we sent a sniper overwatch team—a small number of SEAL snipers, machine gunners, a corpsman, a radioman, and an element leader—into the target area prior to the assault. Their job was to spearhead the operation, sneak in clandestinely, observe the target area for suspicious activity, and provide security when the assault element entered the hamlet. This was critical, as the enemy had an effective early warning network in the area. Sympathetic (or fearful) locals monitored roads and paths going in and out of enemy strongpoints. When coalition forces passed by, the locals passed signals or made radio calls to inform the insurgents we were headed their way. That gave the enemy fighters an opportunity to make a move: either run and evade, hide their weapons and pretend to be civilians, or rally their troops and attack with IEDs, machine guns, rockets, and mortars.

To minimize their exposure for this mission, the overwatch element rode into the COP with a standard U.S. Army logistics convoy so as not to raise any suspicion, while the rest of us—the assault force that would actually clear the village and market—remained at Camp Ramadi, ready to launch.

When darkness fell, the overwatch element quietly patrolled from the COP. They stealthily made their way across flooded fields, through canals, over levees, and through date palm groves, until they reached the target area. The overwatch element observed from a distance for a few minutes and then determined that one of the buildings on the outskirts of the village appeared vacant. The point man pushed a little farther forward, confirmed that there were no signs of any occupants, and then called the rest of the overwatch element to advance. The team entered the building and cleared it, not dynamically as a SWAT team might do, but quietly, like cat burglars. Finding nothing, they put their snipers in place and set their machine gunners in security positions. The radioman passed their position to the tactical operations center back at Camp Ramadi.

Once the overwatch was in position, the next phase of the operation commenced. As ground force commander for the operation, I joined Leif and the rest of Charlie Platoon's SEALs, who would be the assault force for the operation, accompanied by our Iraqi soldiers. The AOIC who had inspired the operation was the assault force commander. We mounted up in our vehicles at Camp Ramadi and drove out to the COP in MC-1 from where the overwatch had launched. Our assault force was about thirty strong, half SEALs and the other half Iraqi soldiers.

With the overwatch element in position, any movement or activity in the village would be observed and passed to the assault force. I anticipated that there might be enemy activity in the area, spurred up when the assault force entered the vicinity and the insurgent early warning network passed the word. Our transit in the Humvees was uneventful. We arrived at the COP, our staging point for the assault. We pulled in and combat parked the vehicles (Humvees were backed into parking spaces to facilitate quick departure), and our team dismounted. I made a quick radio check with the overwatch position.

"Charlie two-six, this is Jocko, over," I said.

"Jocko, this is Charlie two-six, go," the overwatch element leader responded.

I passed a quick situation report: "Assault force is staged at the COP. Any activity when we rolled in?"

"Negative," he responded. "Nothing significant. We saw a few locals moving about. Normal pattern of life. About twenty minutes ago, it got very quiet. When you guys rolled in, no change—it seems like the village is bedded down for the night."

"Roger," I replied. "We will let things continue to settle, then launch in a few hours as planned," I told him, indicating that we would stick to our predetermined assault time late in the night.

I walked out to the vehicles and passed word to the rest of the team. The assault force dismounted the vehicles and entered the COP building. They took off their gear, sprawled out, and waited. Leif, his AOIC, and I had business to attend to, so we made our way to a small tactical operations center (TOC) that had been set up by the 1/109th Soldiers inside their COP. In an age when people usually think a TOC means giant plasma television monitors, coffeemakers, and slick modern furniture, this was the other end of the spectrum. This TOC was bare-bones: a few maps on the wall; a rack-mounted base station radio unit to communicate with elements in the field as well as the headquarters back in Camp Ramadi; some dry-erase boards with names, people, and plans written out on them; and basic communication procedures. That was it.

The AOIC knew the area and the key leaders well and greeted the Army platoon leader and the Soldiers in the TOC.

Leif and I introduced ourselves to the leadership of the 1/109th Infantry platoon that was occupying the COP. "Good evening," I told them as we shook hands. "I'm Jocko, the task unit commander. This is Leif, the SEAL platoon commander."

"Great to meet you guys," the 1/109th platoon commander said. He was a professional Soldier, as were his noncommissioned officers and troops manning the COP. "Thanks for all the support you've been giving us. We've really had some good impact around here. A month ago, we would have been attacked just trying to get to this spot. Now we live here!"

"Outstanding. You guys have done great work," I said. "I'm glad we were able to support you."

With that, the platoon commander talked over the map with us, pointing out danger areas, describing the enemy's tactics particular to the area, and outlining a fire support plan should we need help. Leif and I followed up with some pointed questions about the routes in and out of the target village and then sat down and listened.

Our overwatch element in the target area continued to pass traffic, with no significant change. The area had settled down and there was no remarkable activity in the village.

Inside the COP, we listened to the battalion radio net, the channel that every platoon and every company in the 1/109th battalion monitored. In such a hot area, there was always something happening and radio kept us up-to-date—reports of enemy movement, friendly units maneuvering to contact, U.S. troops wounded and sometimes killed. It was a strange experience to hear the muffled gunfire off in the distance and then hear the radio calls of the men on the ground, in that distant firefight, engulfed in adrenaline, making decisions, passing information, requesting support. Some leaders stayed calm even in bad situations. With others you could hear the panic in their voices. Listening to hundreds of radio calls like this taught me and the rest of the Task Unit Bruiser leadership that staying calm on the radio was a mandatory trait if you wanted to lead effectively.

Then, in the midst of some of the normal radio traffic, we heard a strange radio call from the 1/109th battalion TOC back in Ramadi. It seemed there was another coalition unit that had not deconflicted and was purportedly conducting an operation in the direct vicinity of the Task Unit Bruiser operation. It was not normal for a unit to be out without intensive coordination. But there was even more puzzling information: the report on the radio said the unit "could possibly be dressed in indigenous clothing."

This quickly went from strange to dangerous. Under normal circumstances in this hostile battlespace with multiple U.S. and Iraqi units, which clearly stood out as friendly in their combat gear and weaponry, the hazards from a potential "blue-on-blue" or friendly fire situation were quite high without extensive decon- fliction. But for coalition troops to conduct an operation without identifiable uniforms, when there were U.S. troops in the area who might mistake them for enemy fighters, was completely in- sane. Identifying friend from foe was already hard enough, given the fact that the Iraqi Army dressed in mismatched uniforms, sometimes throwing in elements of civilian clothing. The insurgents sometimes wore a mix of paramilitary gear, mismatched uniforms, and their favorite clothing—tracksuits with a balaclava or kaffi- yeh covering their faces. During my first deployment to Iraq, my platoon had always worn black balaclavas, not only to protect our identities but also because they had a psychologically intimi- dating effect on the enemy. But in Ramadi, no one in Task Unit Bruiser wore balaclavas or anything that covered their faces. A covered face meant terrorist, and no one wanted to be mistaken for a terrorist in this environment. It could result in an American bullet to the head.

Among all this radio traffic, a call came from the overwatch element. "We've got movement," the radioman from the over- watch whispered.

Leif, his AOIC, and I stood up and moved closer to listen to the radio.

"Four to six military-age males, moving tactically," the radio- man described.

"Do you have PID?" I asked. This was a difficult question. PID meant "positive identification"—I was asking if the element could identify if the people they were seeing were friendly or hostile.

"Stand by," the radioman passed. In the SEAL Teams, "stand by" has many meanings, based on how it is used and the tone of the voice. It can mean "Wait a second." Or it can mean "Don't move." It can mean "Don't push me any further." It can also mean "I don't know, let me find out." Additionally, it can mean "Brace for impact, something bad is about to happen."

The tone in the radioman's voice was a combination of "I don't know, let me find out" and "Brace for impact, something bad is about to happen."

Leif and I looked at each other. I nodded to Leif, and he knew what I was thinking. Then he nodded to his AOIC and they grabbed their helmets, hustled outside, and assembled the troops, telling them to gear up and load the vehicles.

I then passed a statement that the overwatch commander didn't expect: "Do not engage unless you confirm an actual hostile act. There could be friendlies in the area."

"What?" the overwatch element leader questioned. This was highly unusual.

"There could be friendlies in the area that have not coordinated with us. And they might be dressed in indigenous clothing," I told him.

"Seriously?" the overwatch element leader responded, his frustration coming through even clearer than his radio signal.

"Seriously. Pass the word," I replied solemnly.

This was a very bad situation. Combat is by nature confusing. It is impossible to know and understand the dynamics of everything that happens on the battlefield. This is classically known as "the fog of war."* The fog is real. Differing reports, differing opinions, differing perceptions, time lags to receive and process information, weather conditions, darkness, terrain, enemy feints and maneuvers, friendly forces moving and reacting—the chaos and uncertainty add up and paint a picture that is foggy at best. When I ran the training for the West Coast SEAL Teams,

---

* A term commonly attributed to Carl von Clausewitz (1780–1831), Prussian general and military theorist, who wrote, "War is the realm of uncertainty," in his book, *On War*. Note: Clausewitz never actually used the term "fog of war."

one of the lessons I regularly taught was that the most important piece of information you could have on the battlefield is the knowledge of where *you* are. Without that, nothing else matters. The next most important piece of information is where other friendly forces are located. Only then does it matter where the enemy is; without knowing where one's own unit is and without knowing where other friendly units are, it is nearly impossible to engage the enemy.

In the scenario unfolding, although the overwatch knew exactly where they were, where the assault force was, and where other 1/109th Infantry units were located, they weren't sure now if there were other friendly units in the area—nor in this case would they be able to positively identify them. It wasn't good.

Tense minutes passed. The assault force had loaded into the vehicles and stood by waiting for the word. Then, without any other prior warning, gunfire erupted from the area of the overwatch. Tracers cut through the sky.

I did not know what was happening. I wasn't sure who was shooting at whom. I asked for a status from the radioman on the overwatch team. Nothing.

Was the overwatch engaging insurgents? Could there be a shootout between insurgents and the local townspeople? Was the overwatch team compromised and under attack? Was the "indigenously dressed" coalition unit there? Was this a blue-on-blue fratricide happening? I simply could not know. The only thing I knew was what we had planned and rehearsed during the mission planning: if the overwatch got compromised, the assault force would roll in "hard," meaning we would drive vehicles right into the target area (normally they would stop several hundred meters away and the assault force would foot patrol in) and "lock down," or set security on the main road that ran through the village. I also knew that if there were insurgents in the village and we gave them too much time, they would either coordinate their defenses and prepare to fight, or run away—neither of which would be good for the assault force. So despite the uncertainty of the situation, I went with the default mode: I got aggressive.

I ran out to the vehicles, loaded with SEALs and ready to roll, jumped into the command vehicle, keyed the mic on my radio, and said, "Execute, execute, execute. We are rolling to Route Duster [the main road in the village] and locking it down."

The lead navigator gave his command on the radio: "Rolling."

The vehicles shifted into gear and started out rapidly down the road toward the village, toward the gunfire, toward the uncertainty.

As the assault force rolled in, the shooting continued but tapered off as our vehicles approached. Although there was a lot of uncertainty in the situation, there were some things that were very well known. The assault force knew where the overwatch was; Leif and his AOIC had gone over that info with everyone. We had also told them that there were possible friendlies in the area—which made everyone nervous and extremely cautious about shooting.

After a few short minutes, the assault force arrived on the road in the middle of the village, came to a halt, and set security. The overwatch had stopped shooting but was positively marking their position so we knew where they were.

"Overwatch: What do you got?" I asked on the radio.

"We had PID on armed military-age males by the river, maneuvering to attack. We engaged," the element leader responded.

"Any enemy movement in the village?" I asked.

"Negative," he answered.

"Roger. Commence assault," I said, staying in our default: aggressive mode. With that, the assault force dismounted, set a cordon on the village, and began a systematic clearance building by building and then through Mav Market, stall by stall. Although the enemy had clearly been alerted, they had not had time to react. As the assault force cleared the village and the marketplace, they found and detained a number of suspected insurgents, who were still dazed from sleep when they were captured. We also discovered a cache of enemy weapons that we destroyed. Despite the confusion and uncertainty during the operation, decisiveness and aggressive action won.

We expected our SEALs to operate with an aggressive mind-set. We expected them to lean forward, maneuver quickly, see opportunities, and capitalize upon them—to aggressively execute to solve problems, overcome obstacles, accomplish the mission, and win.

But of course there is a dichotomy with being aggressive that must be balanced: aggression is not *always* the answer. Aggression must be balanced with logic and detailed analysis of risk versus reward.

In Ramadi, Task Unit Bruiser was honored to support the fifty-six hundred U.S. troops—Soldiers, Marines, Sailors, and Airmen—of the U.S. Army's Ready First Brigade Combat Team of the 1st Armored Division in their efforts to implement the Seize, Clear, Hold, Build strategy and take back the city of Ramadi from insurgents. We formed an exceptional working relationship with the Army and Marine leaders and the men in the platoons, companies, and battalions they commanded. Our relationships were based on trust and mutual respect. The Ready First Brigade commander, a U.S. Army colonel, was an extraordinary leader—aggressive, smart, and with amazing strategic vision. He was a true professional and one of the finest leaders with whom I had the honor to serve. When the brigade commander asked for support, Task Unit Bruiser delivered. We were proud to send in our SEALs and Iraqi soldiers as the lead element of troops on the ground for almost every major combat operation of the Seize, Clear, Hold, Build strategy to emplace U.S. combat outposts in the most dangerous, volatile neighborhoods of the city.

Several months into the deployment, at one of the brigade operation meetings on Camp Ramadi I attended, the brigade commander asked me if our SEALs could help eliminate the threat of enemy mortar teams in an area north of the city called "C-Lake."

The name derived from the area's primary feature, an oxbow lake, formed from the Euphrates River, that was shaped like a "C." It was a relatively rural area that covered about ten square miles with open fields along the river, scattered clusters of houses, and small, unpaved country roads.

But it was also an area utilized by insurgents to launch mortar attacks on U.S. positions. Almost every day, insurgents lobbed mortars at U.S. troops stationed on Camp Ramadi and other nearby bases. Mortars hit our camp on Sharkbase as well, though less frequently. American radar technology could track the mortars' trajectory and deduce the point of origin from where they were launched. Many of the mortars that hit Camp Ramadi came from the C-Lake area. Unfortunately, the enemy understood that we could identify the point of origin of their mortars, so they had modified their tactics. Instead of firing the mortars from one specific location, they constantly moved around the entire area. Furthermore, when the insurgents fired mortars, they rapidly fired only one, two, or three rounds at a time in a matter of seconds, then quickly packed up the mortar tube and disappeared. It was an effective tactic that was difficult to counter.

On top of the mortar attacks, the insurgents were active throughout the C-Lake area emplacing large IEDs in the roads. There were limited roads in the area, which channelized access for U.S. convoys into a small number of routes that insurgents could target. With the open terrain around the roads, enemy fighters could observe U.S. Humvees from long distances and detonate the roadside bombs via radio control from unseen locations hundreds of meters away. The IEDs in C-Lake had taken a deadly toll in recent weeks, with multiple Humvees destroyed and several U.S. Army Soldiers killed.

Since Task Unit Bruiser had been successful in eliminating enemy mortar teams and IED emplacers* in other areas of

---

\* IED emplacer: the U.S. military term for insurgents who planted deadly IEDs, or roadside bombs.

Ramadi, it seemed logical we could help in C-Lake. When the brigade commander asked if we could help out in the area, I told him I would take a look and determine how we could best support the mission. I certainly wanted to help the Ready First Brigade handle the situation, eliminate threats, and ensure more U.S. troops went home to their families. We also wanted to kill enemy fighters responsible for the attacks and make them pay for the deaths of our brother Soldiers who had been killed in the IED attacks. I brought back the request to Leif and Charlie Platoon, and we talked through it. Leif, his platoon chief, Tony, and the rest of Charlie Platoon were always eager to close with and destroy the enemy. So they started analyzing the intelligence, looking at maps of the area, and talking with the Soldiers who had operated around C-Lake. They examined, with the rest of Charlie Platoon and the Task Unit Bruiser intelligence department, the best possible courses of action to accomplish the mission.

Over the next several days, Charlie Platoon launched on other operations in different areas of the city. But upon their return to base, they resumed mission planning for the C-Lake operation. Then, after several days of careful analysis, Leif came to my office to discuss the results of their analysis.

"I don't know about this one, Jocko," he said with a somewhat disappointed look on his face.

"What don't you know?" I asked him.

"The C-Lake operation is a tough one," he replied. "I'm not sure it makes sense."

"Okay. Talk me through it," I said.

At this point Leif and I walked over to a detailed map of C-Lake hanging on the wall. First, we marked the known points of origin from where all the mortar attacks had been launched. No two mortar attacks had come from the same location. Second, there was no discernible pattern to the locations. Finally, there weren't any common traits in the terrain from which the mortars had been fired—some had been fired from roads, some from fields, some from the vicinity of houses or buildings, some in the open, some in areas with foliage for camouflage, some in areas with no camouflage at all. There was no pattern whatsoever that would enable us to position our sniper teams in the right location to observe and engage the enemy mortar teams.

Next, Leif pointed out where the IED strikes had taken place. Because the area was bordered by the Euphrates River and crisscrossed with canals, the means to reach the area by vehicle was limited, with only one major road as our access in and out of the area. With the wide-open and sparse terrain, there were no good vantage points from which we could set up our sniper overwatch positions that would allow us a long access look down the main road to observe and engage IED emplacers. To do that, we would have to expose ourselves out in the open, giving away our position and opening us up for enemy attack. When we were attacked, if we needed help, the only route that U.S. vehicles could utilize to get to us was this main road, where the threat of IED attack was extremely high. It would put the U.S. Army units responding to help us at serious risk—in fact, the Quick Reaction Force might not be able to get to us at all. Of course, the same IEDs would also put our SEALs and Iraqi soldiers riding in the vehicles on the transit in and out of the area at serious risk as well.

"The bottom line is this," Leif concluded. "Any countermortar and counter-IED operations in the area of C-Lake will have a very low probability of success. But the threat to our SEALs and Iraqi soldiers conducting the operation and the U.S. Army troops supporting us will be extremely high."

It was clear Leif, Tony, and the rest of his Charlie Platoon leaders had done their homework on this. I certainly knew they weren't risk averse, as they had proven time and again in the months we'd been in Ramadi. I knew they were eager to put as many enemy insurgent fighters in the dirt as they possibly could, in order to protect brave American Soldiers and Marines from deadly enemy attacks. But I understood from their analysis that there was absolutely no way to predict where an attack would come from, which meant we would be setting up an overwatch in a completely random position—basically searching for a needle in a haystack. Even if we knew where to set up, with so few areas to provide good cover and concealment, the enemy wouldn't have a hard time finding us. Finally, with no ability to overwatch the full length of the main road, we wouldn't even be able to fully prevent IEDs from being planted.

"With all that stacked against us," Leif continued, "and as much as we'd love to support the brigade commander's request, I'm just not sure this makes sense. The risk isn't worth the reward."

He was right. As much as we wanted to execute the operation, take the fight to the enemy, and kill the enemy mortar and IED teams in C-Lake, the operation didn't make sense.

"Yep, you're right," I agreed. "High risk to us and our support with a low probability of reward. I'll talk to the brigade commander."

I held the highest respect and admiration for the brigade commander. He and his staff put tremendous faith and trust in us and appreciated the risks we took continuously to cover his Soldiers and Marines from the high ground with our sniper overwatch positions. I also recognized that in this instance, he was overestimating our capability to eliminate the mortar and IED attacks in C-Lake. That night, I drove across the base and explained the situation to the brigade commander. He completely understood, and we discussed some alternative strategies to solve the problem, like using some persistent air coverage or establishing a permanent coalition presence in the area—a series of checkpoints or combat outposts that could keep things under control. The brigade commander knew, as I did, that while being aggressive is a great default attitude to have, it still must be balanced with caution and careful consideration to ensure it is not a case of excessive risk with limited reward.

### Principle

Problems aren't going to solve themselves—a leader must get aggressive and take action to solve them and implement a solution.

Being too passive and waiting for a solution to appear often enables a problem to escalate and get out of control. The enemy isn't going to back off—the leader must get aggressive and put the enemy in check. The good deal isn't going to deliver itself to a company—the leader has to go out and make a good deal happen. Changes and new methodologies in a team aren't going to implement themselves—leaders need to aggressively implement them.

An aggressive mind-set should be the default setting of any leader. Default: Aggressive. This means that the best leaders, the best teams, don't wait to act. Instead, understanding the strategic vision (or commander's intent), they aggressively execute to overcome obstacles, capitalize on immediate opportunities, accomplish the mission, and win.

Rather than passively waiting to be told what to do, Default: Aggressive leaders proactively seek out ways to further the strategic mission. They understand the commander's intent, and where they have the authority to do so, they execute. For decisions that are beyond their pay grade or above their authority, Default: Aggressive leaders still make a recommendation up the chain of command to solve problems and execute key tasks to achieve strategic victory. In SEAL platoons and task units, we expect this from leaders at every level, right down to the frontline trooper in charge of just himself and his small piece of the mission. But this mentality is crucial to any leader, in any team or organization. It is just as critical to success in business as on the battlefield.

"Aggressive" means proactive. It doesn't mean that leaders can get angry, lose their temper, or be aggressive toward their people. A leader must always deal professionally with subordinates on the team, peers, leaders up the chain of command, customers or clients, and personnel in supporting roles outside the immediate team. Speaking angrily to others is ineffective. Losing your temper is a sign of weakness. The aggression that wins on the battlefield, in business, or in life is directed not toward people but toward solving problems, achieving goals, and accomplishing the mission.

It is also critical to balance aggression with careful thought and analysis to make sure that risks have been assessed and mitigated. The dichotomy with the Default: Aggressive mind-set is that sometimes hesitation allows a leader to further understand a situation so that he or she can react properly to it. Rather than immediately respond to enemy fire, sometimes the prudent decision is to wait and see how it develops. Is it a simple reconnaissance by fire? Is it a feint by the enemy, meant to distract from the real attack? Is the enemy simply trying to lure you into a confined area, where they have a superior force waiting to ambush? A careful moment of consideration might reveal the enemy's true intentions. To be overly aggressive, without critical thinking, is to be reckless. That can lead the team into disaster and put the greater mission in peril. To disregard prudent counsel when someone with experience urges caution, to dismiss significant threats, or to fail to plan for likely contingencies is foolhardy. It is bad leadership.

A chief contributing factor to recklessness comes from what military historians have long referred to as "the disease of victory." This disease takes place when a few battlefield successes produce an overconfidence in a team's own tactical prowess while underestimating the capabilities of its enemy or competitor. This is a problem not just for combat leaders but for leaders and teams anywhere, in any arena, throughout the business world and the civilian sector.

It is a leader's duty to fight against this victory disease so that the team, despite its success, never gets complacent. The risk in any action must be carefully weighed against the potential rewards of mission success. And of course, to counter that thought, the cost of inaction must be weighed as well.

As aggressive as leaders must be, leaders must be cautious that they are not "running to their deaths" simply because their instinct is to take action. The dichotomy between aggression and caution must be balanced. So be aggressive, but never reckless.

## Application to Business

"I am going to build the team *now* so we are ready to handle the growth that will come in the next eighteen to twenty-four months," the CEO told me with great enthusiasm. She was the owner of a small business set for rapid expansion. The CEO had bought the business from the former owner, who had kept it on cruise control for the past five years as he eased into retirement.

Since taking over the business, the new CEO had been getting aggressive—and getting customers. She was working hard and driving her team to do the same. The company was poised for some really big growth in the next couple of years. She knew she needed help with that growth and had brought in Echelon Front to coach her and provide leadership training for her team. It certainly seemed she and her company were on the right track.

However, there were tough obstacles in the CEO's path. First, she had spent most of her personal capital to purchase the company from the previous owner, who had left the business with little cash flow. So between her personal finances and the company's weak balance sheet, there wasn't much operating capital.

Traditional business problems were also present. As with most sales scenarios, this custom manufacturing business had many sales leads that needed follow-up, and only a small percentage of those converted into actual sales. The business had a particularly long turn time from orders placed until payment was received. This included designing, testing, approval, and manufacturing—all of which included transport lag times to and from Asia, where the manufacturing took place. That meant very long and capital-intensive delays between when deals were signed and when final payments were made by the clients.

The CEO continued rattling off her plan to me: "I can see where we are headed right now. The number of leads we are getting, the referrals are increasing, the closing rate for the team is going up. We are going to explode next year and I want the team to be more than ready. Default: Aggressive, right?" she asked me, referring to the combat leadership principle I had discussed with her and her team a few days before.

"Absolutely," I replied. "Default: Aggressive!"

I liked that attitude and always had. That afternoon, she explained the plan to me in more detail, the positions she was duplicating, new positions she was creating, and how she was going to structure the company. It was impressive. She had a great vision of where the company was going and the immense capacity it was going to have to execute orders and deliver results on par with some of her biggest competitors.

In order to house the expanding team, she was looking at new locations for the business—or, at a minimum, expanding her current location to include one of the adjacent spaces. However, she was leaning toward moving to a new location more professional in appearance. The company's current location was run-down from years of declining business, and the building didn't come across as a first-class operation. The CEO knew the value of first impressions and was determined to change that.

"The new location has potential for even more growth," she explained, "which I know we are going to need!"

Hearing this aggressive mind-set was like music to my ears, and the CEO's dynamic and enthusiastic attitude had me completely on board.

"Outstanding," I told her, and then I doubled down on this attitude: "If you set up the right groundwork, infrastructure, and put the right people in place now—you will be ready to take over the world next year."

At that point, filled with fervor and moxie, we literally high-fived each other like a couple of high school kids who had just won the state basketball championship.

What a great way to end the meeting. I walked out of the building that day looking forward to our next meeting the following week.

But as I drove to the airport for the flight home, I sobered up from the excitement and realized I was actually pretty emotional about the company: good emotion, but too much emotion. I realized I was caught up in the owner's enthusiasm and relishing her aggressive mind-set. For that very reason—for the CEO's long-term good and the good of the company—I needed to check myself.

When I got home that night, I sent her an e-mail thanking her for the great meeting. I praised her attitude but then tapered those thoughts. I told her that before she moved forward with any big decisions, we should do a serious and unemotional analysis of the financials, a conservative view of operating capital and growth potential, and forecast how the company's overhead would increase in the near and long term. I asked her to have her team put together these numbers for our meeting next week so we could discuss them.

When I met with her the following week, she was still enthusiastic, which was great to see. But I had to keep myself in check. I had to make sure I didn't get caught up in enthusiasm and the attitude of aggressiveness. I had to ensure that she wasn't being overly aggressive—even reckless.

"I think we are still good to move forward," the CEO said, leading me into her office, where her chief financial officer (CFO) and human resources director were waiting.

"Great," I replied. "Let's look at the numbers."

The CFO presented a few slides explaining the company's financial outlook. When it came to the bottom line, it was tight—too tight for me to feel comfortable. But perhaps doable.

Then I noticed one word on the predictive sales chart: "Stretch."

"I see you have 'Stretch' written there. Are these your stretch goals?" I asked the CEO.

She stumbled a bit, then confirmed, "Well, they are—kind of—but as we expand our sales force, we should be able to hit them."

"You mean a sales force that you haven't hired, haven't tested, haven't trained, and who haven't been proven yet?" I asked, growing concerned.

"Well, not yet, but . . . ," she replied, fading off.

"We both know that none of those are easy with salespeople," I said. "Not the hiring, not the training, and certainly not the proving. New salespeople are hit-and-miss in every industry. And if you are looking at accomplishing your stretch goals based on a stretch sales force, you might have some major issues."

"Well, if it takes a little longer to get there, we can just take a little longer," the CEO pushed back. "We have time."

"Are you sure?" I asked. "Bring up the budget again, will you?" I said to the CFO.

He put the budget slides up on the screen. I took a look in greater detail this time.

"Your stretch goals barely cover your overhead—and as overhead goes up, it won't get any better," I observed.

"But we need to be positioned to dominate next year," the CEO stated, subconsciously appealing to my affinity for being aggressively prepared. I had to check myself—and her.

"I get that," I responded. "But look. Without achieving stretch goals, in six months, you won't break even. As you are sitting waiting for payments to come through, you'll have burned through your operating capital. Now, you could go and get a loan or look for investors, but that is a short-term sacrifice for which you will never stop paying. And if the trend continues without any external money, in a year, you will be upside down. In eighteen months, you could easily be in a position vulnerable to some really bad investor deals, or a forced buyout—or even worse: bankruptcy."

"But what if I do make the goals and then we aren't ready?" the CEO asked. "I thought I needed to be aggressive?"

"Well . . . you do need to be ready and you do need to be aggressive. But being aggressive doesn't mean throwing caution to the wind. It doesn't mean taking catastrophic risk that can and should be mitigated. And it doesn't mean relying on unrealistic stretch goals. You need to get aggressive with risk mitigation and with securing long-term success for the company. You need to get aggressive with you maintaining full control and ownership of the company. You need to get aggressive with budgeting and contingency planning. That's what you need to get aggressive with. Otherwise, you're putting yourself, your hard work, your team, and your company at risk."

The CEO nodded, beginning to understand where I was coming from.

"Look," I continued, "you know how when I explained Default: Aggressive to your leadership team the other day, I explained in detail that I didn't mean getting aggressive toward your people? And how screaming and shouting as a leader wasn't the kind of aggression that helps you lead? Of course, there are times when you have to be firm with people, but it has to be balanced. Aggression is a great attribute, but it can spin out of control. This is a similar situation. Getting aggressive here and growing your overhead isn't going to help you or the company. It is just going to leave you exposed and vulnerable to risk. So. Let's reset, take a look at the end state you are trying to achieve, and come up with a measured, balanced way to get there. Then create a plan that has some embedded checkpoints, triggers, and branch plans so that the risks you take are controlled, calculated, and also provide some exit strategies in case things don't go the way you expect them to."

The CEO nodded and smiled. "I guess I just like being aggressive a little too much. But yes. This makes sense. There is definitely a way to get this done with less risk and more control."

With that, we went to work. We formulated a plan that slowly increased infrastructure and support as the sales team not only grew but proved itself with actual deals closed. The office move was pulled out of the plan, and even the expansion of the existing office was put off until the current space was truly overflowing. She also decided to cut some other expenses: she downsized the warehouse for storing product that wasn't being used to capacity and decided to eliminate one of the three account managers who hadn't built much business yet. When she briefed me on the changes to the plan, I smiled.

"I like it," I told her.

"I do too," the CEO admitted. "And it is a good way to be aggressive: instead of getting aggressive in preparing for an unknown future, I got aggressive cutting costs and managing my P & L*.

"And you know what?" she asked me.

"What's that?" I asked.

"It still felt good," she replied, happy she was able to direct her aggressive mind-set to lead her company by focusing that attitude in the right direction and balancing aggression with clear, unemotional thought and sensible risk mitigation.

---

* Profit and Loss statement.

As lead sniper and an enlisted leader for Task Unit Bruiser's Delta Platoon, J. P. Dinnell also served as point man, the most hazardous, first in line position in the patrol, responsible for identifying forward threats and successfully navigating the team to their target or destination. Delta was attacked and engaged by enemy fighters on a vast majority of the patrols they conducted during this deployment. Here, J.P. courageously leads Delta Platoon and their Iraqi soldiers through the streets after a sniper overwatch mission in eastern Ramadi. Even after grueling hours in the Iraqi heat under constant enemy attack, J.P. maintains his discipline: weapon at the ready with eyes scanning for threats.

(Photo courtesy of Samuel Peterson)

# CHAPTER 7
## Disciplined, Not Rigid

*Jocko Willink*

**CENTRAL BAGHDAD, IRAQ: 2003**

*Why the hell are all the guys in that Humvee smoking?* I wondered.

As I glanced at the Humvee in front of me, it looked as if someone flicked a cigarette out of the vehicle, the glowing red embers creating tiny explosions against the side of the Humvee and the street around it. Then I saw another one. And another one. A few seconds later, reality hit me. Those weren't cigarette embers hitting the Humvee. They were bullets.

It was the first time I had been shot at—and I didn't even know it. Our SEAL platoon was in a convoy of Humvees in central Baghdad, headed toward a notoriously violent part of town. In the early days of the Iraq War, our Humvees had no armor. The vehicles had no doors and were thin-skinned—bullets could pass right through the exterior. They were not meant for urban combat, making the incoming small-arms fire a real threat.

Unfortunately, we couldn't see where the enemy fire was coming from, so we did not return fire. A minute or two later, we pulled into our destination, a small outpost in north-central Baghdad. Once our convoy stopped inside the compound, a radio call came over my headset. One of my guys was hit. Over the radio, the medic asked which vehicle the wounded man was in. The call came back that the wounded man was in vehicle four. I got out of my vehicle, did a quick visual assessment of our current tactical situation. All vehicles were in line on the road on which we had driven into the compound. The road ran parallel to the nearby Tigris River, to our right. We had driven past the main building in the outpost, protected by rows of large wire-and-fabric boxes filled with sand and gravel, called HESCO barriers. The wall of HESCO barriers extended along the bank of the Tigris opposite the main building, but as the road continued past the main building, the HESCO barriers came to an end. It didn't seem like a big concern to me, as the Tigris was fairly wide and small arms would likely not be effective from the bank on the other side.

Once I felt comfortable with our situation, I walked back to vehicle four to check the condition of the wounded SEAL. I had never had one of my men wounded before; I had never even been shot at before, nor had anyone else in the platoon. But I wasn't panicked. I knew my corpsman would quickly assess the wounded SEAL and begin treatment. I also knew that the 28th Combat Support Hospital (CSH) was less than ten minutes away and we could be there quickly if needed, just as we had briefed in our contingency planning.

Luckily, it was not needed. The wound was minor—miraculous, but minor. A single bullet, which must have been a ricochet with greatly reduced power, had hit the SEAL in the head, penetrating the skin but not puncturing his skull. Instead, it had traveled in an arc around his head in between the skin and the skull. The corpsman checked the entry wound, traced it to the bullet, literally pushed the bullet along the track of the wound until it arrived at the entry point, and then simply squeezed the wound as the bullet popped out. No problem.

Just as we were resolving that situation and the corpsman was telling me that we should take him to the CSH as a precaution, I heard a report over the radio.

"We are taking fire!" someone said on our platoon intersquad radio net.

I took a knee behind the Humvee, as did the rest of the guys.

We listened and looked around to try to figure out exactly what was happening. I thought I heard a couple snaps of rounds. But I couldn't tell for sure.

At that point confusion set in. I saw that my guys were looking in different directions. Moving from spot to spot for no reason. Pointing weapons and lasers in every direction. Taking cover behind all sides of the Humvees. Everyone was trying to do something, but it looked as though they weren't sure what they should be doing. This, of course, was my fault. I was the leader. I needed to give some direction. But at this point, even I was unsure what direction to give. So I resorted to a technique I had learned from one of my old platoon commanders: when in doubt, ask. There is no shame in it—especially when compared with the shame of making a bad decision because you were too egotistical to ask a question.

"Where is the contact?" I shouted.

"Across the river!" someone shouted back. That was good. I now had something to work with. But only one person sounded off when that reply came back, which was not the way SEALs operate. In the SEAL Teams, when someone gives a verbal command, everyone repeats that command to ensure that everyone gets the word. But since "across the river" wasn't one of our standard verbal commands—or in the standard format we use to pass information—no one repeated it. This meant that not everyone knew where the contact was. As a result, there was still confusion and a lack of action with the platoon. A few SEALs had dismounted from the Humvees and taken up positions around them; other men, including the drivers and gunners, remained inside the vehicles.

I had to clear up the confusion, and fast. We had parked beyond the wall of HESCO barriers, and most of the Humvees and the men were exposed to the river and the incoming enemy fire.

I needed to get them both, the vehicles and men, behind the HESCO barriers—and I needed to do it quickly. In my mind, for a split second, I struggled to come up with a plan to make that happen. More important, I needed a method to communicate that plan over the radio so everyone would hear it. A long explanation of what was happening would be too complicated for people to pass verbally. I wasn't sure what to do.

Then I realized this was a scenario we had all seen before in training. The training scenarios had been while on foot patrol, in a totally different capacity, but the same procedure could be utilized here—something everyone in the SEAL platoon knew. So I decided to use the same verbal commands that directed our standard operating procedures when we were on foot.

Based on the Humvees' direction of travel, the contact was on our right. So I made the call.

"CONTACT RIGHT!" I yelled. Because this was a standard call everyone was used to hearing and repeating, everyone repeated it. Now everyone knew where the threat was.

Next, I yelled, "ON LINE!" to get everyone's guns facing the threat. Once again, this was a standard call, and everyone repeated it as they executed the action of taking aim across the river. Within seconds, every SEAL was in position, with weapons trained on the threat across the river.

Finally, I called, "SHIFT RIGHT!"—the command to begin to move to the right, based on the direction of the contact, which would move us back behind the cover of the HESCO barriers.

"SHIFT RIGHT!" the platoon members repeated. Immediately, the vehicles and men began moving methodically back behind the cover of the HESCO barriers. In less than a minute, everyone was behind the protection of the HESCO barriers and the contact was over.

It hadn't been much. The incoming rounds were minimal and ineffective. We took no more casualties and none of the Humvees were hit. It was no big deal. The only reason I remember it at all is that it was my first time receiving enemy fire. But I had learned something very important: the power of disciplined standard operating procedures. I had always been told of their importance, especially by the Vietnam-era SEALs. Now, I had experienced it firsthand.

But discipline could be taken too far. While I now fully understood why disciplined standard operating procedures were important, it hadn't yet dawned on me that they could be imposed with too much discipline—too much rigidity.

As task unit commander of Bruiser, I learned that lesson. We were out in the rugged desert terrain of Southern California's Imperial Valley for our first major block of training: land warfare. In land warfare, we learned to shoot, move, and communicate as a team, to close with and destroy the enemy, to Cover and Move, and to utilize our organic firepower to overcome enemy attacks. Land warfare is the foundational training that all other SEAL skills are built upon. But not only was this block of training fundamental, it was also the most physically arduous. It involved long foot patrols across rough desert terrain, carrying heavy loads. During immediate action drills (IADs)—predetermined and heavily rehearsed maneuver reactions that SEALs execute under enemy attack—individual SEALs, performing their role in a dynamic, coordinated scheme of maneuver, have to get up, get down, sprint, crawl, roll, jump, and dive over and over and over again. The maneuvers are physically exhausting. On top of this, the platoon and task unit leaders must also *think*. They have to assess the terrain, identify the location of enemy fire (in training situations, the position of reactive targets during live-fire drills or the location of opposing force role-players during blank-fire drills). Leaders must quickly analyze whether to assault the enemy positions or retreat—can the opposing force be overcome or should the SEALs break contact and depart the area? Once a decision is made between fight or flight, the SEAL leader then makes a tactical call, which indicates the scheme of maneuver the SEALs will execute, much like a quarterback calling a play in a huddle. Only this isn't a huddle on a football field. This is a battlefield with lives at stake (a danger even on the training battlefield during live-fire exercises).

Once the call is made, the team passes the word and executes the maneuver. The maneuvers themselves are fairly mechanical—and they have to be. With live-fire training there are real bullets flying everywhere, and if a SEAL moves beyond his designated area, he could easily be killed by friendly fire. Because of this danger, the standard procedures are closely monitored by the SEAL training instructor cadre and strictly enforced. Failure to follow procedures is reprimanded with written safety violations. Any more than two or three safety violations will likely result in a Trident Review Board and possible loss of the SEAL designator.

During land warfare training, the initial days of IADs are very rudimentary. The squads and platoons maneuver in simple, clearly defined, and premeditated movements on open, flat, even terrain. The first iterations are done without firing weapons, so communication is clear and easily understood. The maneuvers are elemental; the leaders do not take terrain into account and simply move the pieces around a board. It is fairly simple and straightforward, allowing the SEALs to understand the standard operating procedures, which include their individual movements and how those movements fit into the overall scheme of maneuver. As soon as the "dry," non-shooting IADs are solidified, the SEAL squads and platoons graduate to live-fire maneuvers. This adds a layer of challenge, as now the SEALs must listen for verbal commands over the sound of actual machine gun and rifle fire and pass those commands to the rest of the platoon. It doesn't take long to adapt; with the flat terrain, the maneuvers are fairly easy to execute.

That all changes when the training cadre moves the platoons out of the flatlands and into the real terrain of the desert: knolls, ravines, rock outcroppings, dry riverbeds, shrubs, bushes, and other common features of the semi-arid desert. Now, the leaders inside the platoon have to actually think—and lead. The terrain, when read, understood, and utilized correctly, provides an unmatched advantage on the battlefield. Elevated ridgelines offer superior shooting positions; rocks provide cover; ravines or depressions in the terrain furnish exits that allow the platoon to escape from an enemy attack while protected from hostile fire. Once a terrain feature is identified and a plan created, the challenge is then to convey the plan to the rest of the team through verbal and visual signals, both of which become obscured by the noise, dust, and terrain itself.

In Task Unit Bruiser, Delta Platoon initially had some trouble during their IADs. Once the contact started (the simulated attack initiated), the platoon got bogged down. Calls weren't being made. They would remain in position too long, expending ammunition, without advancing or retreating from the enemy. This was bad. As a general rule, it was "flank or be flanked." Either you maneuvered on the enemy or the enemy would maneuver on you. Stagnation on the battlefield will get you killed, and stagnating seemed to be Delta Platoon's reaction to each simulated enemy contact.

As the task unit commander, I was responsible for the platoon's performance. After noticing the issue, I made a point to observe the Delta Platoon commander, Seth Stone, during Delta's IAD runs. Seth was a relatively inexperienced officer. Like Leif, he had done a tour on a ship in the U.S. Navy surface fleet before receiving orders to BUD/S, eventually going through the SEAL basic training program with Leif. They were both from the U.S. Naval Academy, both from Texas, both fans of Johnny Cash and Metallica, extremely hard workers, and very close friends. I was lucky to have them as my platoon commanders.

That being said, the fact remained that they were both inexperienced. Both had graduated from BUD/S only two years prior to being assigned as platoon commanders in Task Unit Bruiser, and each had completed only one pre-deployment workup cycle and one deployment to Iraq, where they spent most of their time not in the field running combat operations but in a tactical operations center, supporting missions in the field from inside the wire. I couldn't expect them to be expert tacticians based on their previous experience. I had to teach them.

Seth required some help, so I began to shadow him closely during his IAD runs. It was easy to shadow him—easier than it should have been. Seth was following the standard operating procedures *without exception of any kind*. Every move he was supposed to make, he made. When it was his turn to stand and move, he stood and moved to the next designated location. When it was his turn to lie down and return fire, he got down into the prone position and returned fire—like a robot. He was executing the SOPs to a tee, without any deviation or thought, and it was fouling him up.

As a leader, you must make it part of your job to see what is coming next, to observe. By observing, leaders can understand the surroundings and the terrain, they can identify enemy positions and observe the locations of their own troops. Once leaders observe all this, they can then make a call.

As I observed Seth, it became clear that his mistake was following the standard procedures *too* closely. If, as the leader, you move and position yourself exactly as the procedure requires, you might not end up in the best spot to actually see what is happening. You might end up in a depression or behind a shrub or a rock, which inhibits your vision, or around a corner out of sight from the rest of the platoon. As a leader, you might end up in a spot where your gunfire is providing critical cover fire for other members of the team, so instead of leading and directing the team, you're shooting. All of these are problematic.

What Seth didn't realize was that the standard operating procedures were general guidelines, not strict rules to be followed. In Seth's mind, the procedures were rigid, and while they certainly were rigid enough to ensure safety, he didn't realize that they were also extremely flexible.

Of course, some parts of the procedures were not flexible at all. For instance, individuals could not move laterally downrange of other shooters or they would cut off other team members' field of fire—or even worse, enter their field of fire and be hit by their bullets. But when behind the line of fire, individuals had the freedom to move around quite liberally, especially the leaders. Leaders could move left or right behind the firing line to observe the location of men and pass the word. They could push back even farther behind the firing line to look for exits. Leaders could even grab other shooters to replace themselves in the firing line, allowing the leader to get up, move around, and look for advantageous terrain features. More important, not only *could* a leader do these things, a leader *must* do them. To not move around, observe, and analyze, in order to make the best decisions possible, was to fail as a leader and fail the team.

On the next IAD iteration, I told Seth I would stay by him and tell him where to move. We rolled out in patrol formation, toward the area where the targets would pop up for the platoon to engage. I stuck by Seth, walking beside him but on the opposite side of his field of fire so I would not interfere with his duties. Delta Platoon patrolled down a ravine with rock and dirt embankments on both sides. This was only a training exercise. But the high-risk live-fire drills in sweltering desert temperatures that induced sweat and fatigue, the SEAL instructor cadre critiquing every move, the suspense of targets that popped up suddenly from unseen positions, and the pressure to make good calls all ensured that tensions were extremely high.

Finally, the automated targets popped up ahead of us and we heard the *pop-pop-pop* of the simulated gunfire they made. Seth hit the ground and started engaging the targets, as did Delta Platoon's point man, J. P. Dinnell, just in front of Seth. J.P. was an outstanding, young SEAL operator, powerful in build and Default: Aggressive to the core. J.P. was something special. Just twenty-two years old, he was a natural leader and always ready to step up and take charge, which he would do many times during the Battle of Ramadi. He was also extraordinarily brave—a fact that would become very clear in combat. During one serious firefight in the Malaab District of eastern Ramadi, he risked his life without hesitation, running into an open street under withering enemy fire to save a U.S. Marine gunnery sergeant who had been wounded, for which J.P. was awarded the Silver Star Medal. But for now, in this training scenario, J. P. immediately opened up with his machine gun to suppress the "enemy" attack. The rest of the platoon dropped into their respective fields of fire, alternating left and right through the whole patrol.

"CONTACT FRONT!" Seth shouted, alerting everyone that the enemy targets were in front of the patrol. Man by man, the rest of the platoon repeated the call, and shouts of "CONTACT FRONT!" rippled down the line of men.

I watched Seth. He knew that they were in a channelized area, the ravine, and with limited firepower up front and maneuverability restricted by the walls of the ravine, he made the call.

"CENTER PEEL!" he yelled. This was the right call and really the only option in this situation. The rest of the platoon anticipated the call and quickly passed the word down the line.

"CENTER PEEL!"

With that call, Delta Platoon began the carefully coordinated drill of Cover and Move. As some SEALs put down heavy suppressive fire, other SEALs got up and bounded back, away from the enemy contact. Everything was going well—until it was Seth's turn to move.

Seth made his way down the ravine past everyone else in the platoon, finally reaching the position where, on paper, he was technically supposed to be, as dictated by the standard operating procedures. Once there, he took a knee facing the ravine wall. I watched him as he stared at the wall of rocks and dirt just feet in front of him.

"What can you see from there?" I asked.

"Not much," he said, shaking his head.

"How can you figure out where to lead your platoon if you can't see anything?" I asked him pointedly.

Seth was quiet for a moment.

"I have no idea," he admitted.

"Well then, move," I told him.

Now he was really confused.

"Move?" Seth asked. The SOPs dictated where he was supposed to take up position, and in his mind he had followed them—in his mind, he didn't have the ability to bend the rules. But those rules had left him staring at a ravine wall, unable to see anything that was happening. If he couldn't see what was happening, he couldn't lead. So I told him to break that procedure.

"Yes. Move," I told him.

"But what about the SOPs?" Seth asked.

Seth was concerned that his movement outside the norm would disrupt the flow of the maneuver. What Seth didn't understand yet was that SOPs weren't meant to be completely unalterable, especially for the leader. So I quickly explained it to him.

"As long as you keep within visual distance of the last man," I told him, "you can move around so you can see what the hell is going on—and figure out where to move next. You're the leader! You have to find an exit."

As a platoon commander, one of Seth's jobs was to find an "exit"—a terrain feature that would allow the SEAL platoon to escape from enemy fire and mask its movement.

"Roger," Seth replied. He then moved another ten yards down the ravine, and as he did, another SEAL came back and filled in the gap, as he was supposed to. This was an inherent part of SEAL maneuvers that allowed the leader to move around, to look and see and analyze the terrain. If the leader moved from the standard position, someone else would fill his spot.

But Seth still couldn't find an exit, and he was almost out of visual range of the last SEAL who had taken his previous position.

"I don't see anything yet, but I'm getting too far away," he observed.

"No problem," I countered. "Wait for the next guy to come back and tell him to fill in the space, then you can go farther."

Seth nodded and cracked a smile at me. He was starting

to understand: leading wasn't about him following the exact procedure—it required him to think and do what made the most sense so that he could best support and lead his team.

"Get down there!" Seth barked, pointing out a position to the next SEAL moving down the ravine in his direction. "I'm finding an exit!"

The SEAL took a knee. Seth bumped a little farther back, scanning for an exit. Still, he saw nothing.

"Fill it in there!" he shouted to the next man coming his way in the ravine, pointing to the general location where the SEAL should take position. Seth then turned again to move ahead and look for an exit to get out of the ravine.

Finally, he found an exit: another ravine broke off to the right and clearly led away from the platoon's current path of travel. It would make a good route to put distance between them and the enemy contact, while protecting them from incoming fire.

He took up a position at the corner of the exit. As the next man came down the ravine, Seth shouted, "EXIT HERE! EXIT HERE!" as he pointed down the ravine off to the right. The SEAL followed Seth's direction, and the rest of the platoon filed by down the new ravine and away from the enemy contact. They continued moving in the new direction for about a hundred meters.

Seth looked at me. He didn't say anything, but his face was speaking loud and clear. He didn't know what to do next.

"Do you think you broke contact?" I asked him, meaning did he think the enemy was still a threat. The guys were now moving without shooting, indicating that they could no longer see the enemy and therefore the enemy was no longer a threat.

"For sure," he answered.

"Okay," I said. "So now what do you need?"

Seth knew exactly what I meant by that.

"Head count," he said.

"Yep. And then?" I asked.

"Put some more distance between us and the enemy," he replied confidently.

"Okay then," I told him. "Get it done."

"Roger," he replied, beginning to grasp his place as a leader with greater confidence.

Seth moved ahead a little farther in the patrol, now no longer bound by the standard operating procedures. He quickly found a little depression big enough to accommodate his entire platoon. He set up in the middle of it and gave the hand signal for "perimeter" as his men started to roll in. They saw him and immediately went to their standard assigned positions. Within a minute, all of Delta Platoon was in position, guns covering every direction. Seth received a thumbs-up signal from both squad leaders, indicating they each had a full head count—all SEALs were present—and were ready to move. Seth got up, moved to J.P., and gave him the signal to patrol out, away from enemy contact.

In the course of a single IAD run, Seth's ability to lead had increased exponentially, and Delta Platoon's excellent performance reflected those results. Seth now understood that standard operating procedures were not fixed, inflexible laws with no room for variation. They were guidelines that needed to be balanced with adaptability and common sense. Balancing that dichotomy was required for everyone, especially leaders.

When he saw Seth's signal, J. P. Dinnell got up from his position in the perimeter and moved out on patrol, scanning for threats. Seth followed in just behind him, taking his position as the patrol leader. The rest of Delta Platoon got up and followed Seth, just as they would over and over again in the streets of Ramadi.

## Principle

While "Discipline Equals Freedom" is a powerful tool for both personal and team development, excessive discipline can stifle free thinking in team leaders and team members. Disciplined standard operating procedures, repeatable processes, and consistent methodologies are helpful in any organization. The more discipline a team exercises, the more freedom that team will have to maneuver by implementing small adjustments to existing plans.

When facing a mission or a task, instead of having to craft a plan from scratch, a team can follow standard operating procedures for the bulk of the plan. As SEALs, we had SOPs for just about everything we did: the way we lined up and loaded our vehicles, our vehicle and foot patrol formations, the methodologies we used to clear buildings, the way we handled prisoners and dealt with wounded SEALs—the list goes on and on. But those SOPs didn't constrain us on the battlefield. On the contrary, they gave us freedom. The disciplined SOPs were a line to deviate from, and we had the freedom to act quickly based on those procedures.

But there must be balance. In some organizations, both in the military and in the civilian sector, there are leaders who put too many standard operating procedures in place. They create such strict processes that they actually inhibit their subordinate leaders' willingness—and ability—to think. This may adversely impact the team's performance and become a detriment to the mission, preventing effective leadership at every level of the organization.

Disciplined procedures must be balanced with the ability to apply common sense to an issue, with the power to break with SOPs when necessary, with the *freedom* to think about alternative solutions, apply new ideas, and make adjustments to processes based on the reality of what is actually happening. If discipline is too strict, team members cannot make adjustments, cannot adapt, and cannot use their most precious asset—their brains—to quickly develop customized solutions to unique problems for which the standard solution might not work.

And when taken to an extreme, too much discipline—too many processes and too many standard procedures—completely inhibits and stifles the initiative of subordinates. Instead of stepping up and making necessary changes, leaders confined to strict procedures will simply follow the procedures even when those procedures are obviously leading to failure.

So as a leader it is critical to balance the strict discipline of standard procedures with the freedom to adapt, adjust, and maneuver to do what is best to support the overarching commander's intent and achieve victory. For leaders, in combat, business, and life, be disciplined, but not rigid.

## Application to Business

The VP of sales was a force to be reckoned with. She was aggressive, smart, and experienced. Having risen through the ranks, she knew the business inside and out. The company's products were solid and provided a true benefit to customers.

But there was trouble in paradise: declining sales for four straight months. The CEO decided they needed some help and reached out to Echelon Front to assess and provide guidance. As soon as I arrived, I was impressed by the VP of sales, but I could also sense her frustration.

"What's been going on?" I asked her.

"Not enough!" she replied. "Not even close!" She was smiling, but she wasn't kidding.

"So I have been told," I said. "What do you think is going on?"

She thought for a minute, then replied.

"Look," she answered, "I'm not a hundred percent sure. Last year was terrific. We couldn't seem to do any wrong. All my regional managers were driving their salespeople hard—training them well and putting up great numbers. The frontline salespeople themselves were on fire."

"Well, that sounds good," I told her.

"It was good," she continued. "Then we hit November—usually a hard month for us—along with December. Our product is practical: home safety, security, and efficiency—not exactly something people ask Santa for."

"Not exactly," I agreed.

"We wanted to maintain sales and profits through that time period, so we got really aggressive as a leadership team—Default: Aggressive, as you like to say," the VP continued.

I laughed, recognizing that she understood the fundamental concepts I often spoke about.

"That's awesome," I told her. "How exactly did you get aggressive?"

"We got aggressive across the board," she replied. "We increased our training for our salespeople. Stepped up our monitoring of their sales calls. We tightened the pricing model to increase margin, and we started tracking—and really driving—the number of outgoing calls that each salesperson made every day."

"And that didn't have an impact?" I asked.

"Not the impact that we wanted it to have," she said. "I mean, it's hard to say. This November wasn't as bad as last November, but it wasn't near where we wanted it to be."

"So then what did you do?" I asked.

"We doubled down," the VP said.

"You doubled down? On what?" I inquired.

"On everything," she admitted. "We improved our scripts and trained even harder on them. We had our salespeople reciting their scripts perfectly. They were all nailing it. We went even harder on our pricing to make sure that every deal we made maximized margin. And we increased the number of calls each salesperson was required to make. We cranked up the discipline across the entire sales force," she explained.

"And?" I asked.

"And nothing," she said.

"Nothing?" I asked, puzzled.

"Nothing," the VP declared. "This December was actually worse than last year. And then, in January, things got even worse. February and March continued down, and April was one of our worst months in three years—and three years ago we were half the size we are now.

"It is bad," she said soberly. "And the market is good. Our competitors are doing fine, but we are losing market share. And yet our product is truly better than theirs. It just doesn't make any sense."

"No, it sure doesn't," I agreed. "Let me do some digging."

Frankly, I was a little worried that I might not be able to figure this one out.

I spent the next week talking with the seven regional managers who led the sales teams. They were located in two centers, and each had sales teams of five to fifteen salespeople. The salespeople were phone pounders—call center grinders following leads from the Internet, print ads, and mailers. They were relatively young, but also motivated. Some of them had made solid six-figure incomes from their commissions over the past several years. The regional managers—so called because their salespeople worked particular regions of the country—were all good people too. All of them except one had come up through the ranks of the call center. The one who hadn't was previously a customer relations representative in the field before transitioning in pursuit of a higher income. So they all knew the business, and they knew it well, from their own experience and from the tutelage of the VP of sales.

I drilled down into the call centers to learn more. At one call center, I brought the four regional managers together in a meeting for some fact-finding.

"What do you think is going on?" I asked them plainly.

"No idea," one of them said.

"None?" I asked.

"Not really," another one replied.

"Any idea at all?" I asked again, likely sounding pretty desperate.

The group sat quietly for a little while. Finally, one of the managers spoke up.

"We have had many ideas. And we've hit every sales driver that we know of," the regional manager said. "We thought maybe our salespeople weren't introducing the product right or overcoming objections effectively, so we really nailed down the scripting and made it bulletproof. And they all know it cold and know not to deviate from it. Then we saw they were giving away pricing too easily; they were giving discounts that they didn't have to and we were losing margins. So we tightened that up too. They have much less leeway in the pricing now. And we have increased the number of outgoing calls they have to make—and they are doing it. They are making about thirty percent more calls every day. They are hammering everything, but we are still just losing traction."

"Everyone?" I asked. "Every salesperson is going backward?"

"Yes. Every one of them," another manager chimed in. "And look—we get Extreme Ownership, we've read the book, but I'll tell you I think we need some new product features . . . we need to up our game from the technology perspective."

"But your VP of sales told me your product is legitimately better than any of your competitors," I countered.

"It is," the manager said. "But there's nothing *new*. We need something new to sell—that's what we need. I'm telling you, our sales force can't do much more than what they are doing. They are like machines out on that floor right now."

I nodded. Something wasn't adding up. I couldn't quite understand what it was. "Alright," I told them. "Let me see what I can figure out. . . ."

The next day, I spent time on the front lines with the actual salespeople who made the calls. I listened in on their calls and asked them some questions. Each salesperson I listened to sounded incredibly professional and polished. Their words were scripted, but they said them so naturally that you could barely notice they were all saying the exact same thing. At first, I was impressed. Really impressed. It seemed as if each one of these salespeople deserved an Academy Award for acting.

But the Academy Award was about the only thing they were winning. I listened as salesperson after salesperson got shot down and failed to close a deal. Their introductions were smooth, but they weren't getting any traction. When they did get some interest from a potential client, most weren't able to get through the client's objections even when giving the proper scripted responses. And those who finally did get through the objections to set up a sale had a really hard time discussing pricing to close the deal. The whole morning, I saw only three deals get closed.

Finally, at noon I offered to take a few of them to lunch. We went to a burger joint, ordered our food, and sat down to wait for it.

"So, what is going on?" I asked, opening the conversation. "You all do such a professional job—but sales are down. Any ideas?"

"I wish I knew!" said one of the younger salespeople. "This is killing me. I might not even be able to continue to work here if I don't start landing some sales."

"I'm in the same boat," another chimed in. "Something has got to change or I won't make it."

Everyone in the group shook their heads.

"What are you doing differently now from where you were six months ago?" I asked.

"I don't think it is anything we are doing—we have just been getting better," a salesperson named Jonathan said passionately. "We are better. We are tighter with our scripts and our pricing and how we overcome objections. We are getting after it. We are like sales machines. But things are just going backward."

Machines—this was the second time I had heard the sales team referred to as "machines." I noticed it, but it still didn't make sense to me.

"If you are doing everything perfectly, then what are you doing wrong?" I asked.

The table sat quiet for a minute. Finally, one of the most senior salespeople, Vijay, spoke up. "That's what we are doing wrong."

"What?" I asked.

"That," he said. "We are doing everything perfectly, like machines, like robots."

*Boom*. It hit me. Right there—Vijay was right.

"Too perfect? What do you mean by that?" asked one of the other salespeople.

I listened to Vijay intently to see if he was saying what I was thinking.

"I mean we do everything too perfectly. We read the script. We answer the questions. We overcome objections. We stick to the pricing model. Let me ask you this: When was the last time you made a person laugh on the other end of the phone?" Vijay questioned the group.

Nothing but blank faces from the whole team. Their silence made the answer obvious. No one had gotten a laugh from a potential client in a long time.

"So then what kind of connection are you making with them?" I asked.

"Exactly," Vijay said. "None."

"Is it possible that in the pursuit of perfection, you all have become too perfect? You have become machines—robots?" I asked.

"And we all know what you do with a robo sales call. *Click*— you hang up," Vijay said.

He was right. That was it. In trying to boost sales, the leadership team had done what they thought was right. They went Default: Aggressive to implement highly disciplined standard operating procedures. And in doing so, they went too far and took away the freedom of their salespeople to adapt on the front lines. Instead of adapting to a potential customer's reaction and making some kind of connection, the salespeople were stuck giving the same script over and over and over again. As good as they were at reading the script and as convincing as they sounded, it didn't matter if they couldn't have a real conversation with the potential client.

And that wasn't the only problem. As I dug down, I found other issues. Because flexibility had been eliminated from the pricing structure, the frontline salespeople couldn't do anything to close deals that had potential but needed a little nudge to get them over the line. Without the ability to offer a special discount or the power to maneuver on price in any way, the salespeople often had to let interested customers walk.

Finally, with the minimum number of calls per day increased and strictly enforced, the salespeople gave up too easily during their calls. If they got one indication that they weren't going to get a deal, they would move on to the next call so they could meet the minimum number of calls required and not be penalized. This was the opposite of what they explained worked better: taking time with a potential client to explain details and build a relationship, thereby increasing the possibility of closing the sale.

With this feedback and information, I went back to the VP of sales and talked her through the problem and the solution.

"Too much discipline?!" she asked with a big smile on her face. "I never thought I'd hear you say that, Jocko!"

"I don't say it too often," I explained, knowing I deserved some ribbing since I touted the benefits of discipline with such regularity. "Because usually discipline is what is lacking. But here, the balance has shifted too far in the other direction. The front-line troops don't have the freedom to make things happen, to maneuver on the battlefield, to adjust and adapt to the situation on the ground—or in this case to the situation on the phone. They aren't making any connections with potential clients. They are responding like robots with no power to offer any pricing concessions to a tough prospect, and with the strictly enforced minimum calls they are required to make, they are being even more transactional on their calls—exactly what they shouldn't be. You're a master salesperson: how would it impact you if you had to stay on script one hundred percent of the time?" I asked.

She was quiet for a moment as the reality settled in.

"It would be very hard to close sales," she admitted, "and I should have known that. Every salesperson is different, and so is every customer—and every call. The ability to connect over the phone is paramount. And I took that ability away from them. It's my fault, and I need to own it."

I smiled. "Yes, you do," I agreed. "That's Extreme Ownership—and it works not because you say you own it but because now you will take ownership of solving the problem."

"Yes, I will," she said.

Over the next few days, we worked on a new plan and training program that emphasized not reading a script but creating a connection with the potential customer—the person—on the other end of the line. On top of that, the company shifted its metrics. They began tracking not the number of outbound calls but the total time spent on the phone with potential customers to help drive good conversations that should translate into more sales. Finally, they loosened the pricing structure, giving more freedom to the salespeople to accommodate interested prospects and get deals closed.

The VP of sales rolled out the plan very quickly and saw the numbers rapidly improve. Balance between discipline and freedom had been achieved—for now—and things were back on track.

SEAL Team Seven Echo Platoon on a mounted patrol south of Baghdad in 2003.
Speed and aggressive posture kept the enemy from attacking . . . most of the time.
(Photo courtesy of Jocko Willink)

# CHAPTER 8

Hold People Accountable, but Don't Hold Their Hands

*Jocko Willink*

**BAGHDAD, IRAQ: 2003**

*Ba-ba-ba-ba-ba-ba-ba-ba-ba!*

The M2 .50-caliber machine gun—which we affectionately called the Ma Deuce—was unleashing fury into the city. And it wasn't alone in its firepower. Our convoy of Humvees had taken some enemy small-arms fire from a building near the highway on which we were driving. We were in Baghdad and it was the fall of 2003, early in the Iraq War. Our Humvees were unarmored. We had completely removed the canvas vehicle doors and modified the seats to face outward so that we could scan with our weapons and engage threats. Facing outward also presented our body armor plates toward potential enemy contact to protect us from the impact of enemy bullets. The Ma Deuce .50-cal was mounted in the turret, the circular hole in the top of each Humvee, manned by a SEAL who stood with his chest and head protruding through the roof. Each Humvee carried SEAL assaulters in the back on bench seats with medium machine guns mounted on articulating swing arms so we could shoot accurately on the move.

As soon as the shooting started, a call came out over the radio.

"Contact right!"

That let everyone know that the enemy attack was to our right. Immediately, everyone who could get their weapon into position returned fire with a vengeance. Dozens of machine guns belched flames and tracer fire, along with M4 rifles. We laid down an overwhelming barrage of firepower that likely compelled whomever had engaged us to deeply regret that decision.

But just because we were shooting didn't mean we stopped the convoy or even slowed down. As we fired, the call came quickly over the radio.

"Blow through, blow through!" Which meant we would actually increase speed to get out of the ambush area. And that was exactly what we did. Within a few hundred yards, we were clear of the ambush, and the call to stop shooting came out over the radio:

"CEASE FIRE!"

We continued on, back to our base on the outskirts of Baghdad International Airport. Upon arrival, we fueled up the Humvees in preparation for the next mission and headed back to our compound for the debrief.

The debrief wasn't critical. Why would it be? We had made it through another attempted enemy ambush, and once again, we crushed them and they didn't hit any of us. In the early days of the Iraq War, we weren't yet facing the well-organized, combat-experienced, and well-funded insurgency that Task Unit Bruiser would come up against in Ramadi three years later. At this time, the enemy consisted of little more than criminals, thugs, and former Saddam Hussein regime elements running around trying to cause problems. They weren't much of a problem for us. We were well trained. We were aggressive. And we were executing missions that gave us a solid advantage over the enemy. Most of the operations we conducted were what we called "direct action" missions, with the objective of capturing or killing the suspected bad guys for planning and executing attacks against U.S. forces, Iraqi security forces, or the new interim government of Iraq.

We would gather intelligence, bounce what we knew off various other intelligence sources, trying to confirm the most important piece of information about the suspected terrorists: their location. Once we had their location, we planned our assault.

The assaults were fairly straightforward. We would stop the vehicles at a pre-designated location and patrol on foot to the target. Once at the target, we used various means to enter the outer walled compound, sometimes going over the walls, sometimes breaching the gates, sometimes both simultaneously. Within a few minutes, we had the entire target building under our control and had subdued all possible threats.

Of course, the planning for every mission was slightly different based on the specific target. We adapted our plans and the tactics, techniques, and procedures to execute operations, but at the same time, we always maintained a solid grip on the fundamental principles of combat leadership: Cover and Move, Simple, Prioritize and Execute, and Decentralized Command.

Cover and Move allowed us to maneuver safely to and from the target. We used this basic but essential tactic for every movement and it was present in every plan we developed. We kept the plans Simple. While it was sometimes tempting to utilize more complex or convoluted tactics, we always chose the most straightforward course of action so that everyone on the team knew exactly how to execute the plan. During the planning phase, we would utilize Prioritize and Execute to ensure the team concentrated our efforts on the most important facets of the target, and we would focus our resources there. Lastly, we would create our plans with Decentralized Command. The junior leaders developed supporting sections, then we would consolidate these into one comprehensive plan.

On top of the Laws of Combat, we used stealth, surprise, and violence of action to ensure we had the upper hand on the enemy whenever possible. It was never our intent to have a fair fight. It was our job to maximize our advantages over the enemy and we did everything in our power to make this happen.

Our tactics and planning usually left the enemy shaken, confused, and unable to intelligently defend themselves. Since no one
in my platoon had been in combat before, the opportunity to exercise everything we had learned about planning and executing
operations was gratifying—not only because we were carrying out
important missions, but also because we had trained and prepared
for so long.

It was awesome. It was awesome because we were getting to
do real work after the long "dry years" of no combat. It was awesome because we had developed sound tactics that made us highly
effective. It was awesome because we dominated the enemy; our
weapons, tactics, and training were far superior. We felt like rock
stars. During the few firefights we found ourselves in, they didn't
stand a chance. So far, only one man had been wounded and it
was relatively minor. We felt unstoppable.

That felt good.

The more missions we handled, the more confident we became. We began to try to push even harder. To complete our missions even faster. To push the envelope.

I noticed that guys started carrying less gear so they could
move faster. Fewer magazines of ammunition since we hadn't been
in any sustained contacts. Fewer hand grenades since we hadn't
had to use them, as the enemy didn't put up much resistance. They
began to carry less water since the missions were quick, and we
always had the vehicles nearby with ample supplies of water in
big five-gallon jugs. This was all done in the belief that if we were
lighter, we could move more quickly. We could bound in and out
of doors and windows and more efficiently chase down bad guys
who had fled from the target buildings. We wanted to be better
and more effective at our jobs, and I agreed with that.

But then arrogance started to creep in. We started to think
that the enemy couldn't even touch us.

One day, before a mission, I talked with one of my guys.

"Let's go get 'em!" I joked with him, slapping him on the back.
But instead of hitting the solid mass of the ballistic body armor

plate we wore in both the front and back, I felt only soft web gear. I grabbed the web gear and squeezed it to confirm—he had no ballistic back plate inserted into his web gear.

"Where's your back plate?" I asked him.

"I took it out," he said.

"You took it out?" I asked, incredulous.

"Yeah. I took it out," he said, indifferent. "It's too heavy. I can move a lot quicker without it."

I was shocked. Of course, at about seven pounds each, the plates were heavy—but they stopped bullets from entering your body and killing you!

"Yeah, but what if you get shot?" I asked him.

"I'm not going to be running," he said defiantly. "The enemy isn't going to shoot me in the back. A lot of us took them out," he told me with a shrug of the shoulders, as if this idea made total sense.

"A lot of guys?" I asked him.

"Yeah. We want to be fast," he said.

Some of my guys weren't wearing body armor—a key piece of lifesaving equipment.

*Idiots,* I thought to myself, *what a bunch of idiots!*

Then, I quickly realized this was my fault. I was responsible for making sure my men had the right equipment every time they went in the field. That was why we held inspections—to make sure they were accountable. But our operational tempo was so fast that I didn't always have time to inspect everyone's gear. Of course, between me, my platoon chief, and our LPO (leading petty officer), gear did get inspected regularly. But we sometimes launched on missions within fifteen to twenty minutes of being tasked; there was no way we could inspect everyone's gear every single time. There had to be a better way than imposed accountability to make sure everyone was carrying all the gear they should be—including the ballistic back plate to help prevent them from taking a bullet to the back. I knew the answer. The solution to this problem wasn't accountability. The solution was the same answer to every problem in every team: leadership. I had to lead.

A few minutes later, we were standing around the magnet board for roll call in preparation for the next mission, before we loaded up the vehicles to launch. Once the LPO had gone through roll call, I said my final piece before launch.

"Remember we are trying to get off the target quickly," I said. "This is a bad area and we don't want the enemy in the neighborhood to have time to set up on us when we leave.

"And—last thing," I emphasized. "If you don't have your back plate in, go put it in. Now. Everyone. Alright? Loading up in five. Let's go."

Only about five or six guys scurried off to their tents to grab their back plate—but that was five or six too many. A few minutes later we loaded up the Humvees and headed out on the operation. It all went smoothly. We hit the target, grabbed the bad guys, gathered the intelligence we needed, and then headed back to base. During the debrief, I addressed the issue of the back plates, not by yelling or screaming or even threatening accountability by constant inspections of everyone's gear. I knew accountability wasn't the answer—we just didn't have time to hold everyone accountable before each and every operation. Instead, I explained *why* it was important for them to wear their plates.

"I know some of you haven't been wearing your back plate. Right?" I looked around the room. A few guys nodded.

"Bad idea," I continued. "Bad idea. Why wouldn't you wear your back plate?" I questioned one of the guys.

"Trying to be lighter," he said. "The lighter we are, the faster we can move."

"I get that," I answered. "But can you move faster than a bullet?" That got a little chuckle from the group.

"Yeah, but I'm not trying to outrun a bullet," one young, confident SEAL said. "In fact, I'm not running away. So the enemy isn't going to see my back." This also got a reaction from the group with some head nods and grins. I even heard "Hell, yeah" from a couple of guys at the back of the room. It was a bold statement. A confident statement. A courageous statement. But it crossed the line from bold, confident, and courageous into cockiness and arrogance.

I understood how the confident young SEAL had arrived at that conclusion and how anyone in the platoon might have arrived at the same thing. We had been winning against the enemy—and winning easily. We had been shot at only a couple of times and nothing very significant. We were dominating and felt untouchable.

"Okay. I'm glad you aren't going to run away from the enemy. I don't think anyone in this room will," I told the group, and I truly believed this. Our platoon was solid.

"But let me ask you this," I continued. "Do you always know where the enemy will be? Do you always think he is going to be in front of you? Don't you think we could get ambushed or flanked from behind and you might get shot from that direction when you hadn't anticipated it?"

The room got quiet. Of course that could happen—at any time.

"Listen. I'm glad we are kicking the enemy's ass," I said, "and we are going to keep kicking his ass. But we cannot get arrogant or complacent. The enemy might never get the drop on us. But at the same time, he might get the drop on you on the next mission. And while being light is good and allows us to be quick, being quick isn't going to stop a bullet from entering your back and killing you. And it isn't just about you; it isn't just you, individually, at risk. If one of you gets shot, that means others have to carry you. Think about how much that will slow us down in a serious gunfight, when we want to be light and fast.

"But it is about much more than that," I said. "If one of us gets killed, it is a win for the enemy. And on top of that—and more important—it is a loss for America, for the Navy, for the Teams, and for your family. And we need to do everything we can to prevent that loss. That includes wearing all the ballistic protection we can. Understood?"

The room was quiet. I had made my point.

As the deployment continued, we still didn't have time to inspect everyone's gear. But we made it a point to make sure everyone understood the bare minimum they needed to carry. They also understood what items were not optional and, more important, *why* they were not optional. Once my troops understood *why* a piece of lifesaving equipment was needed and how it impacted not only them but the mission as well, they made sure not only to have the proper gear with them but also that the gear was ready for use.

This didn't happen because I "held them accountable." It happened because they now understood *why* the particular piece of gear was important for them, for the mission, and for the team. Now they were holding *themselves accountable*. Furthermore, when the troops understand why, they are empowered—and with that empowerment, they begin to police themselves and each other, which provides redundancy and unification of effort.

This is not to say that I never inspected gear. That is the dichotomy: while a leader wants team members to police themselves because they understand *why,* the leader still has to hold people accountable through some level of inspection to ensure that the *why* is not only understood but being acted upon. So my platoon chief, LPO, or I would still regularly inspect gear when able—but that was not our primary tool for accountability. We didn't need to hold the troops' hands to make sure they were accountable. They *held themselves accountable,* which proved far more effective.

Once the platoon realized the importance of executing in accordance with the standard and how violating the required gear list impacted the overall mission, we didn't have to rely solely on gear inspections. Each team member applied peer pressure to keep others in check. And that peer pressure from within the team was far more powerful than any pressure I could apply from above them in the chain of command.

The balance between the troops understanding the *why* mixed with intrusive accountability provides the best possible outcome for a team. As a testament, through the rest of the deployment, I never caught another man without body armor again.

## Principle

Accountability is an important tool that leaders must utilize. However, it should not be the primary tool. It must be balanced with other leadership tools, such as making sure people understand the *why*, empowering subordinates, and trusting they will do the right thing *without* direct oversight because they fully understand the importance of doing so.

Unfortunately, leaders often get the idea that accountability can solve everything—and in a sense they are right. If a leader wants to ensure a subordinate follows through with a task, the leader can inspect repeatedly to confirm that the task gets done. With enough oversight, task completion can achieve 100 percent success. This is why leaders often want to use accountability to fix problems: it is the most obvious and simple method. The leader tells a subordinate to carry out a task; the leader watches the subordinate do the task; the leader inspects the task once it is complete. There is almost no room for error.

Unfortunately, there is also almost no room for the leader to do anything else besides monitor the progress of that specific subordinate in that specific task. If there are multiple subordinates with multiple tasks, a leader very quickly becomes physically incapable of inspecting them all. On top of that, while focused down the chain of command and inward toward the team, the leader will have no ability to look up and out—up toward senior leadership to build relationships and influence strategic decisions and out toward the strategic mission to anticipate future operations and understand developments. Finally, when the leader is not present to provide immediate oversight, the subordinate may or may not continue to properly execute a particular task.

Instead of using accountability as the primary tool of leadership, leaders should implement it as just one of many leadership tools. Instead of holding people accountable, the leader has to *lead*.

The leader must make sure the team understands *why*. Make sure its members have ownership of their tasks and the ability to make adjustments as needed. Make sure they know how their task supports the overall strategic success of the mission. Make sure they know how important their specific task is to the team and what the consequences are for failure.

Now, this does not mean that accountability should never be used. In *Extreme Ownership,* chapter 2, "No Bad Teams, Only Bad Leaders," we wrote that "when it comes to standards, as a leader, *it's not what you preach, it's what you tolerate.*" It is imperative that leaders hold the line and uphold the standards where it matters most. That is another dichotomy nested in accountability: there are absolutely cases when accountability should and must be used. If a subordinate is not performing to standard, despite understanding why, despite knowing the impact on the mission, and despite being given ownership, then a leader must hold the line. That method is accountability. The leader must drill down and micromanage tasks in order to get the subordinate on track. But the leader cannot stay there. The leader must eventually give subordinates leeway to perform based on their own intrinsic drive—not because they are being held accountable, and not based on the micromanagement of the leader, but because they have a better understanding of why.

And that is where balance must be found: use accountability as a tool when needed, but don't rely on it as the sole means of enforcement. A reliance on heavy accountability consumes the time and focus of the leader and inhibits the trust, growth, and development of subordinates.

Instead, balance accountability with educating the team and empowering its members to maintain standards even without direct oversight from the top. This is the hallmark of the highest-performing teams that dominate.

### Application to Business

"They just won't do what we tell them to do!" the national operations manager told me. "They just don't seem to care!"

The company had started using a new software program about three months earlier to track their product as it was installed and utilized by the customers, which consisted of medium- to large-size businesses. It was a well-thought-out system, built on an existing platform that allowed technicians in the field to input what equipment had been installed, the tests that were completed, issues overcome, and shortfalls of the system. It also interacted with the company's customer relationship management system, providing salespeople with information about the customers if they needed to approach them about renewal or upgrades.

"What exactly is it that the field technicians won't do?" I asked.

"They won't use the system. They won't enter the information. They show up on-site with the customer to take care of an install or a troubleshooting scenario, they do their work, then boom—that's it. They enter the bare minimum into the system, but no details."

"What are the details they should be entering?" I asked.

"The details are critical—not for them, but for the follow-on," the ops manager said. "If something else goes wrong and another technician has to go out and troubleshoot, it saves a lot of time and effort if they know what the previous technician did. On top of that, the details really help our salespeople. When they call to offer new services or a renewal of existing services, if they don't know what the customer has been through, they get blindsided. It makes it seem as if no one at the company cares about the customer at all. Try selling to someone that already thinks your company doesn't care about them."

"I can see where that would be problematic," I acknowledged. "So what have you done to get them to do what they are supposed to do?"

"We put a whole bunch of accountability checks into place," he said. "We started with the technicians themselves. We told them they needed to fill in the details. That barely had any impact. Next, we went to the team leaders. We told them we wanted entries in every field of the software—and that we would give bonuses based on the number of fields filled out."

"And how did that work?" I asked.

"It cost us money but didn't get us anywhere," the ops manager replied. "The technicians did as they were told: they filled out every field. But they did so with worthless one- and two-word answers."

"Ouch," I said.

"Yeah. Ouch," the ops manager agreed. "Next up were the regional operations managers. We figured if we held them accountable they would make it happen. So we told them if the technicians in their regions didn't start filling out all the fields—with legitimate details—we were going to drop their volume bonuses by ten percent. We saw a little uptick after that for about two weeks. Then, things went backward—back to where the technicians weren't filling out anything at all, not even a word in most of the fields."

"Not good," I commented.

"No. Not good at all," the ops manager said. "Especially because we reached pretty deep into our budget to have this new software designed, built, and implemented."

"Alright," I declared. "Let me go and talk to some of the team leaders, regional managers, and frontline technicians and see what I can figure out."

Over the next few days, I set meetings and went around talking to everyone involved down the chain of command. I started with the regional managers. It didn't take long to figure out what was going on with them. They had tried to hold the team leaders and technicians accountable for filling in every field—especially when their volume bonus was threatened with a 10-percent cut. But it didn't take them long to figure out that if their technicians spent the additional time filling in all the fields, they couldn't cover as many installations or customer service calls. By not covering as many installations, they made less money, and that cost them more than the 10 percent penalty for noncompliance with the software. Once they realized this, the regional managers backed off holding the front line accountable.

The team leaders had another story. They were busy. They handled the schedules for their teams, and it was a huge job: appointments, cancellations, customers not present, jobs taking too long and interfering with other jobs, and, of course, dealing with absent technicians and getting their jobs covered. On top of that, as the technical experts, they spent a fair amount of time on the phone with technicians troubleshooting more complex problems. Finally, they were also the first point of impact for customer complaints. Any issue with the product or the technician came directly to the team leader first—and those calls had to be handled delicately and tactfully. With all of this on their plates, they didn't have time for much else. And they certainly didn't have time to load individual technicians' screens after every call to ensure that the data was being entered. So even though they understood that it needed to happen, they simply didn't have the time to execute it.

Finally, I got into the field and talked to some of the technicians. They had some significant problems. First of all, entering information into the system took longer than the senior leadership knew. In the field, different customers in different areas had varying levels of cell phone reception. In areas with poor signals, loading each page could take a minute or two—and there were eight pages to load, so this was a huge waste of time. Furthermore, each page started with the need to reenter the customer's name, address, and account number. Copy and paste wasn't a solution because you couldn't copy more than one field at a time, requiring you to flip back and forth between screens, which took forever. Last, instead of having some multiple-choice options for the most common answers, every answer had to be typed in, which wasted even more time. On top of all that, and most important, no one on the front lines really understood how the data was going to help *them*.

When I reported back to the national operations manager with all this information, he was shocked.

"Okay," he said in a depressed voice. "Accountability didn't work. Now what?"

"Now you *lead*," I told him.

He took a moment to let that sink in.

Finally, he broke. "Well then, I am at a loss. How am I supposed to lead here?"

It was a great sign. He was humble enough to admit he needed some help—and what's more, humble enough to ask for it.

"Okay, it isn't that bad," I replied. "Luckily, you have a bunch of good people out there who want to do the right thing. First, you have got to solicit input on how to make the software better. There are some things that would really simplify it. Multiple-choice answers for one. Making the customer information flow from one screen to the next would be helpful—these guys are typing the same information on every page. And there should be fewer pages. Simplify. I know you rarely have to print these things out, so why do they need to be compatible with a paper format? Put more questions on each screen so the techs aren't loading screen after screen—that wastes all kinds of time in the field. Those are just some initial suggestions after talking to only four or five of your techs. I'm sure a broader inquiry would yield even more ideas to streamline the software based on direct feedback from the guys who use it."

"That makes sense," the ops manager replied. "I thought we had gotten enough feedback."

"Maybe you did in the beginning," I said. "But once a complex thing like this hits the field, you need to continually get feedback to make it better. That's just the way it is."

"Got it. Anything else?" the ops manager asked.

"Absolutely," I said. "The biggest thing I figured out in talking to the frontline troops about this is that they have no idea why they are doing this—and, most important, how it affects *them*."

"How it affects them?" he repeated.

"Yes. Right now, they don't get it," I said.

"But they know this data will help us hold on to customers

and allow us to upsell them on better, more expensive products," the ops manager said. "Obviously, that is going to make the company more profitable. What else is there to get?"

"Okay. Think about what you just said," I stated. "If the company makes more money, if the company is more profitable, do you think that a frontline technician cares?"

"I hope he cares! It is his paycheck!" the ops manager yelled.

"Hope isn't a course of action," I said. "And, from his perspective, he has been getting a paycheck consistently for as long as he's been employed here—regardless of how profitable the company is or isn't. It simply doesn't impact him."

"He should still care about it," the ops manager insisted.

"Of course he should," I agreed. "And in a perfect world, every employee would care deeply about the profitability of the company he or she works for. But these folks have other things to care about. Husbands and wives. Kids. Soccer games. Bills and cars and mortgages and the game on Friday night and the broken water heater and the kid heading off to college. They have a ton to care about—and like it or not, the profitability of the company is not high on their list."

"So then what do we do?" the ops manager asked. "If they don't care, why should they give any extra effort?"

"They have to understand *why*—but that *why* has to have a thread that ties back to them, to what is in it for *them*," I told him.

"And how do I do that?" he asked. "How can I make them care about the company's profits?"

"You have to think it through," I said. "It's like this. If you can capture this data that you want, you will be able to better arm both technicians in the field and your salespeople, right?"

"Absolutely. That's the whole point," the ops manager agreed.

"And once the technicians and salespeople are armed, they can do a better job, right?" I continued.

"Definitely," he answered.

"Okay," I said. "Now follow me: Armed with this data, the technicians will be able to provide better and faster customer service, and the salespeople will be able to sell more product to more customers. When we provide better service and sell more products, our business grows. When our business grows, we make more money—"

"That's what I said! But how does that help?" the ops manager interrupted.

"Listen," I told him. "When the company makes more money, we can invest more money in advertising and infrastructure. Once we put more money into advertising and infrastructure, we will gain even more customers and be able to support them even better. The better we perform as a company, the more customers we acquire. The more customers we acquire, the more work there is for technicians, which means overtime and overtime pay. And once the company maxes that out, we will need more technicians. The more technicians we need, the more we have to pay them to be here. So this means down the line, we will increase pay for technicians, especially experienced ones. And lastly, the more technicians and clients we have, the more team leaders and regional supervisors we will need. This opens up a pathway to advancement for every technician at this company. So profitability of the company not only puts money into the pockets of the owners—which the frontline technicians probably don't care too much about—but more important, it impacts the technicians directly: it opens up opportunity for more pay, higher salaries, and a pathway for career advancement. That's the thread that ties all of this together and aligns everyone at the company—the corporate leadership team right down to the field technicians. That's leadership."

The operations manager nodded. The light had come on. It was clear.

Over the next two days, I helped him put together a simple, clear presentation that explained the thread of *why*. We also talked about the fact that he would still have to occasionally inspect people's work to ensure that things were being done—there still had to be some level of overt accountability. But most of the accountability would come intrinsically, from the individual leaders and the field technicians themselves, who were now empowered by understanding the *why*. They would help keep each other accountable, when they fully understood the impact and the direct benefit to them.

A few days later, the national operations manager briefed the plan during an all-hands morning call. He also put one of the tech-savvy regional managers in charge of compiling feedback about the software system so it could be improved. Most important, he drove home how every member of the company would benefit from collecting data to the best of their ability—which would help every employee improve their lives.

The troops now understood that, and they went to work.

# PART III

## BALANCING YOURSELF

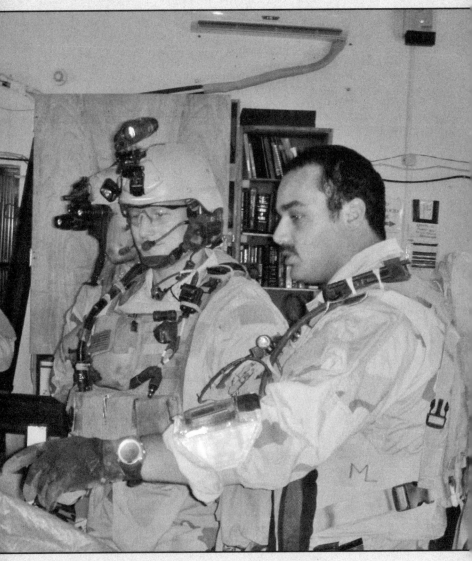

Task Unit Bruiser SEALs from Charlie and Delta Platoons, about to launch on a nighttime direct action capture/kill raid in Ramadi, visit a wounded SEAL brother at "Charlie Med," the Camp Ramadi Medical Facility, as he awaits MEDEVAC transport to major surgical facilities. An exceptional teammate and friend, the wounded SEAL is the brave young man described in the opening pages of Chapter 1. Leif Babin, Charlie platoon commander, at center. Marc Lee, Charlie Platoon assaulter/machine gunner, at right.

(Photo courtesy of the authors)

# CHAPTER 9

## A Leader and a Follower

*Leif Babin*

### SOUTH-CENTRAL RAMADI, IRAQ: 2006

An ominous silence blanketed the slow-moving waters of the canal. The night was dark to the naked eye, with only a few street-lights some distance inland that hadn't been shattered by bullets or shrapnel from roadside bombs. Through the green glow of our night-vision goggles, we saw reeds lining the riverbank on either side. Groves of palm trees and the buildings and walls of the city's urban sprawl were visible beyond the shore. The laser illuminators from our weapons scanned each side of the narrow waterway, looking for enemy fighters lurking in ambush.

Our four boats motored slowly along in formation, careful to maintain noise and light discipline so as not to give away our position. The U.S. Marine Corps Small Unit Riverine Craft (SURCs), and the Marines who drove them and manned their heavy machine guns, carried our platoon of Task Unit Bruiser SEALs and the Iraqi soldiers assigned to us, along with the Marines of SALT 6, the Supporting Arms Liaison Team from the 5th Air-Naval Gunfire Liaison Company. Their commander, Major Dave Berke, was the senior-ranking man of our group. He was an outstanding leader, a Marine fighter pilot who had flown combat sorties in

Iraq and Afghanistan. As a TOPGUN instructor, he could have gone anywhere he chose, but he'd volunteered for a tour on the ground as a forward air controller. Of all the places he could have chosen in Iraq, he chose Ramadi. We were damn glad to have Dave and his Marines along with us for additional firepower and support. They were an outstanding group. Though Dave outranked me, as officer in charge of the SEALs in Charlie Platoon, I was the ground force commander, responsible for all the elements that would land ashore and patrol on foot into one of the most violent neighborhoods of Ramadi. In the event of enemy contact, there were no friendly forces that could come to our aid for several hours. To carry out our objective against untold numbers of enemy fighters, we had only the firepower we could carry on our backs. To mitigate that risk, we brought a large force, one of the largest I'd ever led—nearly fifty personnel. Our strength in numbers would sustain us until Dave could contact aircraft and vector them overhead to support us.

Traveling by boat, we mitigated the risk from IED attacks, the roadside bombs that were heavily utilized by enemy fighters. But on the narrow canal, perhaps fifty yards wide, everyone on the boats was totally exposed, with nothing to hide behind and no way to take cover from any potential onslaught of enemy gunfire the insurgent fighters might unleash upon us. Our only advantage was the darkness and the element of surprise. For now, all was quiet and we observed no movement along the riverbanks. But the tension was extreme. Beyond the reeds, the city on both sides of the canal belonged to al Qaeda. Where we were going, there was nothing but block after block of a war-ravaged city that had seen almost no U.S. or coalition forces in months and was firmly controlled by a brutal and murderous insurgency loyal to al Qaeda in Iraq.

We would be the first U.S. boots on the ground in the area. Our mission was to cover the movement of the U.S. Army Soldiers of Task Force Bandit (1st Battalion, 37th Armored Regiment of the 1st Brigade, 1st Armored Division) in their heavy tanks and vehicles as they drove down the most dangerous road in the world—statistically, it accounted for more attacks from IEDs than any other road in Iraq, or anywhere else. We were the lead element, a small group launching ahead of the main effort—a force of hundreds of American Soldiers and Marines, some fifty tanks, and dozens of heavy vehicles as the spearhead to establish a small U.S. combat outpost in enemy territory. In the early morning darkness, only a few hours after we inserted from the boats, the heavily armored vehicles of the mine clearance team would slowly and meticulously pick their way along the road, identifying and disarming the bombs to clear a path for the M1A2 Abrams Tanks and M2 Bradley Fighting Vehicles. Dave's task was a crucial one: he and his twelve Marines (including a Navy corpsman) accompanied us to control the aircraft overhead, our only means of support for several hours until the tanks could reach us, in the event we came under enemy attack—a likely scenario.

When we arrived at our preplanned insertion point, two boats quietly maneuvered toward the shoreline while the other two covered our movement with their .50-caliber heavy machine guns, M240 medium machine guns, and GAU-17 miniguns.* We stepped off the bow of the SURC onto the muddy riverbank as quietly as possible given the ridiculously heavy load-out—each man carried his helmet, body armor, weapons, radio, and rucksack with enough water, food, ammo, and extra batteries: all essential gear for forty-eight hours of "getting after it" in the most dangerous terrain of the most dangerous city in Iraq. If we lost our air support, we'd be on our own against the onslaught of the hundreds of well-armed, combat-experienced enemy fighters who occupied this section of the city and ruled over its civilian populace in a brutal reign of terror, intimidation, and murder.

We knew they were out there—waiting, watching, and listening. After disembarking from the boats, we moved through the

---

* M134 GAU-17 minigun: a 7.62 × 51mm NATO, electrically driven weapon that fires four thousand rounds per minute through six rotating barrels.

reeds up the slope to the shelter of a date palm grove, allowing the rest of the team room to disembark behind us. Charlie Platoon's point man, Chris Kyle, was in the lead; I followed closely behind. We stopped for a few moments and took a knee, listening for movement as we scanned the area for threats, weapons at the ready. Nothing stirred.

As Chris and I listened for the enemy, I heard someone behind us key the intersquad radio we used to communicate with each other. But instead of a voice, I heard only the rustle of equipment and heavy breathing as the operator toiled under the load of his rucksack and combat gear. It was a "hot mic," an accidental toggle of the radio talk button—what civilians with cell phones might call a "butt dial." But in the field, it was more than just annoying. It prevented us from passing critical communication between the team, and the continuous noise of the radio in our ears also diminished our ability to detect enemy movement.

"Hot mic," I said as quietly as I could, keying up my radio in an effort to talk over the accidental call. "Check your gear."

There was no response. The hot mic continued. It was a liability and it pissed me off. But there was nothing I could do about it.

I waited for the sign that we had a full head count—meaning everyone had successfully disembarked from the boats. When it came, I gave the hand signal to patrol out. As point man, Chris moved out in the lead. He led the patrol around some smaller buildings and through a date palm grove to the edge of a road that ran perpendicular to our direction of travel. It was an open area with no trees or cover and we had to cross it. Across the road was urban terrain: dusty streets and alleyways littered with trash, and the walled compounds and houses of South-Central Ramadi. This was enemy territory. We'd come to take it back.

It was about thirty yards across the open area to the other side of the road and the buildings beyond. We called this a "danger crossing." We'd need weapons to cover the movement of the patrol, which would be exposed and vulnerable to attack while darting across the open terrain. Once we had operators in position to cover us with their weapons, Chris and I nodded at each other and moved together across the street as quietly but as quickly as possible. Once on the far side, we took positions to cover the next element's crossing just behind us. As soon as they reached us, Chris and I bumped forward. Suddenly, Chris held up his hand in a signal to halt the patrol. I moved up to him.

"What's going on?" I asked in a whisper, trying to communicate while making as little noise as possible.

"My battery is out," he answered quietly. The laser illuminator that enabled us to use our weapons in the darkness was no longer functioning on his rifle. It was a critical piece of gear: without it, Chris could not shoot accurately—his essential role as point man.

Still, we had the entire rest of the patrol behind us, almost fifty operators trying to get across the open area before the enemy was alerted to our presence.

"We can't stop here," I said. "Everybody behind us is exposed on the road. We're only three hundred meters from the target buildings. Let's push forward and you can change your batteries there."

Chris wasn't happy. He was at a serious disadvantage. But as the leader, I had the good of the entire team to think about.

Reluctantly, Chris resumed the patrol forward. As we moved out we followed a paved street, a narrow passage between two eight-foot-high concrete walls on either side. Somewhere beyond the danger crossing, the hot mic ceased as the culprit adjusted his gear. But by that point, I barely noticed. We were now deep in enemy territory and scanning for threats in all directions. We knew an attack could come at any moment.

Along the length of the road, in the center of the dust-filled pavement, was a shallow depression where raw sewage drained to a nearby creek. On the left side of the street, piles of trash were stacked against the wall. These trash piles were a favorite hiding place for IEDs, the deadly explosives that were the enemy's most effective weapon. To keep clear, Chris wisely bumped to the right side of the street and moved along the wall, pulling the entire patrol to the right side to mitigate the threat.

Suddenly, I saw Chris freeze. Only fifteen feet ahead of me, his weapon was trained on an apparent threat. It was around the corner and beyond my field of vision, but the unspoken signal was clear: ENEMY. This was Murphy's Law in full effect: without a functioning battery in his laser aiming system, all Chris could do was wait for me to recognize the signal and take action.

Quickly, I moved toward Chris, stepping as carefully and quietly as possible. Immediately, I saw what had stopped him—an armed insurgent fighter, kaffiyeh wrapped around his face, AK-47 rifle at the ready, an extra magazine taped alongside the first for ease in reloading. He was perhaps twenty-five yards away and walking toward us. There wasn't a moment to lose. Though we greatly outnumbered him, if he opened up on us with his automatic rifle, this one well-armed insurgent could kill many of us, particularly in our close patrol formation. He turned his head in our direction, his rifle at the ready—

*BAM! BAM! BAM! BAM! BAM!*

I engaged with my M4: the first round impacted his head and the rest followed as he crumpled to the ground. Chris rushed toward him to ensure he was no longer a threat as I moved to the corner of the wall to provide cover in the direction from which the enemy fighter had come. Where there was one, there very well could be more.

"Need a machine gunner up front," I said, using verbal commands. Our SEAL machine gunner, Ryan Job, always eager and ready to unleash the fury, rapidly pushed forward and bumped me out of my covering position, replacing my rifle with his much more powerful and effective Mk48 machine gun.

"Let's move," I directed. The gunfire, though necessary, had cost us the element of surprise.

Charlie Platoon SEALs surged forward past the prostrate enemy fighter to the target buildings beyond, which we would enter and clear so they could serve as the location for the U.S. Army's planned combat outpost. We boosted SEALs over the gate, and they opened it from the inside. The rest of us entered, rapidly clearing the buildings. Once secure, our snipers established shooting positions and machine gunners set security. Dave Berke and his Marines took station on the roof of the main building with our team.

Our snipers and machine gunners kept watchful eyes in the darkness through night-vision goggles and weapons sights as we waited several hours for the IED clearance teams to cover the half-mile distance from the main road through the city to our position. It was still dark when they arrived, white lights beaming, like something right out of a *Mad Max* movie. The "Buffalo"—a giant armored vehicle with a huge mechanical arm—began digging in the street near the base of the building we occupied. I peered over the side of the rooftop, three stories down, and could clearly see the cylindrical forms of large artillery projectiles, which had been scavenged by insurgents and turned into powerful and deadly IEDs, as the clearance team dug them out of the dirt.

I thought of a phrase I learned in BUD/S: "If you can see the explosive, it can see you." If those artillery rounds detonated, giant fragments of metal would fly in all directions, ripping apart whatever they hit, including my head if I continued to peer over the rooftop. *Not smart.* I took cover behind the roof wall.

As the ground force commander, it was up to me to figure out our next step—where to move to best support the U.S. Army battalion once it arrived. From the rooftop, I observed a large building about three hundred meters to the south, and I pulled out my map to check it out. I talked things over with Charlie Platoon's chief, Tony, and our key leaders.

"I like the look of that building to the south," I said, pointing to it in the distance and then to the corresponding building number on the map. "The rooftop gives us a good position on the high ground and the walls look thick enough to protect us from bullets."

Chris Kyle disagreed. In addition to being our point man and lead sniper, Chris had the most real-world experience of any of us in this type of "sniper overwatch" mission.

"I like that large, four-story building," he countered, pointing out a different building in a totally new direction about 350 meters to the east. We located it on the map and identified the building number.

I was skeptical. I felt the building to the south would put us in position to best support the Army and disrupt enemy attacks and not put us in a bad spot between enemy and friendly positions. To the south, there was another U.S. Army combat outpost several hundred meters away, in a village on the outskirts of Ramadi. But beyond Chris's recommendation to the east, there was only block after city block of enemy territory until you reached the U.S. outposts on the far eastern side of Ramadi in the volatile Malaab District. Chris felt that the majority of enemy attacks would likely come from that direction.

As the IED clearance team finished their work and opened the route in, the Task Force Bandit tanks began to arrive. Main Gun Mike Bajema and his Soldiers from Team Bulldog (Bravo Company, 1-37) were the main effort for this operation. As company commander, Mike was the first to arrive on the scene. The Task Force Bandit battalion leadership, along with Jocko, had ridden in the back of a Bradley. They pulled in just behind.

We debriefed the situation with the U.S. Army units and I turned the buildings we had cleared and occupied for the last several hours over to Main Gun Mike and his Team Bulldog Soldiers.

I still hadn't made a decision about where we were moving next. Since I was the senior man, it was my call. I outranked Chris. Yet I knew Chris had key experience and knowledge that I didn't have. I wasn't a sniper. I hadn't spent my previous deployment supporting U.S. Marine units in the Battle of Fallujah as Chris had.

While I was the leader in charge, I recognized that for my team to succeed, in order to be a good leader, I also had to be willing to follow. "Leading" didn't mean pushing *my* agenda or proving I had all the answers. It was about collaborating with the rest of the team and determining how we could most effectively accomplish our mission. I deferred to Chris's judgment.

"Alright," I told Chris. "Let's go with your plan and move to that building to the east." He smiled.

Just before dawn, under cover of the last minutes of darkness, we patrolled 350 meters down the street and entered the large, four-story apartment building he'd selected. After methodically clearing the building, we put our snipers and machine gunners in place.

Chris's recommendation proved to be the absolute right call. Over the next forty-eight hours, we disrupted scores of enemy attacks on the fledgling U.S. combat outpost and on our combined U.S. Army and Iraqi Army patrols in the vicinity. Our SEAL snipers racked up twenty-one confirmed enemy kills and several more probable kills. Virtually all the enemy activity took place to the east, with almost none to the south. Had we gone with my initial choice—had I disregarded Chris and overruled him because "I was in charge"—we would have been highly ineffective, disrupting virtually no attacks, and that might very well have cost the lives of some of our brethren: SEALs, U.S. Soldiers, and Marines.

There were many times in my Navy career when, in an effort to prove my leadership, I failed to follow. And rather than strengthen me as a leader in the eyes of the team, it undermined my leadership. In those instances, I had to work to recover and build back trust with the team.

As a brand-new platoon commander in Task Unit Bruiser, I'd gotten this wrong during an early training operation shortly after I reported to the SEAL Team. Before we deployed to Ramadi, during our training workup, we practiced our ability to board and take down ships at sea. We called this "Visit, Board, Search, and Seizure" operations.

In preparation for training runs on ships at sea, we planned several hours of rehearsals to dial in our standard operating procedures and practice our movement, tactics, and communications on a ship that was docked pierside in San Diego Harbor. It was great training in preparation for the more difficult task of boarding and clearing a ship that was under way.

With some members of Charlie and Delta Platoons pulled away for other training and qualifications, the group from Task Unit Bruiser that day was a combined element from Charlie and Delta Platoons. I was the senior man in charge, and none of my Charlie Platoon senior enlisted leaders could attend. Instead, the most senior enlisted SEAL at the training that day was a member of Delta Platoon. He was not a chief or a leading petty officer, but he did have several deployments under his belt, which made him the most experienced SEAL there. I had only one prior SEAL deployment.

We launched into movement drills, with SEALs bounding across the open deck of the ship using Cover and Move. All was going smoothly until we observed some confusion with the terminology being used to communicate among the team. Several different terms were being used. It was clear that we all needed to get on the same page.

"This was our SOP from my last platoon," I said. "Let's just go with that."

I put the word out to everyone when we called the troops together to debrief the run.

The experienced SEAL petty officer from Delta Platoon disagreed.

"I think we should do it another way," he said, pushing a different SOP that he was familiar with.

"I already put the word out," I said. "It will be a pain to change. Let's just go with my way for now."

"I don't like your method near as much," he replied. "The way we did it in my last two platoons was better."

To me, the advantages and disadvantages between the two

methods were insignificant. What mattered was that we all were on the same page. And since I'd already put the word out to everyone, I figured it was easiest to just stick with that.

"Let's just go with my method for now," I said. "When we get back to the team, we can talk through it with Tony [Charlie Platoon chief] and the Delta Platoon chief."

"We shouldn't develop bad habits," the SEAL insisted. "My method works best."

Growing impatient, I recognized that this was a test of wills. And being a young, inexperienced platoon commander, I decided that I needed to demonstrate that I was in charge—I was the senior man.

"We're doing it my way," I said. "This conversation is over."

With that, the SEAL petty officer and I got back to the training runs. Soon we wrapped up the runs and headed back to the team. But even in the immediate aftermath, I knew I hadn't handled that situation well. It was the weakest form of leadership to win an argument through rank or position. In the Navy, we called it playing a game of "Rock, Scissors, Rank," like the game of "Rock, Paper, Scissors," except rank wins every time. But every leader I had seen use that form of leadership was not someone for whom I had much respect. It certainly wasn't the leader I wanted to be, and on the ride back to the team, I was embarrassed at how I had handled the situation.

Back at the team, I pulled the SEAL petty officer aside and apologized for the way I had reacted. I told him I should have deferred to his method. He told me he was wrong to have argued with me about it in front of the rest of the task unit. We left the conversation on good terms. I was determined to not let that happen again.

At the time, I had thought that if I gave way and followed the SEAL petty officer's lead, it would make me look weak as the leader. But looking back, I realized the opposite was true. Had I given way to the SEAL enlisted leader with more experience, it would have made me a much stronger leader. It would have shown that I was willing to follow as well as lead. It would have served as a powerful demonstration that I knew I didn't have all the answers and could get behind those with more experience, who were in a better position to lead a particular aspect of the team or the mission.

The minor differences between the two methods we argued about were tactically insignificant. But the missed opportunity to demonstrate my strength as a leader by being a willing follower was a strategic loss. I learned an important lesson from this failure, one that helped me greatly going forward and enabled Charlie Platoon and Task Unit Bruiser to more effectively lead and win.

Every leader must be ready and willing to take charge, to make hard, crucial calls for the good of the team and the mission. That is inherent in the very term "leader." But leaders must also have the ability to follow. This was a difficult dichotomy: in order to be a good leader, you must also be a good follower. Finding that balance is key.

### Principle

Every leader must be willing and able to lead, but just as important is a leader's ability to follow. A leader must be willing to lean on the expertise and ideas of others for the good of the team. Leaders must be willing to listen and follow others, regardless of whether they are junior or less experienced. If someone else has a great idea or specific knowledge that puts them in the best position to lead a particular project, a good leader recognizes that it doesn't matter who gets the credit, only that the mission is accomplished in the most effective manner possible. Confident leaders encourage junior members of the team to step up and lead when they put forth ideas that will contribute to mission success. When the team wins, much of the credit goes to the leader, whether or not that leader was the person driving the operation, tactics, or strategy, and a good leader pushes the praise and accolades down to their team.

At the same time, a good leader must also be a good follower of his or her own senior leaders. As we wrote in *Extreme Owner-ship:* "One of the most important jobs of any leader is to support your own boss." When the debate on a particular course of action ends and the boss makes a decision—even if you disagree with the decision—"you must execute the plan *as if it were your own.*" Only if the orders coming down from senior leadership are illegal, immoral, unethical, or significantly risky to lives, limbs, or the strategic success of the organization should a subordinate leader hold fast against directives from superiors. Those cases should be rare. Chapter 11 of this book, "Humble, Not Passive," elaborates on this dichotomy.

Under normal circumstances, a good leader must follow and support the chain of command. Often, for natural leaders who are eager to step up and take charge, it may be a struggle to follow a leader who is less competent, less aggressive, uncharismatic, or uninspiring. Regardless, when lawful orders from the boss or higher chain of command conflict with a leader's ideas, a subordinate leader must still be willing to follow and support the chain of command. Failing to do this undermines the authority of the entire chain of command, including that of the defiant leader. Failing to follow also creates an antagonistic relationship up the chain of command, which negatively impacts the willingness of the boss to take input and suggestions from the subordinate leader, and hurts the team. Leaders who fail to be good followers fail themselves and their team. But when a leader is willing to follow, the team functions effectively and the probability of mission success radically increases. This is the dichotomy to balance: be a leader and a follower.

### Application to Business

"I need your help," Jim said when we connected via phone. "I've got a serious dilemma."

Jim was the leader of the sales team in the products division of a major corporation. He was a highly competent leader—smart, aggressive toward mission accomplishment, and driven to outperform and succeed where others came up short. Like so many good leaders, he was highly competitive and took pride when his team outperformed the other teams in his division.

Jim had read *Extreme Ownership* and recognized that he needed to make some improvements in his leadership game. He reached out to me to inquire about executive coaching.

"Unfortunately, we aren't able to provide individual coaching anymore," I told him. "That is something we used to offer, but with the high demand for our services at Echelon Front, we only provide executive coaching to our long-term clients now as part of our Leadership Development and Alignment Programs."

Jim was disappointed. At the time, I lived in New York City. Jim lived nearby in New Jersey.

"I'll make this as little impact on you as I can," Jim said. "I'll even jump on a train and come to New York City whenever it's convenient."

"What specific leadership challenges are you struggling with?" I asked Jim. "In what areas are you looking to improve?"

"My relationship with my immediate boss isn't good," he replied, "and I'm not sure what to do about it. I've always been a solid team player, and I've gotten along well with every previous boss I can remember. I'm usually their go-to guy. Now, I seem to be in the doghouse and I'm not sure what to do to make it better."

From our initial conversation, I immediately liked Jim. He was a leader with a Default: Aggressive mentality, and in his struggles with his boss, I saw much of my former self. I made so many of the same mistakes. As I aggressively maneuvered to win the tactical victory, I sometimes created frictions with my leadership that hurt our team in the long run and hindered our strategic mission. I knew that the lessons I'd learned the hard way would be useful to Jim and help him rebuild trust with his chain of command. I also knew that while he likely wouldn't want to hear what I had to say, he was eager to learn and therefore would be more willing to listen and implement my recommendations. I decided to make some time in the schedule for him.

"Okay," I said. "Let's do it. How about we meet up in Manhattan sometime in the next couple of weeks?"

Jim was excited and eager to link up. We arranged a time and meeting place.

The place was a finely decorated New York City social club with a long and storied history, whose members included highly successful business leaders and titans of Wall Street. Having grown up in the country in rural southeast Texas, I was much more comfortable in jeans and a flannel shirt or the clothes I wore while stationed in San Diego: a T-shirt, surf shorts, and flip-flops. But as we often say at Echelon Front, there is no growth in the comfort zone. So I donned the required suit and tie for the venue and went to meet Jim.

My first impression confirmed what I had gleaned in our phone conversation: Jim was a driven leader who truly cared about his job and the team he led. He genuinely wanted to be the best at what he did, earn the respect of his peers and leaders, and he was determined to find ways to improve his leadership game. After some initial conversation, we dove into the leadership challenge with which he was struggling at the company.

"I feel like my boss is being unfairly harsh on me and my team because he doesn't like me," Jim stated. He described how he'd previously been recognized for a particular standout performance by the senior vice president of the division—his boss's boss.

"That recognition seemed to turn my boss against me," Jim continued. "It culminated with a big blowup recently."

"What was the big blowup?" I inquired.

"It happened a few weeks back when I went in for my annual performance review," Jim answered. "Our team had done well overall. I was expecting strong marks, just as I've received in the past, and I was stunned when he handed me the review with a lower rating. I mean, there are some areas where we could have done better. But this rating was far lower than it should have been."

"How did you respond?" I asked.

"I blew up at him," Jim admitted. "I felt it was an insult to me. And, most important, it hurt my team's paychecks. Our bonuses are directly tied to that performance rating. Lower marks meant less money for my team to feed their families. I was furious about this and I told the boss so. Things got pretty heated. He blew up at me and I stormed out of his office."

"That doesn't sound good," I said. "It seems your boss is intimidated by you."

"That's probably true," Jim conceded.

"That means that his ego is getting in the way," I said. "A good, confident leader would welcome any subordinate leader's strong performance and praise from the top. That's great for the entire team. But a weak leader, one who lacks confidence in him- or herself, will be intimidated by strong performers. And that seems to be the case here.

"I understand this situation because you are a lot like me," I explained. "This is exactly the situation I found myself in on multiple occasions throughout my Navy career. And I couldn't figure out why."

I explained to Jim that while it might surprise many who haven't served, there are weak leaders in the Navy and other branches of the U.S. military, just as there are in any facet of leadership in the business world. In fact, from my days at the U.S. Naval Academy to my time on two different Navy surface ships through my years in the SEAL Teams, the number of leaders I deeply admired and respected were relatively few. That is just the way of the world, even in an organization as highly screened as the SEAL Teams: good leaders are rare; bad leaders are common. There were certainly times when I worked directly for a boss I thought was weak, risk averse, or just plain timid. Back then, I was a young and inexperienced but headstrong leader. I would often butt heads with a boss with whom I disagreed over the smallest of things. I would then find myself alienated, as the black sheep among my peer group of junior leaders on the team. It was never where I wanted to be. At the time, I put all the blame on my boss. Looking back, however, I realized that many of the problems that arose for me were self-induced. When I didn't respect my boss, I allowed that to show at times in the way that I spoke and acted. To a boss who clearly lacked confidence, I flexed my ego instead of putting it in check. I failed to recognize that a leader who lacks confidence would be hypersensitive to any perceived slight or lack of professionalism in my communication with him. People often describe such situations as a "personality conflict" or "personality clash," meaning two people of very different mentalities who simply don't get along. But that is merely an excuse. I explained to Jim that there was much I could have (and absolutely should have) done to prevent those frictions from developing. It was yet another recognition of the power that is the mind-set of *Extreme Ownership:* it's not about others; it's about *you.*

"So what do you intend to do now?" I asked.

Jim wasn't sure what his next step should be. He disagreed with the boss's assessment and wanted to appeal the evaluation to the vice president of the division.

"I'd like to go back into the boss's office and set things straight," Jim said. "But I'm worried that it will only result in further escalation and add fuel to the fire of an already bad situation."

"If you go back into the boss's office and tell him he's wrong, that he should change his review, what do you think the results will be?" I asked. "Even if you lay out some quantifiable data to support your argument, is this an argument that you can win?"

Jim recognized this course of action would not achieve the desired result. Without question, it would only further inflame tensions. Even if the highest echelon in the chain of command forced his boss to raise the team's marks in the evaluation, the difficulties this would create for Jim and his team in the long term would be greatly compounded. Changing the evaluation would be a Pyrrhic victory—a tactical win that resulted in a strategic loss.

"Is it good for your team for you to have an antagonistic

relationship with your boss?" I asked. "Does that benefit them? Does it benefit you?"

Jim understood that this wasn't good for anyone. His frictions with the boss hurt him and everyone on his team.

"In order to be a good leader, you must also be a good follower," I said. "And right now, you're failing as a follower."

Jim looked at me, surprised. My response was unexpected. He was a competent leader and not used to failing at anything. I knew it was likely the opposite of what he wanted to hear. But I knew that it was the truth, and it was what he *needed* to hear.

"If you're failing as a follower, then you're failing as a leader. And that means you're failing your team," I explained. "You're telling me that there aren't any areas where you and your team can improve? You are currently at optimal performance and can't get any better?"

Of course there were areas in which he and his team could improve, Jim conceded. And once he admitted this fact, he then acknowledged that some of the critiques in the boss's evaluation, though harsh, were not untruthful. There were a multitude of ways he and his team could improve communication, increase efficiency, and build stronger relationships with their customers and other departments to enable greater mutual support and effectiveness.

"As we wrote about in *Extreme Ownership*," I said, "these things are 'simple, not easy.' And though you've read the book multiple times and understand the basic concepts, the principles can be difficult to implement in your life. Both Jocko and I struggle with this at times, just like anyone—and we wrote the book!

"What you need to do," I instructed, "is recognize your failure as a follower. Go to your boss and take ownership. Accept the critical evaluation and the negative marks. Acknowledge that you must do better. Then, lay out in detail for your boss the major steps you will take to improve in each of the areas where your marks were low. It's not enough to just say it. You have to do it. You must demonstrate through action to improve in each area."

Jim looked back at me in disbelief.

"One of the toughest but most important lessons I learned from Jocko," I explained, "is that you should strive to have the same relationship with every boss you ever work for, no matter if they are good or bad. Whether they are an outstanding leader whom you admire, a mediocre leader who needs improvement, or a terrible leader for whom no one on the team has respect, you must strive to form the same relationship with all of them."

I explained that the relationship to seek with any boss incorporates three things:

1) They trust you.
2) They value and seek your opinion and guidance.
3) They give you what you need to accomplish your mission and then let you go execute.

"Whether they are good, bad, or indifferent as a leader doesn't matter," I concluded. "You must build a strong relationship with your boss founded on trust and support. If you do that, you will succeed as a leader by enabling your team to succeed. And since most of the world can't do this, you will run circles around your peers and outperform everyone else.

"Your mission, going forward," I stated, "is to build a better relationship with your boss. Be a good follower. Repair the trust with your chain of command. So, go and make it happen."

Captain "Main Gun" Mike Bajema and the brave Soldiers that crewed his M1A2 Abrams Main Battle Tank maneuver to support U.S. and Iraqi dismounted troops in Ramadi. Mike commanded "Bulldog"—Bravo Company, 1st Battalion, 37th Armored Regiment (1-37) of the 1st Armored Division. Team Bulldog and his battalion, the "Bandits" of Task Force 1-37, were an exceptional group of Soldiers that aggressively led the "Seize, Clear, Hold, Build" strategy into some of the most dangerous, enemy-held territory in the city: South-Central Ramadi. With so many friendly units, including the Lima and Kilo Companies of the 3rd Battalion, 8th Marine Regiment, 2nd Marine Division, operating in a small city only a few miles across, careful contingency planning was mandatory to deconflict friendly forces on the battlefield and reduce the extreme risk of "blue-on-blue" or friendly fire.

(Photo courtesy of Mike Bajema)

# CHAPTER 10
## Plan, but Don't Overplan

*Leif Babin*

**FIRECRACKER CIRCLE, RAMADI, IRAQ: 2006**

My heart was racing. It felt as if it were pounding out of my chest and I couldn't catch my breath. We were in an all-out sprint, running as fast as we could for a full city block. All I could do was put one foot in front of the other under the crushing weight of the rucksack on my back. A rucksack, or "ruck," was military jargon for what the rest of the world called a backpack. Mine was filled to the brim with a ridiculous amount of gear and ordnance: extra hand grenades, extra magazines for my rifle, flares, spare batteries, 40mm grenades for my M203 grenade launcher, food, and water. It was my first operation into downtown Ramadi—a violent, highly dangerous, enemy-infested area—and I had prepared for every contingency imaginable. I was loaded out for World World III. But while I was supposed to be leading my team, looking out for the good of everyone else in the patrol, I was instead dragging ass and sucking wind. It was all I could do to keep up.

We had planned this operation to accompany two squads of U.S. Marines from Lima Company, 3rd Battalion, 8th Marine Regiment (3/8 Marines), 2nd Marine Division, into a nasty area of central Ramadi near a street intersection known as "Firecracker Circle." It had been given that name not for harmless fireworks like we use to celebrate the Fourth of July but for the massive IEDs that tossed heavy armored vehicles in the air or blasted them into pieces.

Task Unit Bruiser had just arrived in Ramadi, and we learned much from the Marines who had been in the fight for several weeks. The 3/8 Marines were an outstanding unit of professional, courageous warriors. Both Lima and Kilo companies, with whom we worked alongside on numerous combat operations, were tasked with securing some of the most violent sectors of downtown Ramadi. They bravely patrolled into dangerous enemy territory, aggressively engaged and maneuvered when attacked, and endured frequent large-scale, well-coordinated enemy assaults on their outposts that involved dozens of enemy fighters attacking simultaneously from multiple directions with machine guns, mortars, and huge VBIEDs. These Marines fearlessly stood their ground and beat back those attacks every time. We were proud to work with the Marines of 3/8 in Ramadi. They added to the proud heritage and storied legacy of the U.S. Marine Corps earned in places like Belleau Wood, Guadalcanal, Iwo Jima, and Chosin. The Marines conducted "census operations" at night—but while the name sounded like a simple administrative accounting of the civilian populace, the missions were anything but easy. They inserted under cover of darkness and patrolled on foot into some of the most contested neighborhoods of the city. The Marines knocked on doors, entered homes, and spoke with the families living there to find out who occupied the house, learn how U.S. troops could help them, and ask about enemy activity they might have seen. Before sunrise, the Marine squads would occupy buildings and set up sniper overwatch positions, remaining there through the hours of daylight. Once the sun set and it was dark, they would reemerge to continue the census.

For this, my first combat mission into downtown Ramadi, two sections of Charlie Platoon SEALs and our Iraqi soldiers planned to support the Marines in a "remain over day" operation that would last about thirty-six hours—a full night, period of daylight, and through the next night. Before we launched, and as we built our plan for the operation, the Marines advised us to be prepared for significant enemy attacks. We learned that some of the previous attacks they had endured in this area of operations were substantial, with dozens of enemy fighters hammering them with belt-fed machine guns and RPG-7 rockets simultaneously from multiple directions, along with accurate enemy sniper fire. But the Marines would not call for help from the Quick Reaction Force of armored vehicles and dismount troops unless they took serious casualties. The high IED threat in the vicinity of Firecracker Circle made the roads too dangerous to drive—too risky for the vehicles' crew and dismount troops—unless it was absolutely necessary. That meant we would be largely on our own, with only the firepower we carried in with us to beat back attacks from any of the hundreds of insurgents who occupied the area.

*We better be ready to get some,* I thought.

I had learned early in my SEAL career that planning for contingencies was crucial to the success of any mission. Thinking through the things that might go wrong for each phase of the operation and preparing for each contingency would enable us to overcome those challenges and accomplish our mission. I had never been into this sector of Ramadi, but I had listened to frequent calls over the radio net describing enemy attacks and U.S. casualties. I'd read the after-action reports and seen the wounded and dead hauled into "Charlie Med," the Camp Ramadi Charlie Medical Facility. I knew the area was a nasty place. So I got after my contingency plans with a vengeance. Thanks to the insight and experience of Charlie Platoon's exceptional SEAL platoon chief, Tony Eafrati, we had solid SOPs in place for the standard gear load-out each man should carry in his load-bearing equipment on every operation: seven magazines for our primary weapon, the M4 rifle; three pistol magazines; one personal radio, antenna, and extra battery; two M67 hand grenades, which were our standard-issue fragmentation, or "frag," grenades; one battle map; one flashlight; one headlamp; one pair of night-vision goggles; one extra night-vision goggle mount; spare batteries for every device; Kevlar helmet; soft Kevlar body armor for frag protection along with heavy ceramic ballistic plates to stop enemy small-arms fire; food and water as needed; and so on.

Just the standard gear alone was heavy, particularly on a foot patrol in the Iraqi heat. It was late spring and the temperatures were already pushing 110 degrees Fahrenheit at the height of the day. Even at night, temperatures were generally in the nineties.

Beyond the standard load-out, I typically carried additional gear. Attached beneath the barrel of my M4, I carried an M203 40mm grenade launcher. I carried a grenade in the chamber and six additional 40mm high-explosive grenades in my load-bearing equipment. I also carried an extra one-hundred-round box of 7.62mm linked ammunition for our machine gunners and a set of flares to use for marking and signaling to other U.S. troops.

But for this operation, I felt I better go heavy. I opened up my rucksack and thought about what else I could possibly need. Different contingencies raced through my mind, many of them worst-case scenarios.

*What if we are under sustained attack for hours and start to run low on ammunition?* I thought. I threw in four extra fully loaded magazines for my M4. I also added a bandolier with twelve additional 40mm high-explosive grenades.

*What if I need to mark the enemy position for tanks or aircraft?* I thought. I threw in an additional magazine loaded entirely with tracer rounds, whose visible glow sent an orange streak along the bullet path. I also added several smoke grenades to my ruck.

*What if we get overrun during an enemy attack and we need more hand grenades?* I thought. I added three more M67 frag grenades to my ruck.

*What if somebody else needs some?* I added two more frag grenades.

*What if my radio goes down or I burn through my extra battery?* I put an extra radio in my ruck and two more spare batteries. Even if I didn't need them during the operation, perhaps someone else in our squad could use them.

Next, I needed to load-out my water and food. We expected to be gone for about thirty-six hours.

*What if the operation gets extended to forty-eight or even seventy-two hours?* I thought. I didn't want to run out of water, especially in the Iraqi heat. We carried our water in 1.5-liter plastic bottles. I had needed five to seven bottles on previous operations. But just in case we got extended, I increased that to twelve bottles. That equated to about forty pounds of weight just for water alone. I also added some extra food just in case.

I took every precaution, planned for every contingency I could think of. But even before we departed our camp, I knew I had overdone it. My rucksack was jammed so full of gear, I could barely zip it closed. Then, as soon as I "jocked up" in my op gear—put on my load-bearing equipment—and shouldered my ruck briefly to move it out to the vehicles that would transit us to the Marine base on the other side of the river, it felt ridiculously heavy. I began to sense the weight was going to be a problem.

When we launched on the patrol on foot, I learned that the Marines utilized a method of "Sprint and Hold." We used Cover and Move in short bounds. But the Marines' version of Cover and Move required two shooters to hold security while the next two sprinted as fast as they could, all the way to the end of the block. It was a way to mitigate the risk of enemy snipers—they would have to hit a moving target. This process was repeated two by two as the entire patrol moved kilometer after kilometer through the city, block by block, in a series of sprints.

Very shortly into the foot patrol, I knew I was in trouble. The crushing weight of the rucksack bore down on me. My chest heaved from the effort to breathe and sweat soaked my clothes. My "eye pro"—the ballistic glasses we wore to protect our eyes—fogged up completely and I had to remove them just to see.

As SEALs, we took pride in hard physical training and maintaining a high level of conditioning. But I had completely overestimated my ability to carry the weight I'd brought with me. It was far too much. As my BUD/S instructors said when I went through the basic SEAL training course, "If you're gonna be stupid, you better be strong." The heavy load-out was foolish, and now I was paying the price. Time to suck it up and BTF, which stood for "Big Tough Frogman," the unofficial mantra of Charlie Platoon and Task Unit Bruiser. We used BTF as a noun, and adjective, and, in this case, a verb.

I was the senior man, the leader of the entire element of Charlie Platoon SEALs and Iraqi soldiers. But I had become so fatigued from the load I carried, I lost all situational awareness for the greater team and the mission. All I could focus on was putting one foot in front of the other and trying like hell to keep up. When we finally completed the operation the following night, I took with me extremely humbling lessons learned.

Misery can be a remarkably effective teacher. And this was a lesson I would never forget: don't try to plan for every contingency. Doing so will only overburden you and weigh you down so that you cannot quickly maneuver. Yes, contingency planning is extremely important. But I'd gone too far. I should have regulated my planning for contingencies with these questions in mind:

*What if I'm carrying too much weight and can't keep up with the patrol?*

*What if I get so fatigued that I'm focused on myself and unable to effectively lead?*

*What if my gear is so heavy that I can't quickly maneuver and become an easy target?*

Such considerations would have helped me to balance my contingency planning and ensure I didn't overplan and cause a worse situation.

This lesson to not overplan, to not try and tackle every contingency, applies not just to individual leaders but to teams. It was something I learned from Jocko back in our training prior to deployment. We'd get assigned a target package from the training instructors for a direct action raid to capture or kill a specific bad guy. I'd want to stack the assault force with as many SEAL operators as I could to enter and clear the house.

"You don't need that many assaulters," Jocko said, looking over our plan. "It's just going to add to the confusion inside the house."

Jocko had a ton of experience with direct action raids in Iraq. I had none. But it didn't make sense to me. We were going after a known bad guy. He might resist or have others in the house who would resist. Wouldn't more SEALs on the assault force—more shooters inside the house—be better?

Only after Task Unit Bruiser deployed to Ramadi and I gained real-world experience in these missions did I finally understand. After our first few capture/kill direct action raids, I learned that Jocko was right. When we overplanned for too many contingencies and sent a very large assault force to clear the target building, too many SEALs inside the house only added to the confusion and chaos, particularly when Iraqi soldiers were a part of all our combat operations. A smaller number of troops inside the house was far easier to manage, much more flexible, and far more effective. If more troops were needed inside the target building, it was easier and much more controlled to send SEALs who were outside holding security into the house to help out. But it was far more difficult to send SEALs from inside the house to help outside, where we had far less control and a greater array of problems. Once I understood this truth, it was remarkable how much better we performed on target. I now understood that overplanning—trying to solve every problem that might occur—could create many more challenges, put our troops at greater risk, and detract from our ability to most effectively accomplish the mission.

This holds true for planning itself. When I was operations officer at a SEAL Team, I watched as some platoons and task units planned out the microscopic details of a mission—who was moving to what room or exactly where each person would set security on a target. But missions never go exactly how you plan them. So time was wasted on this level of detail, and it caused confusion among the troops when things didn't unfold exactly as they had expected. The lesson learned was that flexibility trumped minute details when it came to planning. The most effective teams build flexible plans.

But on the other side of this dichotomy, thorough planning is critical. Not preparing for likely contingencies is to set the team up for failure.

While combat requires those participating in it to face the possibilities of grave injury and death, you cannot be paralyzed by fear of such things. You must accept that it's dangerous, that you could die. But a little bit of fear—the nervousness felt before launching on a big combat mission, the constant thinking through of contingencies and wondering what might have been missed—is healthy to help fight complacency and prevent overconfidence. Leaders must consider the risks they can control and mitigate those risks as best they can through contingency planning. When proper contingency planning *doesn't* take place, it is a failure of leadership.

In the Battle of Ramadi in 2006, Task Unit Bruiser took extraordinary risks. We volunteered to penetrate deep into enemy-held territory, often where other U.S. forces couldn't respond without great danger and difficulty. Task Unit Bruiser received some criticism from SEAL and other special operations units for the high level of risk that we accepted to support U.S. and Iraqi forces in such counterinsurgency operations in Ramadi. They didn't understand that we took great steps to plan for contingencies and mitigate the risks that we could control. And what the critics didn't know about—what was not discussed in *Extreme Ownership*—were the combat operations that Task Unit Bruiser turned down. We were asked to participate in or support some combat operations, yet when we evaluated the situation in detail, it was clear that proper contingency planning had not taken place. The risk was not worth the reward.

In one such case, another U.S. special operations unit requested support from Charlie Platoon and our Iraqi soldiers.

They needed an Iraqi partner force to help receive the necessary approval to execute a combat operation. The mission was planned to launch into a violent and dangerous area of the city, firmly controlled by enemy fighters. The special operations unit was fairly new on the ground in Ramadi. They had arrived a couple of weeks earlier and were still familiarizing themselves with the battlespace, the U.S. forces that operated there, and the enemy fighters' tactics and capabilities. The unit's leader was motivated and aggressive, eager to get after it and participate in heavy combat operations. I knew that in this battlespace, he would have ample opportunity.

The special operations unit's plan for this mission was bold, to say the least: drive through the city center in broad daylight down a main road known to harbor heavy concentrations of deadly IEDs. As I looked over their plan, I didn't see any contingencies in place for this likely scenario.

"What happens if we lose a vehicle to an IED on the drive in?" I asked the leader.

"We won't," he answered, insisting their armored vehicles and electronic countermeasures would protect his troops from such a scenario.

In Task Unit Bruiser, we learned to set up contingency plans for our routes in and out of the target on every operation. There might be an IED, a roadblock that prevented passage, or a route we thought was passable that turned out not to be once we got there. For every mission, we learned we needed not only a primary route, but also a secondary and tertiary route as well. That way, if the primary route was blocked or impassable, we could quickly shift to the next alternative because of careful contingency planning.

"Do you have a secondary or tertiary route to get to the target as an alternative?" I asked the leader.

The unit's leader shook his head to say "No."

"We don't need one," he said. "This is the best way into the target."

From everything I'd heard about this particular route through the city that the special operations unit planned to travel, it was one of the most dangerous roads in Ramadi—which would place it high in the running for most dangerous worldwide. We'd been told by other U.S. units that had been operating in the area for months in no uncertain terms: *Don't drive on this road or you will get blown up*. Yet the special operations unit did not have a contingency plan for alternative routes. I recommended to the leader that they look at alternative routes, but my input was dismissed.

If one of their vehicles hit an IED, even if it didn't kill or wound any of our troops, it would prevent us from hitting the target, significantly degrading the probability of mission success. Additionally, an IED strike was not the only concern: once an IED immobilized a vehicle, the enemy could engage with small arms and rocket fire to further devastate a patrol, now pinned down and unable to leave the vehicle or its occupants. These were all likely contingencies for which there should have been a solid plan. The whole team needed to understand what to do in such a scenario and how to vector in support. But the leader of the special operations unit was so sure they could make it, he had not planned for any of these contingencies.

*Is there something I'm missing?* I thought. *Am I just being risk averse?*

As planning continued, I drove across Camp Ramadi and consulted a highly experienced conventional U.S. Army company commander who had been on the ground in Ramadi for over a year. The company commander and his troops had a wealth of experience. They were Army National Guard, which meant back in the States they were reservists: part-time Soldiers who trained one weekend a month and two full weeks every year. In the civilian world they were carpenters, salesmen, schoolteachers, store managers, and business owners. But having been on the ground in the most violent battlefield of Iraq for fifteen months, they had been transformed into hardened combat warriors. We trusted their experience and leaned on them for guidance.

I knocked on the company commander's door. He welcomed me and ushered me in.

Over the map, I talked through the special operations unit's proposed plan, pointed out the intended route, specified the target buildings, and asked for his opinion.

He just shook his head and remarked: "You won't make it half-way down that road before you hit an IED. You will never reach the target."

"I didn't have a good feeling about this one," I said, appreciating his candid feedback.

"Leif," he continued, in brutal honesty, "if I wanted to get a bunch of my guys wounded or killed, this plan is exactly what I would do."

There it was. My suspicions were confirmed. I knew this company commander was a bold leader. He was aggressive and well respected. I knew that he would not—and did not—shy away from danger or risk. He and his Soldiers were the definition of courageous warriors. They had supported us on several high-risk missions that put his men in harm's way. So if he was telling me this, I had better listen.

I drove back across Camp Ramadi to speak with the leader of the special operations unit. After walking into his office, I told him what the National Guard company commander had said. I urged him to revise his plan and explore alternative routes to the target area. I stressed that the IED threat was a highly probable contingency for which he and his team needed to be prepared. But the leader of the special operations unit was unfazed, still confident in his plan.

"Those National Guard guys," he responded, "they're risk averse. We roll in heavy with our armored vehicles and we've got massive firepower."

Special operations units such as this one, SEALs, and others had far greater training, better equipment, and a much larger budget for gear than the National Guard. Yet the National Guard unit, despite their lack of high-speed training and equipment, had accomplished a great deal on this toughest of battlefields. They had earned the utmost respect from us and the other U.S. units operating in the area. And the National Guard had something far more valuable than high-speed training and the latest gear: fifteen months of arduous combat experience in Ramadi. Because of that experience, from daily gun battles with insurgents to the devastating carnage of IED attacks, these National Guard Soldiers were now battle tested, combat proven, and still humble enough to respect the enemy and his capabilities.

I continued to try to convince the special operations unit leader to come up with an alternative plan that included contingencies for likely scenarios or perhaps wait for a better opportunity to nab the high-value target. But I could not dissuade the leader from launching on the operation.

I told him that our SEALs and Iraqi soldiers would not participate. I hoped that the lack of an Iraqi partner force might inhibit his ability to get mission approval. Unfortunately, they were granted permission to execute the mission, and despite the warnings, the special operations unit leader went forward with the operation. A few days later, in broad daylight—right in the middle of the day—they launched on the operation.

They never made it to their objective.

We learned later what happened: their convoy of armored vehicles had traveled only a short distance down the road on which they'd been advised not to drive when an IED exploded under the lead vehicle. With the heavy armored vehicle disabled and on fire, several of their troopers inside were wounded. Unable to abandon the vehicle or the men inside, they were pinned down under withering enemy gunfire for several hours as they waited for help. Finally, a nearby conventional army unit was able to respond and tow their vehicle. It was a miracle no U.S. troops were killed, though several were seriously wounded. But it was a close call and a humbling lesson that careful planning is essential. Had the special operations unit's leader listened and thought through the likely contingencies, he never would have taken that route. Instead, he and his team would have come up with an alternative that would have prevented his men from being wounded and their vehicles destroyed and given them a much greater chance to successfully accomplish the mission.

### Principle

Careful planning is essential to the success of any mission. In *Extreme Ownership*, chapter 9, "Plan," we wrote that mission planning meant "never taking anything for granted, preparing for likely contingencies, and maximizing the chance of mission success while minimizing the risk to the troops executing the operation." While the risks in combat are obvious, there are also significant risks in the business world. Livelihoods are at stake: jobs, careers, capital, strategic initiatives, and long-term success. Leaders must manage this risk through careful contingency planning for the things that can be controlled. But not every risk can be controlled.

For planning, there is a dichotomy within which leaders must find balance. You cannot plan for every contingency. If you try to create a solution for every single potential problem that might arise, you overwhelm your team, you overwhelm the planning process, you overcomplicate decisions for leaders. Rather than preventing or solving problems, overplanning creates additional and sometimes far more difficult problems. Therefore, it is imperative that leaders focus on only the most likely contingencies that might arise for each phase of an operation. Choose at most the three or four most probable contingencies for each phase, along with the worst-case scenario. This will prepare the team to execute and increase the chances of mission success.

It is important, however, that leaders manage the dichotomy in planning by not straying too far in the other direction—by not planning *enough* for contingencies. When leaders dismiss likely threats or problems that could arise, it sets the team up for greater difficulties and may lead to mission failure. At every level of the team, leaders must fight against complacency and overconfidence. Nothing breeds arrogance like success—a string of victories on the battlefield or business initiatives. Combat leaders must never forget just how much is at stake: the lives of their troops. Business leaders, too, must never become callous with the livelihoods and careers of their employees and associates or the capital invested. Each risk requires careful evaluation, weighing, and balancing the risk versus the reward—the benefit to the team and to the strategic mission of a successful outcome. Careful contingency plans that are focused are key to managing such risks and achieving victory. It is difficult to balance the dichotomy between these two extremes. But it is critical for every leader to understand that in order to be successful, he or she must plan, but not overplan.

## Application to Business

"I don't believe we have fully looked at the contingencies," said the chief operating officer (COO). "I've voiced my concerns. But they don't seem to be taken seriously."

Jocko and I sat in the COO's office. We were there to kick off a Leadership Development and Alignment Program for the company's senior executive team and midlevel managers. The company had delivered a string of successes in recent years, owing in large part to a smart and aggressive leadership team eager to establish the company as a major player and take on the dominant competitors in the industry. The company's successes drove an additional capital raise, which they had recently secured. As a result, the company now had the resources to invest in expansion.

Victory upon victory had built confidence in the company's executive team and its department leaders—and none were more confident than their CEO. The CEO was determined to grow, and he had no shortage of grand ideas. The company's COO urged more caution and a careful evaluation of the risks involved.

"What risks are you most concerned about?" Jocko inquired.

"We are trying to grow in multiple directions simultaneously," the COO responded.

"Launching a single subsidiary company is expensive and carries risk," the COO replied. "We are launching two different subsidiary companies at the same time. We are also expanding the corporate office, hiring dozens of new administrative staff, and locking in a long-term lease on three more floors of the corporate headquarters building. That's over a hundred more offices and a significant long-term expense. These plans seem to make sense right now, but if the market takes a downturn or we have a significant manufacturing problem, all those plans would be in jeopardy."

"Well, those are real possibilities," I said. "It sounds like your team is in need of some detailed contingency plans."

"Look," the COO continued. "I'm willing to accept that we will have to take some risks as we expand. But we need to think about how to handle those risks. I'm concerned that we are over-leveraging ourselves."

"Why do you think the CEO is pursuing these initiatives concurrently?" I asked.

We had worked with a number of companies in rapid expansion mode. Some had aggressively launched new initiatives that achieved extraordinary results. Others had taken on too many simultaneous risks that burned huge amounts of capital with little return, and they had to pull back and pursue a more careful growth strategy.

"I get that there are significant opportunities in each of these efforts," the COO answered. "I am all about the need for us to grow and expand our market share. But we really haven't done the contingency planning you're talking about—and that's the problem. Look: If the market took a downturn or we had a major recall of a product, and one of these subsidiary companies failed, the loss would be significant but it wouldn't be catastrophic. But if both of these subsidiary companies failed simultaneously, it would be a major blow to our company's bottom line. It might shut the whole thing down."

With careful contingency planning, the CEO and the company's leadership team would have taken steps to mitigate such a possibility. If they focused their efforts to launch only one subsidiary initially, and once its success was established launched the next one, that would be a much safer bet.

"What about the additional administrative support?" I inquired. "Is that something you feel isn't needed?"

"I understand the need for additional administrative support," the COO replied. "We've had a number of requests from our department heads for more support. I understand that. But taking on a multiyear lease of expensive office space large enough for a hundred additional offices is, I think, excessive. Why can't we just expand to a single additional floor instead of three? Who knows what the economy will look like a year or two from now? This company has only seen good times. We haven't been around long enough to experience hard times. What if the economy takes a turn for the worse and we lose significant business? Our company will be on the hook for these additional salaries, and even if we let employees go, we will still be locked in to the long-term lease for empty offices and burning major capital that we may not have."

His concerns sounded reasonable. It was clear that he wasn't totally risk averse, but he knew things might not go as planned and he urged caution about the level of risk the company was taking and the lack of steps taken to mitigate that risk. This was precisely the reason that planning for contingencies was so critical to mission success.

"When we were in combat," I told the COO, "it was crucial to carefully evaluate risk and develop contingency plans for the things that were likely to go wrong. Once we analyzed those risks, we recognized that there was much we could control to reduce risk. Contingency planning helped us take the steps necessary to prepare for the uncertainty of outcomes during combat operations. And that's no different for you or your team here.

"In Ramadi, when we went into enemy-held neighborhoods where the threat was extremely high," I said, "we took steps to mitigate risks from attack. The roadside bombs or IEDs were the biggest threat, so in the worst areas, we didn't drive. We walked in via foot patrol. We set up sniper overwatch positions in buildings, where the chance of enemy attack was high, and we set up multiple positions that could support each other. Planning for these contingencies helped us manage the risk—even extreme risk in that environment."

Jocko added: "You might think that in the SEAL Teams, we are all Big Tough Frogmen who run to the sound of the gunfire no matter what. And for many situations, that is exactly what we did. We have to show courage under fire and be willing to risk our lives. But we can't be foolish. We can't take needless risk that prevents us from accomplishing our strategic mission and endangers our troops," Jocko continued. "As leaders, we have to do that smartly by mitigating the risks we can control. Careful evaluation of the risk enables us to develop contingency plans so we can execute in the most effective manner to accomplish the mission with the least amount of risk to our troops."

Jocko explained to the COO that in training, we put SEAL leaders to the test to humble them and hopefully prevent them from having to learn such lessons in combat when real lives were at stake.

"We utilized a 'kill house' to practice maneuvering through hallways, entering doors, clearing rooms. We often conducted such training using simulated fire with paintball or Simunition rounds against role-players—SEAL instructors or volunteers acting as the bad guys or opposing force," Jocko said.

Jocko described how many of the scenarios were designed to lure the SEAL unit into a dire situation, where the leader must step back and analyze the risk.

"In one such scenario," Jocko said, "our SEAL instructor staff would place a bunkered 'enemy' machine gun position covering a long hallway, where the role-players simulating bad guys could engage the SEAL platoon from a protected position from which they couldn't be easily hit by the SEAL assault force trying to clear the building. The SEAL leader would send two shooters forward down the hallway toward the enemy fire. The two SEALs would encounter devastating fire, the sting from dozens of paint rounds hitting their bodies at high speed. The instructor staff would put them down—they'd be told to lie on the floor of the hallway simulating that they'd been killed. The SEAL leader would usually send two more of his SEAL shooters forward. The results from attacking a hardened position would inevitably be the same: two more SEALs 'killed.' Then the SEAL leader would send two more shooters, until the hallway was littered with dead—thankfully only simulated dead."

"That's when we would have to step in," I added, "and ask the SEAL leader: 'Do you think this is a good idea to continue sending more of your troops to their death?' When the leader responded in the negative, I explained that charging forward into enemy gunfire was courageous but foolhardy. It would only result in the destruction of his entire force. And worse, they were no closer to accomplishing the mission of eliminating the threat and clearing the house. I instructed him to contingency plan—to think of another way to attack the problem: 'Can you send two of your SEAL shooters outside the building and attack from a different direction? Is there another entrance, a window or doorway, where we can attack the enemy from behind?' I would ask."

"We watched the lightbulb go off in that SEAL leader's head as he realized that not only could he do this but he absolutely must do this if he was to succeed as a leader," said Jocko. "It is a leader's duty to mitigate the risk you can control."

"I struggled with those same problems in the same type of difficult training scenarios," I told the COO. "In the moment it was difficult to see what needed to be done. But when I recognized this, I realized that we could perform much better if we took the time to develop careful contingency plans. If, before we even launched on the operation, I thought about how we might best react to a likely scenario, I could more easily make that decision when I encountered it. Even better, if I briefed the team on what to do in the event we encountered such a scenario, they were ready to execute and the team could do so even without immediate direction."

"But best of all," Jocko added, "when SEAL leaders thought through a likely contingency—like a bunkered enemy machine gun position in the house—and carefully planned how to handle that situation, they came up with alternative ways to get the mission accomplished while reducing the risk to the SEAL assault force. This meant they might enter the building from a direction that the enemy role-players hadn't anticipated and catch them off guard. When this happened, the SEAL platoon decimated the enemy fighters, accomplished the mission, and didn't lose a single man."

"That's where you need to be," I said. "All business ventures will inherently carry some element of risk. Thorough planning, understanding and creating action plans for likely contingencies, will help you mitigate that risk. While you can't plan for everything—and you shouldn't get bogged down with too much planning—you must still use solid planning to mitigate the risks you can control. Finding the balance between planning and overplanning is critical, and it sounds like right now you need to lean toward more planning so that you are fully prepared to react properly should some of these possible contingencies occur."

With that, Jocko and I encouraged the COO to lead up the chain of command and put together a comprehensive plan that included a clear assessment of the risks and the contingency plans to help mitigate them. The COO moved forward, aggressively planning to achieve the CEO's goals, but with thorough contingency plans in place to ensure the highest probability of long-term mission success.

The "ammo table"—ammunition storage in the Charlie platoon mission planning space, which also served as the Task Unit Bruiser Ready Room. SEALs are taught from day one that violence of action and superior firepower are what wins in a gunfight. Task Unit Bruiser agreed.

(Photo courtesy of the authors)

# CHAPTER 11

## Humble, Not Passive

*Leif Babin*

### ROUTE MICHIGAN, SOUTH-CENTRAL RAMADI, IRAQ: 2006

Everyone in the convoy was on edge as our Humvees rolled through downtown Ramadi on the main road, known to U.S. forces as "Route Michigan." It was broad daylight, and as insane as it might seem, despite the frequency of violent attacks, there were some locals along the roadside and civilian vehicle traffic on the road.

Every pothole, every piece of trash that littered the road, might be an IED delivering fire, shrapnel, and death. The frequent bomb craters and charred remains of vehicles along the roadside were a grim reminder. Ambushes, too, were a huge threat. Insurgent fighters with RPG-7 rockets and belt-fed machine guns might be concealed in nearby buildings, ready to unleash an attack at any moment.

Our SEAL turret gunners manned their heavy machine guns and scanned relentlessly for threats. They stood with chest and head exposed through the roof of the Humvees above the vehicles' armored plates. Each turret had armor protection on three sides but still left the gunner vulnerable. Those of us inside the vehicle also kept a sharp eye out for any potential attack as best we could through the thick, dust-covered glass of the armored windshield and windows. But the best protection for the turret gunners—our convoy's best defense—was our posture: ultra-aggressive, weapons pointed in all directions manned by vigilant gunners, ready and eager to unleash the fury at the first sign of a threat. We aimed to make any potential attackers hesitate, to think twice about whether they wanted to suffer the consequences, and wait for an easier target. The *muj*\* were keen to talk about martyrdom, but they never wanted martyrdom on *our* terms. The possibility that they might be slaughtered before they could do any real damage to us was a substantial deterrent.

So far on this patrol, our aggressive posture—combined with a little luck—proved successful, and no visible threats appeared. Our convoy rolled on through the center of downtown Ramadi, past the Marine outposts at the Ramadi Government Center and another called "OP VA"† that stood as small bastions of hope and security in a vast sea of violence and savagery. The brave Marines who manned those outposts, from Kilo and Lima Companies of the 3rd Battalion, 8th Marine Regiment, endured frequent vicious and well-coordinated attacks from large numbers of insurgent fighters. Their heavily fortified guard posts, hidden beneath blankets of camouflage netting to protect against the threat of enemy snipers, concealed vigilant young Marines manning their weapons in a state of constant alert. We loved and admired those Marines.

We felt the same admiration and bond of brotherhood with the Soldiers of Team Bulldog—Bravo Company, Task Force 1/37—with whom we conducted scores of combat operations. Our convoy had just departed Team Bulldog's base of operations, Combat Outpost Falcon, where "Main Gun" Mike Bajema and his Soldiers lived and worked, battling insurgents deep in the volatile neighborhood of South-Central Ramadi. The SEALs of Task Unit Bruiser's Charlie Platoon and the Iraqi soldiers who accom-

---

\* *Mujahideen:* Arabic for those who waged jihad; the term Iraqi insurgents called themselves. U.S. forces shortened this to *muj*.

† OP VA: Observation Post Veterans Affairs; the location of the U.S. Marine outpost in the former Iraqi Veterans Affairs building.

panied us had spent the previous twenty-four hours on a sniper overwatch mission and a series of presence patrols in this dangerous area of Ramadi. There had been some solid "Big Mix-It-Ups"—Charlie Platoon's term for a substantial gunfight. We had wrapped up another series of violent combat operations in the brutal Iraqi summertime heat. It was always a great day when we took out a number of enemy fighters and disrupted their attacks and freedom of movement—and when they didn't get any of us. Though we had completed our tactical objectives in South-Central and departed COP Falcon, the combat operation wasn't over until we made it back to base. With IED attacks against vehicles accounting for the vast majority of U.S. casualties in Iraq, our travels off base and our return home via convoy were statistically the most dangerous part of the operation.

As our Humvees continued at high speed, civilian vehicles that also shared the road pulled to the side to give us a wide berth. Though most carried civilian passengers, any one of these vehicles could have been a car bomb ready to explode in a massive, deadly blast. Our drivers maneuvered past the civilian vehicles, giving them as much distance as possible. We continued on across the bridge that spanned the Habbaniyah Canal, the demarcation line that separated downtown Ramadi from the western Ramadi neighborhood of Tameem. We were almost home.

Everyone was tired, worn out, and exhausted. The punishing summertime Iraqi heat had taken its toll, and the profuse sweating through our heavy gear for the past twenty-four-plus hours left our faces sunken with dehydration. We longed for the creature comforts that would soon be ours upon arrival at our home base: air-conditioning, showers, hot food, and the temporary reprieve from concern about immediate wounds and death.

Soon, we approached the turnoff from Route Michigan toward Ogden Gate, the back gate of the major U.S. base in the area, Camp Ramadi.

"Right turn, right turn," came the lead navigator's call over the radio. The vehicles slowed down on the three-hundred-yard approach to the gate. It was wise to proceed cautiously toward Ogden Gate. The Soldiers who manned the machine guns covering us couldn't be seen, hidden behind camouflage netting draped over heavily fortified security towers. These Soldiers withstood frequent attacks from insurgent forces, regularly receiving sniper fire, machine gun, and mortar attacks. Off the pavement of Route Michigan, the entrance road to the gate was pulverized from the constant transit of heavy U.S. tanks and armored vehicles entering and exiting. Fine sand billowed into thick clouds of dust that penetrated the air inside the vehicles. The "moon dust" made it difficult to breathe and obscured our vision both inside the vehicles and outside. It prevented us from seeing the next vehicle in the convoy only a few yards in front, as well as the vehicles behind.

Our convoy came to a halt in front of the huge M88 tank recovery vehicle that served as the gate. When a sixty-eight-ton M1A2 Abrams Main Battle Tank or twenty-seven-ton Bradley Fighting Vehicle broke down, it needed a massive vehicle to tow it. The M88 was designed for just such a purpose. But here, at Ogden Gate, the M88 was used to block the path from any potential attack from the enemy's most devastating weapon, what we called a VBIED (vehicle-borne improvised explosive device)—what civilians called a "car bomb." We checked in with Soldiers at the main gate, gave them our call sign and total head count. Once we'd been cleared, a Soldier hopped into the big M88, fired up the engine, and, tank tracks clattering loudly, motored the behemoth out of the way so that our convoy could roll onto the base that was our home.

Once on base, the turret gunners and everyone in the vehicles could relax. Every moment outside the wire, up until the second we entered the gate, was game on. But once inside, it was purely an administrative drive across the base to the section of Camp Ramadi where we lived and worked: Sharkbase*. With the pressures of combat temporarily lifted, there was always some jok-

---

* We later changed the name from Sharkbase to Camp Marc Lee, after Marc
  was killed in action on August 2, 2006.

ing and lighthearted banter over the radio. Our route across the base took us past the vehicle graveyard, where the twisted and burned-out hulks of U.S. and Iraqi armored vehicles were dragged and deposited after an IED attack. It was a grim reminder of the dangers just outside the wire and how fortunate and blessed we were to have survived another operation, another convoy through that treacherous city.

As we made our way across Camp Ramadi and out a side gate, the road led us around to Sharkbase. We pulled our vehicles up and came to a stop in the street out front of two tin-roofed wooden buildings, our chow hall and Charlie Platoon's planning space.

"All stop, all stop," came the call over the radio.

Mission complete. I opened the heavy armored door to the Humvee and stepped out. After ensuring my weapons were clear and safe, I dropped them and my helmet on the desk in our platoon space and headed off to see Jocko.

His office was in the main building, a large, columned structure that had once been an ornate residence for elements of Saddam Hussein's regime in pre–U.S. invasion Iraq. The building was now our tactical operations center. I walked through the kitchen and into the TOC, greeting our Task Unit Bruiser watch standers there—the information systems technicians and operations specialists with whom we communicated when out in harm's way. These non-SEAL support personnel were a critical part of our team. I walked into Jocko's office and greeted him.

"God is Frogman," I said, a statement I uttered frequently upon our return. "We had some close calls on that one, but we got everybody back in one piece."

I informed Jocko that all personnel and gear were accounted for and safely back on base.

"Right on," responded Jocko with a smile. "Welcome back."

The more we operated in Ramadi, the more I realized that despite the most careful planning and meticulous effort to mitigate risk, the chances of horrible wounds or death were very real and ever-present on all our operations. Only through divine providence did we not lose men on every operation. Because the Almighty looked out for us so often and led us through many close calls, we were convinced that God must be a SEAL—or, in reference to our forefathers in the Underwater Demolition Teams, a Frogman.

Combat is a harsh teacher, and the battlefield in Ramadi was brutal. We were constantly humbled by the dangers and immense challenges of continuous urban combat. I was the platoon commander for Charlie Platoon, and often the ground force commander—the senior leader—for many of the combat operations. When we pulled off a great success and I got a little cocky, I'd quickly find myself getting humbled once again when the enemy employed an innovative tactic we hadn't yet anticipated or hit us in a manner for which we were unprepared. Most of all, I was continuously humbled by everything that I realized I could and should have done better: the recognition that I should have more carefully deconflicted with other U.S. forces we were supporting; made my commander's intent even more simple, clear, and concise; or empowered junior leaders to an even greater degree. In this battlespace, it was "be humble or get humbled."

Jocko sat at his desk, in front of a computer screen. He was heavily engaged in combat of a different nature. He and the task unit staff handled legions of requests from our higher headquarters, answered their continuous questions, and generated mountains of paperwork at their direction. To Jocko's credit, he largely shielded us from much of this, allowing me and the rest of Charlie Platoon, as well as our task unit brothers in Delta Platoon, to focus on our operations.

"The task group is hounding us to provide an E6 to cover down on a special assignment," Jocko informed me.

I didn't like the sound of that. The task group, our immediate higher headquarters located about thirty miles down the road from us in the city of Fallujah, wanted us to provide an experienced SEAL, a noncommissioned officer with the minimum rank of first class petty officer, to fill a role for them.

"What's the assignment?" I asked.

Jocko explained that the assignment was a sensitive one, highly classified but with a substantial profile and visibility from several levels up the chain of command.

"This one is coming from the CJSOTF," he said.

The "CJSOTF" was the Combined Joint Special Operations Task Force,* our boss's boss, responsible for all special operations forces in Iraq. I understood there were pressures from above on our task group to provide a body to fill the billet. I understood that this was important, but I was still concerned that it also appeared to be an attempt for higher headquarters to grab precious personnel from my platoon. My protective instincts kicked in.

It can be difficult for any leader to detach from a situation and see beyond the immediate mission of his or her team. It is a natural reflex for leaders to resist sharing resources or critical personnel because it makes their immediate job harder, even if it ultimately benefits the greater team and the strategic mission. But an important part of being a leader is to be humble enough to see beyond his or her own needs. I had learned from Jocko that humility was the most important quality in a leader. In Task Unit Bruiser, there was no room for arrogance and big egos. The importance of humility that Jocko talked about had been confirmed time and time again since we had arrived in Ramadi.

I had learned that the world did not revolve around me and my immediate team—Charlie Platoon. We were only a small part of much larger operations that were happening on a vast scale in Ramadi and the surrounding areas of Anbar Province. We were honored to support the thousands of Soldiers and Marines of the Ready First Brigade in their efforts in Ramadi.

Being humble also meant understanding that we didn't have it all figured out. We didn't have all the answers. It meant we must

---

* In U.S. military terminology, "combined" meant multinational and "joint" meant multiservice, including different branches of the U.S. military.

learn from other units that had been in Ramadi longer and work with them to support our chain of command and support the mission. It wasn't about how many operations we conducted or how many bad guys we dispatched. The true measure of success in the large-scale counterinsurgency operations we supported lay in the stabilization and security of the city over the long term. We needed the humility to understand that our higher headquarters, the task group and the chain of command above us, had strategic insight that we likely did not have.

Being humble meant understanding the importance of strategic direction from our boss. It meant doing all we could to support the conventional forces we worked with, the Iraqi soldiers we trained and combat advised, and of course our chain of command. Being humble meant we put our heads down and got the job done as directed to the best of our ability.

But at the same time, there was a dichotomy to being humble: being humble didn't mean being passive. It didn't mean not to push back when it truly mattered. While I didn't have the visibility or complete understanding of the strategic picture that the boss and his staff at the task group had, they also lacked understanding of how strategic direction or requirements impacted our tactical operations on the front lines. And it was up to me to push that information up the chain of command. Humility has to be balanced by knowing when to make a stand.

I had witnessed a good example of this when we'd been directed to work with Iraqi soldiers. As Jocko wrote in detail in chapter 3, "Believe," of *Extreme Ownership*, upon Task Unit Bruiser's arrival in Ramadi, the CJSOTF required us and every other U.S. special operations unit in the theater to operate "by, with, and through Iraqi security forces." That meant working alongside poorly trained, poorly equipped, and often untrustworthy Iraqi soldiers. After much initial pushback, we thought through the reasons we were being directed to do this. After fully understanding and disseminating the *why* to the platoons, Task Unit Bruiser accepted this mission and took it on, despite its inherent difficulties and dangers.

But there were many other U.S. special operations units, including SEAL units, that did not. Instead of embracing the spirit of "by, with, and through" Iraqi troops, these U.S. units embraced the literal guidance to "put an Iraqi face" on U.S. operations. In some cases, that meant a single Iraqi face: many American units had only one or two Iraqi soldiers on combat operations where the assault force consisted of twenty or thirty Americans. The Iraqis stood in the back and contributed little to the missions.

To overcome this mentality and enforce the spirit of the directive, the CJSOTF further imposed a specific ratio of U.S. special operators to Iraqi soldiers (or Iraqi police) that had to be met on each operation. For every American special operator, they required that there be seven Iraqi soldiers. This seemed reasonable enough in many parts of Iraq where there were plenty of Iraqi soldiers and the threat level was far less significant. But in Ramadi, the Iraqi Army units that Task Unit Bruiser worked with were undermanned and overtasked. There simply were not enough Iraqi soldiers to go around. The limited number of Iraqi soldiers available for any one operation meant that compliance with the required ratio would allow us only two or three SEALs total on most operations. In far less hostile parts of Iraq, a combat operation with only three or four American special operators and another twelve or sixteen Iraqi soldiers could be executed without endangering the lives of the entire force. But this was Ramadi, a violent, terrorist stronghold and the epicenter of the deadly insurgency in Iraq. We didn't have that luxury. Against a combat-experienced, well-armed, and determined enemy, the Iraqi troops didn't count for much in a firefight. If an enemy force of twenty or thirty insurgent fighters attacked us, it was highly probable that an element made up of mostly Iraqi soldiers with only a few U.S. special operators would be overwhelmed and everyone killed. This horrific outcome was not just a theory. It had happened in Ramadi to U.S. units that were unprepared for the level of violence.

As task unit commander, Jocko understood the importance of "by, with, and through Iraqi security forces." In fact, he directed the opposite tack from most every other SEAL and special operations unit: he required that we take Iraqi soldiers on every operation. We embraced that. But when the ratio directive was issued, I talked it over with Jocko and explained what this meant to Charlie Platoon, how the number of Iraqi troops we had available were limited and how it would endanger our SEALs and our mission.

Jocko recognized that this was a time when he must push back for the good of the mission and the safety of his men.

"We can't comply with this directive," Jocko told our commanding officer at the task group via a phone call. "I understand the reason for it. I can assure you that we will take as many Iraqi soldiers with us as we possibly can on every operation. But here in Ramadi, for the types of missions we are conducting, in such dangerous territory, if we comply with this ratio we will likely have one of our elements completely overrun. There is a high probability that they will all be killed."

Our commanding officer and his staff at the task group understood. They certainly didn't want to endanger our SEAL operators or the missions we were a part of. And because we rarely pushed back on anything and had the reputation of humbly complying with direction from senior leadership, we had built trust up the chain of command. So when our task group explained the circumstances to the CJSOTF, they waived the ratio requirement for Task Unit Bruiser.

As Charlie Platoon commander, I saw the requirement to provide one of my experienced first class petty officers for another mission in much the same way. No matter how important the new tasking might be, if Charlie Platoon gave up a key leader for the duration of deployment, it would cripple our combat capability and remove crucial leadership experience.

I talked it over with my Charlie Platoon chief, Tony. We had only two men of that rank in the platoon: one was our leading petty officer, who played a vital leadership role in the platoon; the other was Chris Kyle, our lead sniper and point man, whose experience and skill were integral to the success of our sniper overwatch missions. Worse, because we often split into smaller elements led by inexperienced leaders who were out on their own, operating independently with no oversight from Tony or me, the experience of our two first class petty officers was crucial. The loss of either would not only hurt our performance on the battlefield and make us less effective, it would significantly increase the risk to our forces, which already operated in an environment of extreme danger.

It was pretty clear to me, and to Tony, that we simply could not comply with the directive. This was an area in which I must push back.

I spoke with Task Unit Bruiser's senior enlisted advisor, who was responsible for the actual assignments of all our task unit's enlisted troops.

"We can't comply with this directive," I told him.

"Charlie Platoon needs to cover down on this," he insisted. "This is coming from our commanding officer. We don't have any choice."

I tried to explain the impact this would have on Charlie Platoon, but he again told me we didn't have a choice. But it still made no sense.

So, I went to speak with Jocko. I had made up my mind that we could not, in good conscience, comply with the directive. I knew if I could make a good case to Jocko, he would do everything in his power to support me and Charlie Platoon.

I explained to Jocko how I understood that the project was important. I understood it bore strategic significance and had substantial visibility from senior commanders in the theater. But we would have to curtail the strategically critical operations in support of the Seize, Clear, Hold, Build strategy that were our main focus if we complied.

"I cannot comply with this and set our team up for failure with potentially deadly consequences," I said.

The loss of an experienced SEAL leader during intense combat operations at the height of the Battle of Ramadi would have been catastrophic to Charlie Platoon's operational capability. It meant we would be far less effective on the battlefield and that our platoon would be at far greater risk.

Jocko pushed back to the task group and passed along my concerns. Under pressure from the CJSOTF, our task group insisted that we comply. While I understood the need and the pressure on my chain of command to comply with the request, I could not passively comply with the removal of one of my key leaders to my team's detriment. Even if it meant I might be fired, I was determined not to allow this to happen.

Finally, Jocko intervened to explain up the chain what the loss of such an experienced SEAL meant and the negative strategic consequences of the move. As a result, an alternative plan was formed to fill the billet, relieving Charlie Platoon of the need to sacrifice a critical member of the team.

But while a leader can't be passive, a leader must also carefully prioritize when and where to push back. Leaders have an obligation to support their chain of command and carry out the orders that come from above (see chapter 9, "A Leader and a Follower"). Pushing back against an order or task from the boss should be the rarest of exceptions and definitely not the rule. To go against the chain of command when you don't have to is unnecessary and unwise. If challenging and questioning orders becomes routine, junior leaders damage their relationships up the chain of command, which undercuts the ability to push back against direction from above when it truly matters.

In Task Unit Bruiser, we were successful in the two examples above only because we had built a strong relationship with our commanding officer and his staff at the task group through humility. When they had asked us to complete paperwork, we did it—on time and well-edited, quality work. When they asked us to take photos of our Iraqi soldiers in training and on combat operations, we did that and strove to do it better than anyone else. When the task group asked for serialized inventory lists of all equipment before departing on operations, we took the extra time and effort and made it happen. The list of seemingly unimportant requests we dealt with was significant, and with the high operational tempo of violent urban combat day in and day out, it was not easy to comply with these requests. But in Task Unit Bruiser, we didn't complain about the little things that others might have pushed back on. Instead, we understood that there were important reasons for these administrative requirements and got them done. More important, we knew that in doing the seemingly small things well, we built trust that strengthened our relationships with our chain of command and enabled us to challenge an order in the rare circumstances when there truly was a strategic detriment to our mission and increased risk to our troops.

Staying humble was the key to developing trust with the chain of command. It was also crucial to building strong relationships with the U.S. Army and Marine Corps units we served so closely with in Ramadi—units we depended on for our survival and mission success.

We had formed an exceptional working relationship with Captain Mike Bajema and his U.S. Army Soldiers from Team Bulldog. As Bulldog's company commander (Bravo Company, 1/37), Main Gun Mike led nearly two hundred Soldiers and a hundred more Iraqi soldiers stationed at Combat Outpost Falcon, located deep inside enemy-held terrain in the heart of South-Central Ramadi. He and his Soldiers risked their lives for us constantly, and we risked ours for them. It was a relationship built on trust, mutual respect, and admiration. But the relationship hadn't started out that way.

I first met Mike in the planning phase, before the launch of the first major U.S. operation into South-Central Ramadi to implement the Ready First Brigade's Seize, Clear, Hold, Build strategy. It was a massive operation. Our SEALs would patrol into the area as the first U.S. boots on the ground. Mike's tanks and infantry troops would follow us as the main effort of the operation. As the planning took place, we were gathered outside his battalion headquarters, the home of Task Force Bandit, on base at Camp Ramadi. I walked up to him and introduced myself.

"Captain," I said to Mike, using his Army rank, "I'm Lieutenant Leif Babin, SEAL platoon commander. We're looking forward to working with you and your team."

Mike looked back at me curiously.

"What are SEALs doing in Anbar Province?" he asked. "Shouldn't you guys be riding a ship in the Persian Gulf?"

It was a jab. He was joking, but it was a jab nonetheless. It wasn't the way I had anticipated the conversation going. But I just smiled back.

"Probably so," I responded. "But we're here in Anbar to support your efforts."

Mike was a professional Soldier. He wasn't being rude. But he had a lot on his plate leading a reinforced U.S. Army company of tanks and infantry Soldiers. He was likely unfamiliar with the capabilities of a SEAL platoon and thus unsure how we could support his efforts.

Besides, many of the conventional Army and Marine units had had bad experiences with special operations forces (SOF). SOF units, including SEALs, could be arrogant and egotistical. I found out later that Mike and his guys had experienced this with another SOF unit they had worked with previously. The SOF unit had treated him and his Soldiers unprofessionally. They refused to share intelligence with them or include them in the planning process, and they carried themselves with an arrogance that made working alongside them problematic. It's likely that Mike expected the same from me, from our Charlie Platoon SEALs, and from Task Unit Bruiser. But I was determined to demonstrate the opposite and forge a strong relationship with him.

Unlike other SEAL and SOF units, we were clean-shaven, wore squared-away uniforms, and kept our hair short. Jocko knew that a professional appearance among the conventional forces was important—and he demanded that we remain well within regulations. That went a long way and made solid first impressions. But more important, we treated Mike and his Soldiers with the respect they deserved, just as we did with every Soldier and Marine. Team Bulldog and the other companies we worked with were outstanding Soldiers, aggressive and determined to close with and destroy the enemy. The armor units were skilled in maneuvering their tanks. The infantry troops were fearless in their patrols and clearance operations. All it took to build a relationship with them was to not act like arrogant jackasses; to not carry ourselves as though we thought we were somehow better because we were SEALs. That humility went far to solidify the relationship.

Two weeks later, the Ready First launched the next series of operations into a different neighborhood, to establish Combat Outpost (COP) Falcon. Mike and Team Bulldog were the main effort. We were again the lead U.S. element on the ground that forged the way and set up on the high ground to protect his Soldiers as they infiltrated the area.

With the COP Falcon operation, Mike understood who we were and how we contributed to his mission success. Our SEALs took great risk to push forward into the most dangerous areas, set up our overwatches on the high ground, and provide cover for his Soldiers as they built the COP and patrolled the streets around it.

But it was the smallest, seemingly insignificant things that truly solidified our relationship with Main Gun Mike and his Soldiers. We had been out in sniper overwatch position in a large building down the street from COP Falcon. After two days in that position, we needed to resupply. We patrolled back to COP Falcon to rest and refit and prepare for the next operation. As our SEALs and the Iraqi soldiers with us made our way inside the compound to the relative safety of the combat outpost, we saw team Bulldog Soldiers hauling sandbags from a semitrailer parked on the street up the stairwell to the third-story rooftop of the main COP Falcon building. Our guys were exhausted and ready to sit down, drop their helmets and body armor, and grab some water and an MRE (meal, ready to eat).

But there were thousands of sandbags on that semitrailer. It just didn't seem right to me to sit down and rest while these Soldiers were laboring. So I asked Mike if we could help.

"We're good, brother," Mike replied. "I know you've been getting after it for two days. And you're going to launch on another operation soon. Y'all get some rest. We'll take care of the sandbags."

I looked at my platoon chief, Tony Eafrati. He was always ready to BTF—Big Tough Frogman. That meant we would take on something extremely dangerous or physically challenging. Tony nodded at me. It was a nonverbal signal: *Let's do this*.

"Negative," I responded to Mike. "We'll help with the sandbags."

I told the rest of Charlie Platoon and some other SEALs who were with us to drop their combat gear and grab sandbags. There was some grumbling among the platoon. They were hot, tired, and ready for a break. Likely there were some SEALs among us who felt they were above carrying sandbags—that somehow they were "special" and "elite" and we should leave this work to the "conventional" forces. They were wrong.

These Soldiers were outstanding warriors worthy of respect and admiration. They had already launched tanks with heavy firepower to rescue Charlie Platoon SEALs and our Iraqi soldiers from a deadly enemy attack. These Soldiers had our back. And mutual support was the key to building relationships that enable teams to Cover and Move for each other. Besides, as I thought about it, the rooftop machine gun positions we were reinforcing with the sandbags directly supported us. They covered for us as we moved, as we departed and then returned to the safety of the COP from combat operations deep into enemy-held neighborhoods. The more secure those machine gun positions were, the better they could lay down fire for us as we maneuvered through the streets.

We hauled sandbags up and down the stairs for the next forty-five minutes. It was a solid workout, but the extra hands helped shorten the time it took to complete the task and assisted Bulldog in securing their rooftop machine gun positions.

It seemed like a small thing, but it was clear that it went a long way in helping us build an exceptional relationship. Mike and his Bulldog Soldiers saw that we didn't hold ourselves above them or above the manual labor tasks. It demonstrated humility and solidified an already strengthening relationship.

Going forward, Team Bulldog Soldiers put themselves at great risk over and over and over again to render assistance and fire support to our Charlie Platoon SEALs. They came to our aid and rescued us every time we called for help—*every single time*. I loved those Soldiers and their courageous commander they called "Main Gun" Mike, and I will never forget them.

I will also never forget the importance of humility for a leader. A leader must be humble, must listen to others, must not act arrogant or cocky. But a leader must balance that and know that there are times to question superiors, to push back, to stand up and make sure the right things are being done for the right reasons.

### Principle

Humility is the most important quality in a leader. When we had to fire SEAL leaders from leadership positions in a platoon or task unit, it was almost never because they were tactically unsound, physically unfit, or incompetent. It was most often because they were not humble: they couldn't check their ego, they refused to accept constructive criticism or take ownership for their mistakes. The same is true in the business world. We dedicated an entire chapter of *Extreme Ownership* to this subject (chapter 4, "Check the Ego"). Humility is essential to building strong relationships with others, both up and down the chain of command, as well as with supporting teams outside the immediate chain of command.

Some leaders took this too far and became humble to a fault. But being too humble can be equally disastrous for the team. A leader cannot be passive. When it truly matters, leaders must be willing to push back, voice their concerns, stand up for the good of their team, and provide feedback up the chain against a direction or strategy they know will endanger the team or harm the strategic mission.

This is a difficult dichotomy to balance. But as with all the dichotomies—being strong, but not overbearing, for example—just the awareness of these two opposing forces becomes one of the most powerful tools at a leader's disposal. Leaders must be humble enough to listen to new ideas, willing to learn strategic insights, and open to implementing new and better tactics and strategies. But a leader must also be ready to stand firm when there are clearly unintended consequences that negatively impact the mission and risk harm to the team.

### Application to Business

"You guys haven't given it a chance," said the CEO, exasperated. "No one has fully implemented the new software system. You're all complaining about it and telling me it won't work, and you haven't even used it. I need everyone to get on board with this."

There were some unintelligible mumbles around the room. But nobody countered the CEO's claim or made an overt objection. I could clearly see that many of the company's key leaders disagreed with the plan, but nobody stepped up to push back against the CEO, at least not in a public forum.

We sat in a large hotel conference room, with thirty key leaders of a successful technology company. The CEO and many of the company's senior leaders had read *Extreme Ownership* and been deeply impacted by the book. Bringing the book into the company's leadership training, the CEO strove to implement the principles within his team. The company had brought their key leaders together for a leadership off-site and asked me to provide leadership training.

I presented a leadership brief on the Battle of Ramadi and the lessons that we learned, as detailed in *Extreme Ownership*. After an hour or so of the presentation, I opened it up to the room for questions and discussion, to aid them in direct application of the principles to their business.

"Extreme Ownership," I said, repeating the topic just covered in detail. "Let's talk about where you are taking ownership of problems and getting them solved. More important, where is this *not* happening? Where can you take greater ownership? Where are you casting blame or waiting for others to solve problems that you should be solving?"

The CEO was eager to answer. He jumped right in.

"I'm a little frustrated at the lack of ownership to implement our new software system," he said. "We've talked about it for months. And yet, no one is taking ownership. All I'm hearing is a whole lot of excuses."

I took mental note that his comment was itself a lack of ownership, casting blame on the team for poor, ineffective implementation of the new system. True Extreme Ownership meant looking at yourself to examine what you could do better. That is what made it "simple, not easy." Human nature was to blame others, to allow frustrations with a problem to see everyone else as the issue and not yourself. But his comment wasn't Extreme Ownership. Such blame casting and excuse making only created more.

It was a common problem we saw with many leaders: A good leader might have read the book many times and loved the concepts, but still struggle with implementation falling back on old habits. As a result, problems never get solved.

"Is there a reason that you all are purposely not utilizing the new software?" I asked the room.

There was an uncomfortable silence.

"You guys haven't given it a chance," the CEO interjected. "You're all complaining about it, but no one has implemented it. I think it's just a matter of resistance to change, any change—even if the change is for the better."

The CEO was obviously frustrated with his leaders. It was clear he felt they were not supporting his direction on a key initiative to improve the company's performance.

"We have already invested a ton in this new program," the CEO continued. "It's been years in the making. We've hired consultants, we've looked at the options. The decision has been made, and now it's time to execute."

"Does everyone understand the *why*?" I asked the other leaders in the room. "Are you clear about why the company is shifting to the new software system?"

There were a few head nods, but over half the room didn't answer. They just sat there or shrugged their shoulders. It was clear that the *why* needed to be explained in far greater detail.

"It seems a greater explanation of the *why* is warranted," I said, directing my comment at the CEO.

"I've explained this many times, but I'll explain it again," said the CEO. "As our company grows and we expand the number of clients and projects, we need to be far more efficient in managing, supporting, tracking, and following-up. Our antiquated software system is far behind what our biggest competitors utilize. It is a big selling point for them, and if we don't upgrade, we will continue to forfeit business to competitors.

"Does that make sense to everyone?" the CEO asked. The others nodded around the room. Realizing he needed to demonstrate ownership, the CEO continued: "I thought I had been clear as to why, but obviously it wasn't clear to all of you."

The explanation answered the questions that some in the room harbored about the new system, though clearly at least a handful of the company's senior leaders had understood the reasons behind the need for a new system.

"I get the *why*," one of the department leaders replied. "I'm totally on board with the need to find a better system."

"Then why is the new program not being implemented?" I asked. "What's the problem?"

"I think it's because you're all comfortable with the way we've always done things," the CEO chimed in. "Change is always hard. And no one wants to change."

"No, I'm open to change," the department leader countered.

"I know we have to change. I just don't think that this new software system you have selected is the answer. It solves a handful of problems, but it creates even greater issues for us."

This was a start. But the CEO couldn't help himself and began to weigh in on the discussion.

"I don't think that's—" the CEO began.

I cut him off.

"Hold on," I interjected. "This is good feedback. It's why I am here, to help you generate these discussions. Let's hear what he has to say."

The CEO understood and complied, nodding to the department head to continue.

"Can you explain how the new software system creates greater issues for your team?" I asked the department head.

The department head did so, launching into detail about the negative impact of the new program on some of his most lucrative and high-profile projects. He wasn't merely complaining. He had clearly done the research and found major flaws with the new system that could be a serious detriment to the company's strategic mission.

Another department head added, "We feel the same way on my team. The new software seems great in theory, but in practice it is hugely problematic. Two of my trusted frontline leaders pointed out some major flaws to me a couple of weeks back when we discussed implementing the new system."

The CEO's face showed a look of concern. "This is the type of feedback that I need to hear," he said.

"We tried to tell you," the department head insisted. "Several of us tried to push back."

"You may have," I responded. "But it's clear that you didn't effectively raise the arguments as you have done just now."

I explained that the issue for them wasn't humility. They clearly had the humility piece down, recognized the boss's authority and strategic insight.

"But none of you stepped up to collectively push back on

the new software. You may have spoken out initially, but you've backed down from the authority of the CEO," I continued. "Yes, he's the boss. Yes, you need to execute his direction. But do you think he wants you to implement a system that would fail?

"Of course not," I answered. "This is a time to lead up the chain of command, as we wrote about and most of you have read in *Extreme Ownership,* chapter ten."

I explained to the company's leaders that they must carefully prioritize where to push back. It can't be for everything. If they did, their concerns would not be taken seriously when it truly mattered. But when the strategic mission or the ultimate good of the team was at risk, those were the times that a leader *must* push back. To not do so, I told them, was to fail as a leader; to fail the team and the mission.

"This is not a new concept," I explained. "Over two hundred years ago, Napoléon Bonaparte addressed this very issue. In his *Military Maxims,* Napoléon states:

> Every general-in-chief who undertakes to execute a
> plan which he knows to be bad, is culpable. He should
> communicate his reasons, insist on a change of plan,
> and finally resign his commission, rather than become
> the instrument of his army's ruin.*

"If you're passive, if you don't push back," I said, "you aren't leading up the chain of command. The boss needs and wants your honest feedback on this. He may not even know it," I said jokingly.

The rest of the group chuckled. The CEO also smiled. He clearly realized he had been overbearing in this situation. In his zeal to provide a strategic solution for the team, he hadn't fully

---

* *Military Maxims of Napoléon,* translated from the French by J. Akerly (New York: Wiley and Putnam, 1845), Maxim LXXII.

heard them, answered their questions, or investigated their legitimate concerns.

"Honestly," the CEO said, "I thought you all were just pushing back on this because you were resistant to change. Not because you had concerns about the new system.

"I realize now I should have asked for your input with a listening ear," he continued. "Rather than shut you down the first time I heard pushback."

It was a huge learning point for the CEO and a big lesson learned going forward for the team. For the sake of the company and the mission, the CEO needed to seek feedback and address the concerns of his key leaders. He needed to encourage his department heads to voice their opinions and express their disagreements. The CEO had made the common mistake of not fully recognizing the power of his position. He was the boss. He held the power. And most people wouldn't exercise the courage to confront that head-on. It was important the CEO fully recognize the power of his position and the reality of a general reluctance to confront it.

For the department heads and other key leaders on the team, it was a wake-up call that they were failing the team—they were culpable if they didn't push back and provide clear and direct feedback up the chain to fully explain the negative impact to the company's strategic objectives. Once the CEO understood their causes for concern, he relented and empowered the frontline leaders to develop their own solution for a new software system.

Delta Platoon commander, Lieutenant Seth Stone (*center left*), leads a joint patrol of Task Unit Bruiser SEALs, U.S. Marines and Soldiers, along with Iraqi Army troops through the Malaab District of eastern Ramadi. While the surrounding team members lock down potential threats, Lieutenant Stone detaches mentally and scans the area, plotting the team's next measures.

(Courtesy of the U.S. Navy. Photograph taken by Mate Second Class Sam Peterson.)

# CHAPTER 12
## Focused, but Detached

*Leif Babin*

### WESTERN RAMADI, IRAQ: 2006

*YAK-YAK! YAK-YAK! YAK-YAK!*

The unmistakable sound of AK-47 fully automatic gunfire echoed with deafening blasts around the small, smoke-filled room as bullets ricocheted off the concrete floor and walls.

*We're taking fire through the door,* I thought. *It's on.*

We no longer had the element of surprise, having just blasted in the outer door with an explosive breaching charge that woke up the neighborhood with a thunderous boom. Clouds of dust and smoke choked the air and made it difficult to see as we entered the building, scanning for threats. But once inside the room, we realized it was only a small foyer that led to another locked door, which led to the main house. Shattered glass and debris were strewn across the floor as Charlie Platoon SEALs and Iraqi soldiers stacked up in the "train"—a line of shooters ready to make entry once the locked door was breached.

Our intelligence indicated that within this home lived an insurgent who had planned and carried out multiple deadly attacks on U.S. and Iraqi troops. The latest attack was well planned and well orchestrated: insurgents had hit an Iraqi Army outpost (which contained a handful of U.S. military advisors) with machine gun fire from multiple directions. Next, they lobbed mortars into the compound with deadly accuracy. While the Iraqi soldiers manning the guard posts panicked and took cover, another insurgent drove a truck packed with explosives—a VBIED (vehicle-borne improvised explosive device)—into the compound, detonating in a gigantic fireball of death and destruction. Only through the extraordinary bravery of the U.S. Marine and Army military advisors who stood their ground and returned fire was anyone in the compound saved. Tragically, a U.S. Marine and a Soldier were killed, along with six Iraqi soldiers, and several others wounded. The well-fortified outpost was reduced to a shattered wreck. But the strategic damage to morale of the Iraqi troops proved even greater than the death and destruction inflicted. In the days following the attack, nearly the entire battalion of several hundred Iraqi soldiers deserted. The insurgents had dealt a crushing blow. Now, Task Unit Bruiser had the opportunity to capture or kill one of the ringleaders of that attack. We aimed to accomplish our mission.

As we waited to make entry through the next door, the sudden full-auto burst of gunfire instantly got everyone's attention. It was without question an AK-47, the Iraqi insurgents' primary weapon.

"They're shooting at us through the door," another SEAL said in a calm but loud voice. "Stand by to get some."

He had quickly come to the same conclusion that I had—that we all had. It was a contingency for which we were well prepared. The terrorist we were after was likely armed, certainly willing and eager to kill us, as was just about everyone associated with him. The SEAL shooters in the front of the train pointed their weapons at the closed and locked door, ready to engage any threat that emerged. The next SEAL back in the train reached down to his gear and pulled out a hand grenade—an M67 fragmentation grenade (or frag grenade) in preparation to neutralize the threat. If the enemy was shooting at us, we needed to be Default: Aggressive to solve that problem. It was the commonsense thing to do, rather than enter a room where a hostile enemy waited to gun us down.

But as the SEAL operator removed the grenade from his gear pouch and unwound the tape we used to secure the pin, I sensed that something wasn't right. Stepping out of the train, I looked around. There were enough weapons covering the potential threats in the room. I was the assault force commander, the senior leader on the assault team that entered the house to capture our primary target—or, if he was shooting at us, kill him as justified under the rules of engagement.

But the most important place I could point my weapon was not at threats. I had plenty of SEAL shooters whose primary job was to handle such threats. As the leader, I trained my weapon away from the threats and toward the ceiling, what we called "high port"—the weapon pointed to the sky. With my weapon at high port, I no longer looked down the sights with tunnel vision. Instead, I looked around—I observed everything that was going on. That gave me maximum vision: I could see what was actually happening and assess the situation.

As I did so, I observed one of our *jundhis** in the train, with a bewildered look on his face, staring down at his weapon, an AK-47. I could see where bullets had chiseled holes in the concrete floor at his feet, just behind the SEAL operator only inches in front of him. It was suddenly clear the gunfire had not come through the door ahead of us, but from behind us, from this *jundhi* within our own shooter train. He had had what we called an "accidental discharge," or AD. Like an idiot, he'd taken his weapon off safety and placed the AK-47 selector switch on full auto. At the same time, he'd improperly had his finger on the trigger and, in his nervousness, squeezed off a burst of automatic gunfire. The rounds had missed one of our Charlie Platoon SEALs just ahead of him in the train by only a few inches.

---

* *Jundhi or jundi:* Arabic for "soldier," the term Iraqi soldiers called themselves and commonly used by U.S. military advisors in Iraq.

Meanwhile, we were about to breach the door and toss a frag grenade into the next room, killing anyone on the other side within range of its deadly blast of shrapnel.

"Put that frag grenade away—it was an AD!" I shouted, loud enough so that everyone in the room could hear.

"What?" a SEAL operator in the back of the train responded in disbelief. "Who?"

He quickly saw me and the other SEALs next to me glaring at the offending *jundhi,* whose face showed a mix of terror, surprise, and guilt.

As the first shooters in the train held their weapons on the locked door, the SEAL holding the frag grenade returned it safely to the grenade pouch on his gear. A SEAL breacher quickly came forward and placed a small explosive charge on the locked door. Everybody backed up a safe distance.

*BOOM.*

The door popped open and the first two SEALs entered, quickly followed by the rest of our SEALs and Iraqi soldiers.

In the next room, just on the other side of the door, we encountered a military-age male, the head of the household and his entire family—his wife and four young children. He was not armed and made no effort to resist. Like most of the *muj* we captured, they glorified jihad in public, but when rough men with weapons broke down their door in the night, they cowered in fear behind women and children. We detained the prisoners and the train moved on.

As our assault force cleared the rest of the building, I heard Jocko's voice on the radio net.

"Leif, this is Jocko," he said. "Heard shots fired. You good?"

Jocko, the ground force commander in charge of two separate assault forces (including ours) and the mobility element of Humvees, was outside our building with the vehicles. He had heard the gunfire and recognized it as an AK-47. Assuming we had encountered resistance from armed enemy fighters, he was waiting patiently for an update, knowing that I had my hands full and would update him when I could.

"Jocko, this is Leif," I replied. "It was an AD. An Iraqi soldier."

"Roger," Jocko responded simply. While other bosses might have asked for more information, such as why it had happened and who had the AD and if there were casualties and if the target was secure, Jocko trusted that I had the situation under control—and that if I needed help, I would ask for it.

While the rest of the assault force cleared the last rooms in the building, one of my most trusted SEAL enlisted leaders, serving as the assault chief for this operation, confronted the *jundhi* who had accidentally discharged his weapon. This SEAL leader happened to be the one who had nearly been hit by the Iraqi soldier's errant bullets, and he wasn't happy. The SEAL ripped the AK-47 out of the *jundhi*'s hands, removed the magazine, and cleared the weapon. He grabbed the bewildered Iraqi soldier and unleashed a verbal tirade on him. The *jundhi* spoke no English, but from the SEAL's demeanor and gestures, the message was clear: he had screwed up royally and could have seriously wounded or killed some of us. He had also nearly caused us to employ a grenade that would have inflicted some horrific civilian casualties.

As we still had work to do, I intervened before things could escalate further.

"Let's get him outside," I said. After calling over an interpreter, who translated the order into Iraqi-dialect Arabic, I told the *jundhi* to sit and wait in the back of a vehicle outside. A SEAL escorted him, AK-47 rifle now empty, out to the truck to ensure he complied.

Once the target was secure, I passed the word over the radio to inform Jocko and the other SEALs in the mobility element.

I followed up with our prisoner-handling team, which was in the process of identifying the military-age male. The prisoner soon proved to be the insurgent ringleader we were looking for.

Jocko made his way through the front door and into the target building to see what we had found and if we needed any support.

"We got him," I said, giving Jocko a thumbs-up as he entered the room. "Here's our man." I pointed at the prisoner.

The insurgent's hands were cuffed with zip ties and he had been thoroughly searched.

"That was a close one," I told Jocko.

"Yeah," Jocko said. "I heard some AK fire just after you breached. And I thought, *Oh, you guys are gonna get some,*" he said with a smile.

"I thought we were taking fire through the door," I explained. "We were just about to toss a frag grenade into the next room. Had we done so, we likely would have killed or horribly wounded the woman and her young children. That would have been a disaster."

*Scary,* I thought, contemplating just how easily something like that could happen in the chaos of combat. Had it occurred, it would have been a heavy burden for each of us to carry on our conscience. It would have also served as significant propaganda for our insurgent enemies, who already tried to paint us and other American troops as butchers in order to dissuade the local populace from siding with us and the government of Iraq against the insurgency. This would have had major negative repercussions on the strategic counterinsurgency mission.

"Thank God you didn't let that happen," Jocko said.

I literally said a quick mental prayer of thanks to God for sparing us from such a horrific outcome.

Immersed in the chaos of the scene—the smoke, dust, and bullet ricochets—it was perilously easy to get sucked into the details, unable to recognize the initial conclusions as false and unmindful of the tragic consequences of getting it wrong. While in the train and focused on the threat at the next entry door, I had a hard time seeing the bigger picture and understanding what had happened. But as soon as I detached, from the moment I took just one step out of the shooter train and looked around, I immediately saw what had happened. It was a profound lesson: leaders must be detached, must pull back to a position above the fray where they can see the bigger picture. That was the only way to effectively lead. Otherwise, the results could be disastrous.

This was but the latest reminder of the same lesson I'd learned on one of our first combat operations in Ramadi. I'd been too immersed in the details and lost track of the strategic picture.

Shortly after Task Unit Bruiser's arrival in Ramadi, our intelligence shop handed me our first target package, with details on a suspected insurgent, his associations, and where he was believed to be located. This would be my first real-world operation as an assault force commander on a capture/kill direct action raid. I shared the target package with Jocko and informed him of our intention to launch on the operation that night. Jocko had extensive experience leading such missions from his previous deployment to Iraq. He let me and my key leaders run with the tactical planning and helped us get the wheels in motion to receive the necessary approvals through our chain of command. Getting the operation approved required an immense amount of paperwork: a Microsoft PowerPoint presentation of several detailed slides and an extensive Microsoft Word document several pages long. Additionally, we had to coordinate with the U.S. Army unit that owned the battlespace—the real estate where we planned to conduct the operation. We also needed approval through the Iraqi soldiers' chain of command so that they could accompany us.

We had most of the day to plan the operation and get all the necessary approvals. But I hadn't detached. I'd gotten bogged down, obsessed with the details. I spent too much time on the approval paperwork and not enough on the plan. It was a failure to properly Prioritize and Execute. Having been pulled too far into the weeds, I was unable to see where the team needed to focus our efforts in the limited time we had available. As the time for launch neared, our mission brief was not yet complete and I wasn't confident that we were ready. Besides, we hadn't yet received approval for launch. With the pressure mounting, I vented my frustrations to Jocko.

"I don't believe we will be ready in time to launch," I told him. "I think we should delay the operation and wait until tomorrow night."

Jocko disagreed.

"Leif," he said in a reassuring tone, "this isn't that hard. You and the platoon are more than ready. You will see. We will get the approvals. Go ahead and brief the mission, and we'll launch as soon as it's approved."

While I became fixated on the immediate tasks to plan and execute this mission, Jocko was detached. He saw the bigger picture and why it was critical for us—for Task Unit Bruiser—to launch on as many operations as possible in those first few days on the ground.

"We need to generate momentum," Jocko said. "We need to do as many operations as we can here at the beginning of deployment so that we develop the experience and build the task group's confidence in us. If we can generate enough momentum early on, that will set the tone and carry us throughout our time here."

Overwhelmed by the myriad details of the approval and planning process, I'd lost sight of the strategic vision. I now realized that in the bigger picture, it was important that we launch this operation that night and not delay.

Once I gained that perspective, I was determined to make it happen. We finalized our brief, quickly filled in the remaining holes in the plan, and delivered the mission brief (the operation order or OPORD) to the team. Shortly after the OPORD concluded, we received approval and launched on the operation. As Jocko predicted, it wasn't that hard. I hadn't needed to overthink it. We captured the insurgent, gathered some intelligence, and returned to base without incident. When we got back, I walked into Jocko's office.

"You were right," I said. "It wasn't that hard."

Going forward, I recognized that I needed to better Prioritize and Execute. To do that, I needed to detach—to not get so focused on the details but instead be mindful of the broader aspects of the planning and approval process. My platoon would handle the details, and I trusted them to do so. Otherwise, time would slip away and the critically important things could get overlooked.

I understood why it was critical to keep my eye on the strategic picture and pass that perspective on to my platoon. But I could do that only if I didn't get dragged into the tactical details.

There was a dichotomy here, and finding the equilibrium was difficult. I learned to detach myself from the details so I could more effectively lead. But a few weeks later, I learned the hard way that if a leader became too detached—too far removed from the details—critical steps were missed and the team's performance suffered.

I'd been slammed by this reality upon our return from one combat operation in Ramadi. We had been back at our camp, Sharkbase, for several hours when our leading petty officer approached me with bad news: Charlie Platoon's lead SEAL communicator (or radioman) had informed him that we were missing a very sensitive piece of communications equipment.

I was taken aback. "How can that be?" I asked, stunned. There were strict procedures in place to ensure we had proper control of such highly classified and essential gear at all times. These procedures applied to all branches of the U.S. military.

I went to speak to my lead SEAL communicator.

"What happened?" I asked him. He told me how he discovered the gear was missing. It was clear that he and our other SEAL radioman had not followed proper procedures. This was a serious incident and a major embarrassment for Charlie Platoon. Worse, it cast a negative light on Task Unit Bruiser and our entire SEAL Team.

I had to go tell Jocko what had happened. He wasn't happy. As a former SEAL radioman himself, he understood the strict procedures that must be followed and the clear lack of discipline Charlie Platoon had shown in violating them.

I was furious with my SEAL communicators. They knew better. But more important, I was furious with myself. *I was to blame.* Casting blame on my radiomen was the opposite of Extreme Ownership. This was my fault, and I knew it. I had become too detached. I'd given my radiomen far too much leeway. I hadn't periodically checked on them and ensured that proper procedures were being followed. I'd stepped too far back from the details of Charlie Platoon's communications department.

Initially, as Charlie Platoon began our training cycle the year before, I'd kept a much closer eye on our communications equipment procedures. But after a single early misstep, which we quickly rectified, my lead SEAL communicator routinely demonstrated he was on top of things. I felt confident in his ability to run his department, and I let him run it. I focused my attention elsewhere. And frankly, once we were on the ground in Ramadi, I had been pulled in too many different directions. I had gotten so busy that I hadn't made time to check in with my lead communicator to ensure that he and the other SEAL radioman were in compliance with proper radio equipment–handling procedures.

In *About Face,* Colonel David Hackworth wrote that he had learned this fundamental truth from his U.S. Army mentors: "An organization does well only those things the Boss checks." Regularly checking up on procedures showed the team what I found important. Had I done so with our radio equipment, my SEAL communicators would have never gotten lax and they would have ensured proper procedures were followed. I hadn't reminded them how critical it was for us to do so and what was at stake if we didn't.

Now, Task Unit Bruiser had to own this failure—my failure. There were also strict procedures to follow in the event such gear was lost, and I ensured we followed them to a tee. We immediately passed the word up the chain of command and told our higher headquarters what had happened. We sent out a military-wide electronic message informing everyone that we had lost the critical communications equipment. It was a big black eye for us—for Task Unit Bruiser, for Charlie Platoon, and for me in particular. But I had to own it. Most important, I had to make sure we would never let it happen again.

We canceled Charlie Platoon's combat operation for that evening. It would have been a good one, a mission we'd been planning for a couple of weeks, and I was disappointed not to be able to execute it. We almost certainly would have gotten into some Big Mix-It-Ups, killed a number of enemy fighters, and likely had substantial strategic impact in a volatile area of the city. Instead, we loaded up in our Humvees and returned to the U.S. combat outpost where we'd last utilized the missing equipment. A thorough search found nothing within the confines of the outpost's perimeter defenses of concrete barriers and concertina wire. We then launched a foot patrol along the route we had taken previously—a road that suffered frequent vicious attacks from insurgents. It made for difficult searching, but we had enough SEALs covering with their weapons so others could scan the pavement and trash piles. After an extensive search of several hundred yards, we turned around to head back to the combat outpost.

As we patrolled back, suddenly:

*YAK-YAK YAK-YAK YAK-YAK.*

Two insurgents opened up on us with AK-47s from an alleyway that ran perpendicular to the main road along which we patrolled. Several SEALs immediately returned fire, sending the insurgents running. Marc Lee, Chris Kyle, and I gave chase down the alleyway, using Cover and Move. But by the time we reached their previous location, the insurgents were long gone. They disappeared into the walled residential compounds of the congested urban neighborhood.

It was time to wrap up and head home. We never found the missing equipment.

As for me, I had learned a valuable lesson about this dichotomy. In order to effectively lead, I had to detach. But I must never become too detached. I couldn't obsess over the details, but I should nevertheless be attentive to them. It was a humbling lesson learned that I would never forget.

### Principle

Naturally, leaders must be attentive to details. However, leaders cannot be so immersed in the details that they lose track of the larger strategic situation and are unable to provide command and control for the entire team.

In combat, when you look down the sights of your weapon, your field of view becomes narrow and focused. Your vision is restricted by the small aperture of your weapons sight. You cannot see what is happening around you or the team. It is critical, then, to ensure that a leader's default weapon position should be at high port—gun pointed at the sky, standing back to observe with the widest field of vision possible. This enables a leader to look around and even move around, where he or she can best provide command and control for the team. Most important, it allows a leader to keep the larger, overarching goals of the mission in perspective. The analogy applies directly to non-combat situations. It is no different in the business world, where leaders must ensure they don't get sucked into the tactical details but maintain the ability to detach.

In *Extreme Ownership,* chapter 7, "Prioritize and Execute," we wrote:

> When confronted with the enormity of operational plans and the intricate microterrain within those plans, it becomes easy to get lost in the details. . . . It is crucial . . . for leaders . . . to "pull themselves off the firing line," step back, and maintain the strategic picture.

This key concept resonated with many readers and helped them improve their leadership skills. Detachment is also an ongoing issue with which many leaders struggle. Leaders cannot allow themselves to get so obsessed by the details that they lose focus on the bigger picture. It is essential for leaders to understand that this should be their default mind-set, so they can always be aware of it. If they don't maintain a position above the fray, then leaders are failing their team and failing the mission.

What we didn't clearly articulate in *Extreme Ownership* is the need to balance somewhere between understanding the details and becoming completely submerged and overwhelmed by them. Leaders can't get so far away—so detached—that they lose track of what's happening on the front lines. Leaders must still be attentive to the details, understand the challenges of the teams executing the mission at the front echelon, and position themselves where they can best support their teams. This is the dichotomy that must be balanced: to become engrossed in and overwhelmed by the details risks mission failure, but to be so far detached from the details that the leader loses control is to fail the team and fail the mission.

### Application to Business

"For some reason, I wasn't thinking about this in my office yesterday," said Rob. "But sitting here in the classroom today, it's all of a sudden very clear where we as a company should be focused to improve our process and increase profitability.

"Modularization," Rob continued. "We need to be thinking modularization in everything that we do. This will help us reduce extensive man-hours on-site that generate huge costs. It will increase our efficiency and help project managers cut down operating expenses."

"That sounds promising," I remarked. "It's a great observation and one I'd like to dive into in more detail with everyone here. But before we do that, let's pull back for a second and analyze why this is all of a sudden clear to you. Why do you think you weren't thinking about this yesterday? Why is it so easy to see now?" I asked Rob.

For the leaders in the room, understanding the answer to this question was paramount. The recognition and understanding of the Dichotomy of Leadership—the opposing forces that must be balanced—served as a powerful leadership tool to help each of them lead and win.

I stood in front of a classroom of fifteen senior leaders of a highly successful company. Echelon Front had been hired to run a

Leadership Development and Alignment Program for their senior leaders. Most of the participants were division managers, with a wealth of experience and knowledge in their industry. The company had generated a record of success and built a solid reputation that enabled them to make substantial gains on competitors and increase their market share. As the company grew, the senior executive team wisely noted that they had no formal leadership training program for their senior leaders, and one was warranted. They asked Echelon Front to develop a program to help build into the culture of their team the principles of *Extreme Ownership* they'd read about. After an initial assessment with one-on-one interviews of participants and discussion with each participant's boss, we launched the kickoff with an intensive, full-day training session. We then scheduled follow-on training events at rotating locations throughout the company's operating region every few weeks.

Here, at the third training session, a number of the leaders had traveled from their territories and the home offices where they spent much of their time. Independent of the content I presented and the questions and discussions generated, the requirement for each participant to pull away from his or her daily grind brought significant benefits. It forced them to detach. Removed from the details, pressures, and pressing deadlines of the front lines, they found it easier to see the strategic priorities with clarity and how best to achieve them. This concept of detachment was a critical leadership skill on and off the battlefield, in business, and in life.

I repeated the question to Rob and for everyone else in the group: "Why do you think you weren't thinking about this yesterday? Why is it all of a sudden clear now?"

"Yesterday, I was making phone calls, dealing with immediate fires on a couple of different projects, and pretty much buried in my e-mail in-box," Rob answered.

"You were immersed in the details, down in the weeds," I said in agreement. "And you have to be attentive to those details. You can't pull back too much. But you can't obsess about the details.

Your job as a leader is to detach—stand back and see the bigger picture.

"Attending this training session has pulled you away from those details," I continued. "And as you sit here in the classroom, you're detached. Now, what needs to be done is much clearer. It's a key lesson that you must learn."

I relayed how I had learned this lesson in the SEAL Teams.

On the battlefield, as a leader, when you look down the sights of your weapon, I explained, your field of vision is reduced from a hundred and eighty degrees or more around you to only what you can see through the small aperture of your scope or aiming device. The narrow view isn't the leader's job. The leader's job is to look around and see the bigger picture. I recognized that in a SEAL platoon, which carried a massive amount of firepower, my rifle didn't count for much. But if I wasn't looking around, who was? No one. It was up to me.

"Leadership in the business world is no different," I explained. "All of you, as senior leaders, should be striving to detach so you can stand back, gain perspective, and recognize where your priorities should be focused.

"But this is something you have to balance," I continued. "You have to detach. But you can't be so detached that you don't know what is going on. Because if you don't know what's going on, you can't help your team; you can't lead."

To illustrate this dichotomy for the class, I told them how, as a SEAL platoon commander, I found myself struggling with where to position myself in the kill house during our close-quarters training, where the team practiced clearing rooms and hallways in an urban environment. In my previous platoon, I'd been told that as an officer, my role was to stand in the back of the train.

"Why are you in the back of the train?" Jocko asked me, observing Charlie Platoon's runs through the kill house from the catwalk above.

"I thought that was where I was supposed to be," I answered.

"Can you tell what's going on with your guys at the front of the train?" Jocko asked.

"I have no idea what's going on up front," I admitted. If I didn't know what was going on up front, how could I lead? I certainly couldn't help the team solve a particularly challenging problem, vector more resources to my shooters, or provide proper command and control.

"If you don't know what's going on, you can't lead," Jocko told me. "You can't be in the back, because you don't know what's happening up front. You can't be all the way up front, because then you get sucked into every room clearance, and then you're too far into the tactical details to provide proper command and control. Your position should be somewhere in the middle, with the bulk of your forces, close enough to the front to know what is going on, but far enough back that you aren't in the weeds doing the tactical work."

It made sense. It was simple, but Jocko's guidance was illuminating. I gained confidence and fully understood where I should be as a leader. Most important, I realized I wasn't stuck in a particular position. I could move around to see what was happening and assist the team members where they needed it the most. It was an important lesson that I never forgot.

"To find that careful balance," I told the company's senior leaders, "make sure you don't go to the extreme in either direction. I've seen SEAL leaders and a number of business leaders who have gone too far. You must maintain the balance: detached, but not so detached that you don't know what's going on and can't lead.

"Any leader, when things are going very badly for the team, has to step in and help them solve problems. I have seen some leaders who felt they were above solving problems. This is an extreme form of detachment, one we call 'battlefield aloofness.' It's not a good thing. It can result in epic failure."

I told the class how Jocko had used the term to describe an

overly detached SEAL leader while we were observing a SEAL task unit during a training operation.

The SEAL was a task unit commander, serving as the ground force commander during a field training exercise in a MOUT (military operations in urban terrain) facility. His platoons were heavily engaged in a difficult tactical problem inside one of the large cinder-block buildings, with multiple role-players attacking them with paintball rounds. The task unit had pulled its vehicles to a stop outside of the target building, and their assault force had dismounted and entered the building. Immediately, they were heavily engaged by a number of well-entrenched "enemy fighters"— actually SEAL instructors and role-players. Quickly, several SEALs were hit and the training instructors put them down, meaning they were simulated killed or severely wounded. The rest of the SEAL assault force was pinned down inside the target building. They needed help, resources, guidance, and direction. Jocko and I, inside the house observing the SEAL platoons in action, waited for someone to step up and assist, but it never came.

"Where is the task unit commander?" Jocko asked, after several painful minutes of watching the problem escalate. I looked around but didn't see him.

"I think he is still outside in his Humvee," I observed.

Jocko and I walked outside of the target building. The task unit commander was nowhere to be seen.

Finally, we approached the line of Humvees parked on the street outside the target building. We found the task unit commander inside, sitting comfortably in his seat. We opened the heavy armored door of his Humvee.

"What's crappening?" I said, borrowing a favorite phrase from our brother and former Task Unit Bruiser Delta Platoon commander, Seth Stone. The TU commander said nothing.

"What's going on in there?" Jocko asked the task unit commander, motioning toward the target building where his team was pinned down.

The task unit commander didn't have an answer. He looked down at his map but never moved from his seat in the back of the Humvee.

"I'm waiting for a status update," he responded, as if he were perfectly on top of things.

He keyed up his radio. "What's your status?" he asked, directed at his platoon commander—the assault force commander in the house. Jocko and I both wore radios and monitored the task unit's communications network so we could listen in on their radio traffic and evaluate the leadership's communications between one another.

There was no answer over the radio. The platoon commander and much of his team were pinned down in a horrific gun battle inside the house. They had several simulated casualties and were trying to pull them out of a hot hallway—meaning bullets were flying down the hallway. The platoon commander was not in a position to even hear the radio transmission, much less respond to it.

"I need a status update," the task unit commander repeated on the radio net.

No status update was sent. Another half minute of silence passed.

"So, what's going on?" Jocko asked again.

"I don't know," the task unit commander replied. "I'm waiting for a status update."

Jocko turned and looked at me, puzzled.

"Maybe you should move toward your assault force commander and go get a status update," I said. "You aren't stuck in the vehicle. Move around to wherever you can best provide command and control. Or, you can sit here in your Humvee and wait for everyone to die."

With that, the TU commander got out of the vehicle and moved toward the target building to try and figure out what was happening.

"Battlefield aloofness," Jocko said. "That's the best term I can think of for that level of detachment." It meant that the leader was so detached, he had no idea what was going on. If there were problems, he expected someone else to solve them. This task unit commander actually seemed annoyed that he had to step out of the Humvee and lead. But he quickly learned that when the team is on the verge of disaster, it's time for the senior leader to put detachment aside and step into the fray, to solve problems and help the team. It's time to *lead*. Once those problems are getting solved, the leader can then step back to a position of detachment.

With this, I illustrated for the classroom of leaders how it was essential to balance the dichotomy: to remain focused, but also detached. Now, the class understood how they could best apply this concept, find the equilibrium, and lead their teams to victory.

Task Unit Bruiser SEALs from Charlie Platoon patrol on foot back to friendly territory following the first major operation of the Ready First Brigade Combat Team's (1st Brigade of the U.S. Army's 1st Armored Division) "Seize, Clear, Hold, Build" strategy to take back Ramadi from enemy insurgents. Task Unit Bruiser SEALs and Iraqi soldiers supported the "Seize, Clear" portion of that strategy with sniper overwatches, patrols, and clearance operations alongside the courageous Soldiers and Marines of the Ready First Brigade. Once back in friendly territory, they would quickly reload, refit, and plan the next operation for Task Unit Bruiser. This photo was taken on the day following the events described in the opening of Chapter 3.

(Photo courtesy of the authors)

# AFTERWORD

The dichotomies we have highlighted in this book represent only a small portion of the many dichotomies in leadership that must be balanced with every move or decision a leader makes. The list of dichotomies is endless. Each one could fill a chapter in this book. Leaders can be too reliant on metrics and not pay enough attention to the hearts and minds of their employees or customers—or they can do the opposite: pay too much attention to people's feelings while ignoring the data. Leaders can be too direct in their speech and intimidate their teams and subordinate leaders or put them on the defensive; but they can also not be direct enough with their words and fail to convey their message clearly. Leaders can invest too much capital or not enough. They can grow their team too quickly and allow performance standards to slip or grow too slowly and leave the team undermanned and overwhelmed. Leaders can let their personal life suffer because they focused too much attention on work and not enough on their family, or they can neglect work to spend time with their family and end up losing their job and their means of supporting their family. Leaders can joke around too much and not be taken seriously, or they can never joke around and spread a culture of humorless misery in their team. Leaders can talk too much to the point where their team stops paying attention or not talk enough so their team doesn't know where the leader stands.

The list of dichotomies is infinite. Because for every positive behavior a leader *should* have, it is possible to take that behavior to the *extreme,* where it becomes a negative. Often a leader's greatest strength can also be his or her greatest weakness. But knowing and understanding that these dichotomies exist is the first part of keeping them from becoming a problem.

The second part requires paying careful attention so that a leader can tell when things are out of balance. If a team has lost its initiative, the leader is likely micromanaging. If a team is clowning around and not getting things done, the leader has joked too much. When leaders sense that their leadership is ineffective, it requires a careful examination to see where they are out of balance. Then action can be taken to bring equilibrium back to the dichotomy.

When a leader moves to rebalance, however, caution must be exercised not to overcorrect. This is a common error: when leaders sense they have gone too far in one direction, they can react by going too far in the other direction. This is ineffective, and can make the situation worse. So instead, make measured, calculated adjustments, monitor the results, and then continue to make small, iterative corrections until balance is achieved.

Once balance is achieved, a leader must recognize that equilibrium will not last. Circumstances change: subordinates, leaders, employees, the enemy, the battlefield, the market, the world—it all changes. And those changes will upset the balance of the Dichotomy of Leadership. The leader must continue to monitor the situation, readjust as changes happen, and restore balance.

Like so many of the challenges in leadership, finding and maintaining balance is not easy. But as we wrote in *Extreme Ownership,* it is the immense challenge of leadership that makes the reward of success so fulfilling. A deeper knowledge and understanding of the Dichotomy of Leadership unleashes the highest levels of performance, enabling the leader and the team to dominate on any battlefield, to Lead and Win.

So, take the challenge. Become the most effective leader possible. And while you should absolutely take Extreme Ownership of everything in your world, you must also absolutely strive to be extremely balanced in everything you do: with your subordinates, your superiors, your peers, your decisions, your emotions, and your life. In leadership, you will find challenges, you will find rewards, you will find struggles, and you will find fulfillment. But as a leader, if you can think and act with balance, you will achieve the goal of every leader and every team: Victory.

Lieutenant Leif Babin *(Left)* and Lieutenant Commander Jocko Willink *(Center)* with Task Unit Bruiser in Ar Ramadi, Iraq, 2006. On the right is Lieutenant Seth Stone, the Delta Platoon Commander and dear friend of Jocko and Leif. After this deployment, Seth took command of Task Unit Bruiser, deployed back to Iraq, and led aggressive SEAL operations during a highly successful campaign to pacify Sadr City, Baghdad in 2008. On September 30, 2017, Seth was killed in a training accident. We will never forget him.

(Photo courtesy of the authors)

# INDEX